MAN IN PROCESS

By Ashley Montagu

MAN IN PROCESS

HUMAN HEREDITY

THE CULTURED MAN

MAN: HIS FIRST MILLION YEARS

COMING INTO BEING AMONG THE AUSTRALIAN ABORIGINES

EDWARD TYSON, M.D., F.R.S. (1650-1708): AND THE RISE
OF HUMAN AND COMPARATIVE ANATOMY IN ENGLAND

MAN'S MOST DANGEROUS MYTH: THE FALLACY OF RACE

STATEMENT ON RACE

THE DIRECTION OF HUMAN DEVELOPMENT

THE NATURAL SUPERIORITY OF WOMEN

THE REPRODUCTIVE DEVELOPMENT OF THE FEMALE

ON BEING HUMAN

THE BIOSOCIAL NATURE OF MAN

DARWIN, COMPETITION AND COOPERATION

ON BEING INTELLIGENT

IMMORTALITY

EDUCATION AND HUMAN RELATIONS

ANTHROPOLOGY AND HUMAN NATURE

INTRODUCTION TO PHYSICAL ANTHROPOLOGY

HANDBOOK OF ANTHROPOMETRY

PRENATAL INFLUENCES

ASHLEY
MONTAGU

Man in Process

THE WORLD PUBLISHING COMPANY

CLEVELAND AND NEW YORK

PUBLISHED BY The World Publishing Company
2231 WEST 110TH STREET, CLEVELAND 2, OHIO

PUBLISHED SIMULTANEOUSLY IN CANADA BY
NELSON, FOSTER & SCOTT LTD.

Library of Congress Catalog Card Number: 61-6651

FIRST EDITION

WP561

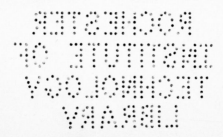

To Chauncey
and Elizabeth Leake

Contents

CONTENTS

Introduction

MAN IN PROCESS of evolution, of development, physically and culturally, constitutes an object lesson in the method of trial and error. In both dimensions of his development, the physical and the cultural, he has been, on the whole, spectacularly successful. Physically he is remarkably resourceful at adaptation. What he cannot accomplish by means of his purely physical endowments he can through the agency of his behavioral ones. Having no wings with which to fly he invents them and flies faster and higher than any bird. He has mastered the art and science of living and finding his way underwater as well as he has in his natural medium on the surface of the earth. He is only a few decades, at most, away from creating life itself. He has established a mastery over nature which is unique in the three billion years of this earth's history, without establishing anything like a comparable mastery over himself. This has been so often remarked in recent years that it has become something of a cliché. The danger of a truth too often repeated lies in the fact that it may become wearisome, a bore, something to avoid and evade. Like a hackneyed melody it palls upon the ear.

The truth, like the melody, nevertheless lingers on. Man controls virtually the whole of nature. The only part of it which he does not control, to anything approaching the same degree, is his own. This is no cause for despair. It is, however, at this stage in man's development certainly cause for concern. Even more so it is cause for serious and sympathetic understanding. To reverse Pope's apothegm, the proper study of man is mankind. To learn to understand ourselves we need to pay more attention to the illuminating variety of ways in which human nature expresses itself in different societies. We need to do this in order to understand to what a major extent human nature is custom-made, tailored according to the specifications and requirements of a particular society. It is in this way alone possible to learn that what we so often take to be biologically determined differences in the expression of human nature are, in fact, only socially determined differences.

It is important to arrive at a sound view of these matters in a rapidly shrinking world in which peoples who are just beginning to emerge from nonliterate tribalistic cultures are increasingly going to demand an equal role with other peoples in the government of world affairs and in their relations with other human beings. Political developments in Africa and in other parts of the world, as well as in the southern United States, underscore the pressure of what is no less than a profound moral obligation on the part of every thinking citizen to make himself acquainted with the facts concerning the nature of human nature. Each of the chapters in this book, in one way or another, constitutes a contribution calculated to assist the reader to that end.

Man is the most educable of all living creatures. This means that he can not only learn what is sound, but also what is unsound. An important measure of his progress lies in the degree to which he has learned to distinguish between the sound and the unsound, between verifiable facts and traditionally received prejudgments, between reason and rationalization, between measured weighing of evidence and myth. The fact is that no society has ever achieved thoroughgoing progress in this direction, and few individuals have ever done so. It would, however, be a mistake to see in this dichotomy a division between the rational and the irrational. It is true that these elements are deeply involved in the system of beliefs held by every human being, but the irrational beliefs may have been arrived at in a manner and with a motivation profoundly more rational than those in which the rational ones were arrived at. For example, many of the factually demonstrable beliefs held by men in the Western world are, in fact, no more than superstitions—the superstitions of the day which they have derived from the secular religion to which they happen to subscribe, the religion of science. I do not think that this is reprehensible. There is nothing else that most of us can do. There are innumerable things that we have to accept on faith. The trick is to know how to distinguish between those things that we may accept on faith and those that we should not.

I have myself never met anyone, however distinguished intellectually, who did not subscribe to a good many beliefs which were demonstrably untrue. The truth has to have a pick and shovel taken to it if we would discover it, and the world is full of so many things to know that it is quite impossible for any one man in his lifetime to dig them all out and confirm them for himself. All of us simply have to take on faith most of the truths to which we subscribe, on the basis of the assurances of those who should know. This is what men do in all societies. And a myth is nothing more than a belief in something as true, and upon which men act as if it were true, but which is in fact not true. Man's myths are his attempts to explain the world in which he lives. In a very real sense man may be defined as the myth-making animal. Everywhere his fertile imagination, working with the materials of reality, has created the most beautiful myths. But he has also created some that are not so beautiful, and for this modern man has an especial penchant. The modern myth of "race" is a particular example. That is why it is dealt with at some length in this book.

Human societies may roughly be divided into two kinds: those which attempt to solve the problems of real existence by absconding from them, and those which attempt to solve those problems by mastering them. In the first kind, myth will prevail; in the second, method will be a dominant motif.

And so it is with individuals in every society. There are those who want to live by the pleasure principle exclusively; solutions which minister to their comfort are what they value. Any idea or act which challenges the beliefs which keep them comfortable are regarded as hostile to their welfare and are therefore to be combated. Those, on the other hand, who tend to adhere more closely to the reality principle are comparatively few in any society, for an addiction to critically weighing the evidence is likely to result in the discovery that some things are wanting and that others are not what they are believed to be. This is likely to challenge established values and threaten the security of those who subscribe to them. The troublemaker is not likely to find himself blessed. The deviant character, the eccentric, the maverick, is not encouraged in any society. But to the extent to which he is, we have a measure of the advancement toward increasing humanity. A society that has to have a legislative committee to investigate unorthodox beliefs or beliefs calculated to subvert the government returns to the days of the medicine man and the voodoo doctor who by divination sought out the offender and by that very act condemned him. Incantation rather than ratiocination is likely to become the dominant motif of such an irrational society.

The object of these remarks is to make it clear that as members of civilized societies we differ from the members of nonliterate—the so-called "primitive"—societies to the extent only that we have developed the ability to weigh the evidence critically for ourselves. Technologically our societies are vastly more advanced than those of nonliterate cultures, but most of us have no more contributed to that technological advancement than we have to the great literature and the scientific discovery of our society. How many of us could build a television transmitter or receiver, or a dynamo, or even a simple fuse, or any one of a hundred thousand other technically simple devices? How many of us can write a tolerably good poem or good novel? Our society bequeaths these things to us, but very few of us are ever involved as contributors to the making of that literary, scientific, and technological tradition. We are most of us consumers, not makers. And yet each of us is more or less educable enough to be able to learn to distinguish between the probable and the improbable, the possible and the impossible.

This book is concerned with man's educability. It shows man in process—in process of learning to be a more rational human being. It descants on his nature and on the interpreters of his nature, and it endeavors to show how those interpreters fall into error by maintaining traditional views and analyzing the facts in the light of those views instead of in the light of the facts. Indeed, the traditional view of man's nature is still so strong that my defense of the facts has been met with either a contemptuous shrug of the shoulder or with complete silence. But facts have a way of prevailing, even of asserting themselves once they are brought out into the open, for if they are not facts they will eventually surely return to the well-merited obscurity from which they have been retrieved.

Is man innately a bestial creature? Shall war always be with us because man is innately warlike? Is man innately depraved, as our Victorian and earlier ancestors told us? Is man a cannibal? What is "race"? Do varieties of man differ from one another to such an extent as to render it necessary to deal with them differently as human beings? What are the facts? What are the fancies? What can a rational man believe?

The chapters of this book are so designed as to cause the reader to rethink the foundations of some of his own most taken-for-granted beliefs: the belief in "blood," for example, the meaning of "puberty" in the female (adolescent sterility), and the like. Here are things in which practically every one of us believes, which condition our conduct, and which are codified in our language, our literature, and our statute books.

Finally, I am concerned with showing the reader how rational some of the seemingly irrational beliefs of nonliterate peoples are; that they are not as irrational as they may appear to be, but are at least as rational as the majority of our own rational beliefs. The difference between the "savage" and ourselves is only skin deep. Mankind has yet some distance to travel before it achieves the fulfillment of genuine humanity. Perhaps these essays may clarify the way.

ASHLEY MONTAGU

Princeton, New Jersey
April, 1961

MAN IN PROCESS

ACKNOWLEDGMENTS

I am indebted to the editors and publishers for permission to reprint the articles which form the chapters of this book from the journals in which they originally appeared. The sources are given at the foot of the first page of each chapter. Each article has been thoroughly revised and brought up to date.

A. M.

1

The Sociobiology of Man

WHAT IS MAN as a biological being? What is man as a social being? What is man regarded as a function of both a biological and a social structure in interaction? These are the questions to which an attempt to return an answer will be made in this book.

I propose to make no vague generalizations concerning the social and biological functions of human beings, but rather to attempt to relate the more fundamental of man's biological and social functions, concerning which reliable knowledge is available, to the world in which human beings exist at the present time; to indicate what the nature of those functions is; to point out how they have been understood and formed up to the present time; and finally, to suggest the nature of the principles which must be recognized if "Nature's sole mistake," as one unsympathetic philosopher has termed man, is to be turned into a success.

In the study of any organism it is always desirable to remember that the organism exists as a whole and not merely as a series of parts which may be studied in dissociation from one another in atomistic fashion—as if such parts had any meaning apart from their relation to the whole organism. Yet this is a principle which has often been forgotten or neglected

From *The Scientific Monthly*, vol. 50, 1940, 483-490.

by numerous investigators in the pursuit of their studies, and its neglect has been the occasion of much confusion in scientific thought. Nowhere is the confusion thus engendered more apparent than in the fields of study relating to man in society. An instance of this, with which many will be familiar, is the practice of drawing inferences concerning the native ability of individuals on the basis of ratings derived from intelligence tests without taking into consideration the very necessary factors of the social and economic history of the individuals tested in this way. Or, to cite another instance, there is the oft-repeated assertion that so-called primitive peoples are mentally inferior to ourselves because they have not developed a culture which can compare with ours. These are typical examples of inferences which are drawn from particular aspects of phenomena without any reference to the framework as a whole of which they form a part. When the whole, in such connections, is considered and understood, the real significance of the integrated part becomes unequivocally clear, and that significance is very different from what is attributed to the part when it is not so considered in relation to the whole.

So here we shall take mankind as a whole for our province and consider its fundamental social and biological functions as a whole, or series of whole frameworks. Where we encounter significant differences—as we shall—we shall attempt to explain them in terms of the whole to which they relate. In this way we may perhaps arrive at some common principles which may apply to man universally and in all societies.

The first point concerning which it is necessary to be clear is the position of man in the world as an animal organism. Upon this elementary point there strangely seems to exist a considerable amount of confusion. It is often stated that man is descended from a monkey or, variously, from the gorilla or the chimpanzee. In such statements there is not an ounce of truth. Man, in common with these animals, belongs to the same Order of Mammals, the Order of Primates, but his kinship with the monkeys is very remote, while his relationship with the African anthropoids, the chimpanzee, and the gorilla is collateral and not linear. That is to say, though the anthropoids and man were probably derived from the same stock, their evolutionary history has proceeded along disparate and divergent lines. Thus, man is not descended from any existing anthropoid ape, but from the same stock as that from which the anthropoids also originated; hence, they may be regarded as, at most, collateral relatives or very distant cousins and, from the standpoint of the modern zoologist, members of the same extended family.

Fossil remains of an animal from which man and the anthropoids may have originated are known from the Miocene horizons of the Siwaliks of India, namely, the remains of *Sivapithecus sivalensis. Sivapithecus* is known only from some fragments of upper and lower jaws and a good assortment of teeth, but these represent among the most valuable of the remains of any animal. Comparison of these remains with the similar parts of anthropoids on the one hand and with human beings on the other suggests that man has become a less specialized form, while the anthropoids have become, by comparison, excessively specialized. The moderately developed canine teeth of *Sivapithecus* have in man been replaced by a tooth the tip of which is almost level with the biting surfaces of the rest of the teeth, whereas in the anthropoids these teeth have been replaced by great tusk-like structures.

There is a lesson which suggests itself here, and it is, I believe, a perfectly legitimate one to draw from the evidence. The lesson is that specialization is achieved at the cost of general efficiency and leads to a constriction of the process of living or experiencing, whereas a general and well-integrated distribution of energies leads to an increase in general efficiency and an enlargement of the capacity to live and experience. And this, essentially, is the difference between the apes and man. The apes have pursued a developmental course which will ultimately lead to their extinction. They are too narrow, too specialized. They cannot compete with man. The human species, on the other hand, has pursued a developmental course which has been characterized by its plasticity and adaptability, a plasticity and adaptability which have led mankind to the position in the world in which it now finds itself—not "Nature's sole mistake," at least, not yet, but nature's most spoiled brat, perhaps; unquestionably nature's most promising child. It need hardly be pointed out that spoiled brats and promising children are conditions frequently found together in the same individual.

In terms of zoologic time, and in terms of experience, mankind is still in the childhood of its development. Of the future we can say very little. As a friend of mine, a garbage collector, once appropriately remarked, "If we take care of the present the future will take care of itself." The time for lamentation and jeremiads may safely be postponed to the end of the next half-million years, when the original readers of this book and its author may possibly figure in the cases of the university museum as the fossil representatives of a race that failed to understand the situation!

This plasticity and adaptability which so conspicuously endows man, beyond all other animals, with the ability to control so much of the world in which he lives, is reflected both in the structure of his body and of his mind. Both are the least specialized of any to be found in the Order of Mammals to which he belongs. Now, this is an extremely important point to grasp; that is, that man biologically is both structurally and mentally the most plastic and adaptable animal in existence. Structurally, this plasticity has enabled him to adapt himself to an untold variety of conditions. Upon his inner genetic resources he has been able to draw for combinations of physical characters which have met the requirements of natural, sexual, and social selection, which, as factors operating in geographically isolated localities, have been instrumental in producing the varieties of man with which we are acquainted. Whether these varieties of man represent the effects of the action of mutant genes, of natural, sexual, or social selection, or any combination of such factors, the outstanding fact remains that the group has varied in the way it has structurally without in any way losing its plasticity; indeed, there seems to have been a very definite gain in plasticity and adaptability.

And here the important fact requires to be stated that all varieties of man belong to the same species and without a doubt have the same common human ancestry. This is the conclusion to which all the relevant evidence of comparative anatomy, hematology, and genetics points. On genetic grounds alone it is virtually impossible to conceive of the varieties of man having originated separately as distinct lines from different anthropoid ancestors. Genetically, the chances against such a process ever having occurred are in mathematical terms of such an order as to deny the suggestion even so much as a glimpse into the universe of possibility. On anatomical grounds the evidence is quite clear. The physical differences which exist between the varieties of mankind are, from the anatomical standpoint, so insignificant that when they are properly evaluated they can be defined only in terms of a particular expression of an assortment of genes which are common to all mankind. And this one may say very much more definitely and with much greater justice than one may say it of the differences exhibited by any of our domesticated varieties of cats, dogs, or horses. There are numerous varieties of cats, dogs, and horses, and these represent highly selected strains of animals which have been bred as more or less pure breeds and domesticated by man. Man, too, is a domesticated, a self-domesticated, animal, but unlike our domestic animals the varieties of man are quite mixed and are far from representing pure breeds. The range of variation in all human varieties for any character is very much more considerable than that which is exhibited by any group of animals belonging to a pure breed. All the evidence indicates that the differences between the so-called "races" of man merely represent a random combination of variations derived from a common source which, by inbreeding in isolated groups, has become more or less stabilized and hereditary in a large number of the members of such groups. Furthermore, the evidence indicates that such selection of variations as has occurred in different groups has been restricted entirely to physical characters. There is no evidence among the varieties of mankind that any process of mental selection has ever been operative. The conception of selection for mental qualities seems to be a peculiarly modern one, adapted to modern prejudices.

Man has bred dogs for certain temperamental qualities

useful in the hunt—dogs like the Irish setter, for example. The Irish setter is always red-haired, but his red hair has no connection with his temperamental qualities. Yet his hair color is often used as a tag or label for his temperamental qualities. The Irish setter has the same kind of temperament as the English setter, but the hair color of the English setter is white-and-black. The only difference between white, black, white-*and*-black, and red setters lies in their coat color and not at all in their mental or temperamental qualities. No one ever asks whether there are temperamental differences between white, black, or brown horses; such a question would seem rather silly. But when it comes to man, the prejudice of anyone who has ever made the statement that skin color is associated with mental capacity is accepted as gospel. For such an assumption there is about as much justification as there would be for the assumption that there exist substantial mental differences between the differently colored varieties of setters. We know this to be false for setters *only* because we have paid more attention to the character of the mental qualities of dogs than we have to those of human beings. But those of us who have paid some attention to the character and forms of the mind of peoples belonging to different varieties of mankind and to different cultures have satisfied ourselves, by every scientific means at our disposal, that there exist no significant or demonstrable innately determined mental differences between the varieties of mankind. There is every reason to believe that such mental differences as we observe to exist between the different varieties of man are largely due to factors of a cultural nature, and are in no significant way related to biological factors.

A question often asked is: Why do the cultures of different varieties of man differ so considerably from our own? The answer is really quite simple. Cultures differ from one another to the extent to which their experience has differed. No matter with what variety of mankind we may be concerned, or with what groups of a particular variety, culture is in its broadest and fundamental sense not merely an aspect but a function of experience. By "experience" I mean anything that an individual or group of individuals has undergone or lived, perceived or sensed. The reason why the cultures of different varieties of man are so different from our own is that these varieties have been exposed to experiences which differ as considerably from our own as do the cultures in question. If you or I, with our present genetic background, had been born and brought up among a group of Australian aborigines, we should have been, culturally, Australian aborigines, though physically we would remain members of our own variety. For experience is determined by the place and culture in which groups and individuals live, and it is for this reason that groups and individuals belonging to different cultures will differ mentally from one another. Our physical structure would not have varied, because it was genetically determined by our present parents, but our cultural equipment would have been that of an Australian aboriginal. Why? Because culture—and by "culture" I understand social behavior and all its products—because culture is something which one acquires by experience, unlike one's physical appearance, which one acquires through the action, for the most part, of inherited genes. And the culture of individuals, as of groups, will differ according to the kinds of experience which they have undergone.

The culture of different peoples, as of different individuals, is to a very large extent a reflection of their past history or experience. This is a point which is worth more than laboring, for if the cultural status of any variety of man is merely determined by the kind of experience which it has undergone, then it is evident that by giving all people the opportunity to enjoy a common experience—supposing for the moment that this were desirable—all would become culturally and mentally equal; that is, equal in the sense of having benefited from exposure to the same kind of experience, always allowing, of course, for the fact that no two individuals can ever be alike in their reception and reaction to the same experience and that there will always, very fortunately, continue to be great differences between individuals. There can be very little doubt that genetic differences in temperament and intellectual capacity exist between the individuals comprising every variety of mankind, no two individuals in this respect ever being alike, but it takes the stimulus of a common experience to bring these out and to render them comparable.

It is because of differences in cultural experience that individuals and groups differ from one another culturally, and it is for this reason that cultural achievement is an exceedingly poor measure of the value of an individual or of a group. For all practical purposes, and until evidence to the contrary is forthcoming, we can safely take cultural achievement to be the expression merely of cultural experience. Obviously, all learned activities are culturally, and not biologically, determined, whether those activities be based upon instinctive urges or traditional practices. The generalized urges which all human beings in common inherit continue to be present in all human beings in all cultures, but how these urges are permitted to operate and how they are satisfied are things which are determined by tradition and which vary, not only in different cultures, but in different groups within the same culture. For example, one of the fundamental urges which we all inherit is the urge to eat. Now, different human groups to whom the same foodstuffs may or may not be available, not only eat different foods but prepare them in unique ways and consume them with or without implements in a variety of different styles, and usually for no better reason than that it is the customary practice to do so. The faculty of speech is biologically determined, but what we speak and how we speak is determined by what we hear in the culture in which we have been culturalized. Human beings everywhere, when they are tired, experience a desire to rest, to sit down, to lie down, or to sleep, but the manner in which they do all these things is culturally determined by the custom of the group in which they live. Many other instances will doubtless occur to the reader's mind. The point to grasp here is that even our fundamental biological urges are culturally controlled and regulated, or culturalized, and their very form and expression, not to mention their satisfaction, molded according to the dictates of tradition.

In view of the tremendous number of different cultural variables which enter into the structure and functioning of different groups and the individuals comprising them, it is surely the most gratuitous, as it is the most unscientific, of procedures to assert anything concerning assumed genetic conditions without first attempting to discover what part these cultural variables play in the production of what is predicated. Obviously, no statement concerning the mentality of an individual or of a group is of any value without a specification of the environment in which it has developed. The introduction of the *deus ex machina* of genetics to account for the cultural differences between people may be a convenient device for those who must do everything in their power, except study the actual facts, in order to find some sort of support for their prejudices, but it is a device which will hardly satisfy the requirements of an efficient scientific method. Such devices must be accepted in a charitable spirit as the misguided efforts of some of our misguided fellows to conceal the infirmities of their own minds by depreciating the minds of others, John Stuart Mill in his *Principles of Political Economy* (1848) put the stamp upon this type of conduct very forcibly when he wrote: "Of all the vulgar modes of escaping from the consideration of the effect of social and moral influences on the human mind, the most vulgar is that of attributing the diversities of conduct and character to inherent natural differences." While the number of people guilty of this vulgar error have greatly increased since Mill's day, the fraction of people who know it to be false has also greatly increased, and there is no need of despair for the future. The facts which are now available concerning the peoples of the earth render it quite clear that they are all very definitely brothers under the skin.

It would perhaps be too much to expect those who have been educated in the contrary belief to accept such a view, but the least we can do is to provide the children in our schools with an honest account of the facts instead of filling their guiltless heads with the kind of prejudices that we find distributed through so many of the books with which they are provided. Surely, a sympathetic understanding of people who behave "differently" and who look "different" cannot help but broaden one's horizons and lead to better human relationships all round? Socially, this is of course greatly to be desired, but it can hardly be said that much has yet been achieved in this direction. There is here, obviously, a great deal of work to be done.

But let us return to our main discussion, for, though school children and others have frequently heard of physical relativity, few if any children, and hardly any others, ever encounter the concept of cultural relativity. From the standpoint of the well-being and happiness of mankind the latter is a vastly more important conception to grasp than the former. By "cultural relativity" I mean that all cultures must be judged in relation to their own history, and all individuals and groups in relation to their cultural history, and definitely not by the arbitrary standard of any single culture as, for example, our own. Judged in relation to its own history each culture is seen as the resultant of the reactions to the conditions which that history may or may not record. If these conditions have been limited in nature, so will the culture reflecting their effects. If the conditions have been many and complex in character, then so will the culture be. Culture is essentially a relation which is the product of the interaction of two correlates, the one a plastic, adaptable, sensitive, biological being, the other simply experience. If we agree that mankind is everywhere plastic, adaptable, and sensitive, then we can account for the mental and cultural differences between the varieties of mankind only on the basis of a difference in experience. And this, when everything is taken into consideration, seems to be the true explanation of the mental and cultural differences which exist between the varieties of man. Let me give one or two examples of cultural relativity, as it were, in action.

Five thousand years ago the ancestors of the present highly cultured peoples of Europe were savages roaming the wilds of that continent. The ancestors of the modern Englishman were living in a Stone Age phase of culture, painting their bodies with woad and practicing all sorts of primitive rites, and culturally about equivalent to the Australian aboriginal —a state in which they continued for more than three thousand years until their discovery and conquest by the Romans in the first century of our era. Five thousand years ago, at a time when the kingdoms of Africa and the Babylonian empire were at their height, Europe was inhabited by hordes of savages. Babylon has long since passed into history, and the kingdoms of Africa have undergone comparatively little change; but five thousand years ago, and less, the natives of these great cultures could have looked upon the Europeans as savages equal to beasts and by nature completely incapable of civilization—and, hence, better exterminated lest they pollute the blood of their superiors! Well, whatever sins the Europeans have since committed, they have at least shown that given a sufficient amount of time and experience they have been capable of civilization to a degree not less than that to which Babylon and the kingdoms of Africa attained.

Here we have an example of cultural relativity. If we use time as our framework of reference and say "The Africans have had a much longer time than we have had to develop culturally as far as we have—why haven't they?" the answer is that time is not a proper measure to apply to the development of culture or cultural events; it is only a convenient framework from which to observe their development. Cultural changes which among some peoples have taken centuries to produce are among other peoples often produced within a few years. The rate of cultural change is dependent upon a multiplicity of different things, but the indispensable and necessary condition for the production of cultural change is the irritability produced by the stimulus of new experiences. Without the irritability of such new experience cultural change is exceedingly slow. Hence, if new experience is the chief determinant of cultural change, then the dimension by which we may most efficiently judge cultures is that of the history of the experience which has fallen to the lot of the cultures observed. In other words, to evaluate cultural events properly one must judge them by the measure of experience viewed through the framework of time. We of the Western world have packed more varieties of experience into the past two thousand years than has probably fallen to the lot of the Australian aborigines and other peoples throughout their entire history. Hence, any judgments of value we may attempt to make between our own culture and that of other peoples will be quite invalid unless they are made with due regard to the differences in the history of their experience. Bearing this cardinal principle in mind we shall be able to steer a clear course.

If, then, the essential physical differences between the varieties of mankind are limited to superficial characters such as skin color, hair form, and nose form, and the cultural and mental differences are due largely if not entirely to differences in experience, then from the sociobiological standpoint all the varieties of mankind must be adjudged as fundamentally equal; that is to say, biologically as good and as efficient as one another and, culturally, potentially equal. All normal human beings are everywhere born as culturally indifferent animals and they become culturally differentiated according to the social group into which they happen to be born. Some of the culturally differentiating media are neither as complex nor as advanced as others; the individuals developed within them will be culturally the products of their cultural group. As individuals they can no more be blamed for their cultural status than an isolated villager in any land can be blamed for the parochialism of his views. Culture, the culture of any group, is more or less determined by accidental factors which the group, as a group, has usually done little to bring about. The more advanced cultures have merely been luckier in the breadth of their experience and their contacts than the less advanced cultures.

Culturally, most people have solved the problems with which they have been confronted very satisfactorily—and the chief difference between a primitive and an advanced culture seems to lie in the number of problems which have been created and in the number and variety of the attempts made to solve them. Quantitatively, the number of problems with which the average individual in Western civilization has to grapple are far more numerous than those with which any member of a simpler society must deal, but it is doubtful whether he is for that reason to be regarded as a better human being than a member of a less advanced society. The average product of the Machine Age is hardly an achievement of which to be proud.

In judging cultures it is not so much the *quantity* of experience that matters as the *quality*. A little experience of the right quality is vastly more important for human happiness than a large amount of experience of the wrong quality. When the quantity begins to outstrip the quality there is a serious danger of quality going under altogether. We of the Machine Age are faced with such a danger. In spite of our enormous technological advances we are spiritually, and as humane beings, not the equals of the average Australian aboriginal or the average Eskimo; we are very definitely their inferiors. But stressing superficial differences between peoples only serves to maintain the illusion that there may be more fundamental differences behind them. What in truth and in justice requires to be done is to stress the fundamental kinship of all mankind, to stress the likenesses which we all bear to one another, and to recognize the essential unity in all mankind in the very differences which individuals of all ethnic groups display. Unity neither implies nor necessitates uniformity. It is important that human beings shall be united, but not that they shall be uniform. We must learn to recognize the all-importance of our common humanity and the triviality of the things that divide us. The world must be re-established as a vast co-operative community in which every ethnic group, every people, is freely permitted to give as well as to receive. Such an ideal will never be achieved by the continued misunderstanding of the meaning of those differences among peoples which are, in fact, the very marks of that strength which has enabled the human species to survive all the challenges of the environment to which it has thus far been exposed. We stand much in need of a broader, saner, more sympathetic utilization of those differences to strengthen each other even more fully, in living a fuller, a more varied, a more interesting, and a more peaceful life.

2

The Future of Man

WHEN WE SPEAK of the future of man I think it is his progress that we have mostly in mind and, as someone has remarked, the belief in progress is the wine of the present poured out as a libation to the future. The truth is that within man's new zone of adaptive evolution, namely what the anthropologist calls culture (that is, what remains of man's past working on his present to shape his future), change has been proceeding at such a rapid rate during the last fifty years that, as one wit remarked, even his future isn't what it used to be.

You have heard the definitions of an optimist and a pessimist, the optimist being defined as one who believes that this is the best of all possible worlds, and the pessimist as one who is very much afraid that the optimist is right. Now some wit has improved upon this for our own immediate times by defining an optimist as one who believes that the future is uncertain. There are, however, one or two things about man's future of which I think we can be certain. One is that things will not come out all right in the end if we merely sit by and let them happen. The other is that things will most probably

From symposium on *The Future of Man,* Joseph E. Seagram & Sons, Inc., Sept. 29, 1959, 27-31.

turn out well for man if he conscientiously works at the task of making them do so.

Virtually every great advance that man has made toward whatever humanity he has achieved has been at the cost of toil and sweat and persistence in the face of all discouragement. If we would insure the future of man, the present is the time to work for it, however discouraging the prospects may at the moment seem.

The first, most important, and most immediate end toward which we must work is the preservation of man. War must be outlawed forever. However gradually this end may be achieved, it is the necessary and sufficient condition of our continuing to be. Political or any other kinds of differences must be settled, not by force, but by humane discussion and mediation. It was Plato who said that civilization is the victory of persuasion over force. That was two thousand years ago.

As a student of man's evolution I view him as the most extraordinary of all nature's performances: a most improbable creature, brash and bright, a spoiled brat, in fact—full of promise, only a small part of which has been realized. Of this creature, because of his unique educability, it is possible to say as it is of no other that he is potentially capable of anything—but there's the rub. By virtue of the fact that man is born substantially without instincts and has developed into the creature most capable of learning, he has become adept at learning not only more sound things than any other creature but, by the same means, more unsound things than any other creature. The result of this is not intelligence but confusion.

The proper appellation for man as a species, from a classifier's point of view, is not that premature and rather oafishly arrogant definition of him that was offered by Linnaeus, namely *Homo sapiens,* the "wise guy"—but rather "Homo sap," for the dissonance of sound and unsound relations between symbols which reverberate in the pool of electrical circuits which serves him for a mind produces at one and the same time behavior that is both intelligent and unintelligent. We must frankly recognize, as Lord Bacon pointed out over three centuries ago, that truth grows more readily out of error than it does out of confusion.

The approach to this particular problem, it seems to me, must be through education; education conceived as the science —that is, the theory—and the art or practice of human relations, plus the ability to use one's mind critically. This would require a thoroughgoing revaluation of our present modes of instruction, which are too often confused with education. Education, in the only sense in which it can have a humane meaning, is nothing more nor less than the humane discipline of the whole person.

If we will labor in this direction I believe we may be confident of a happy outcome for man. But these words, as all others, will amount to no more than an ineffectual address to the supersonic layers of the atmosphere unless it is fully understood that the meaning of a word is the action it produces.

3

Anthropology and History

HISTORY IS MADE by man, and anthropology is the study of man's own history from his earliest origins to the present day. For the teacher of history, anthropology should be an indispensable study which will add depth and greater objectivity to his understanding and will arm him with facts and viewpoints which should assist him greatly in the teaching of his subject.

The anthropologist studies the history of each people as a self-consistent whole. One of the principal lessons learned by students of anthropology is that of cultural relativity, or the ability to evaluate the behavior and institutions of another people in terms of its own social organization without introducing the distortion of one's own biases as a member of a different culture. Each people must be understood in terms of its own history of experience and not that of the external observer. Anthropology shows why it is unsound to compare different peoples and their ways of life, their cultures, without first clearly comprehending the differences in the history of their experience. These are most valuable lessons for the teacher of world history. His ability to convey such lessons to his pupils may well play a substantial part in determining the future course of world events.

As a distinguished anthropologist has said, "Anthropology

holds up a great mirror to man and lets him look at himself in his infinite variety." It is an understanding of that infinite variety which, more than anything else, the world stands in need of today. In order to understand the nature of that variety it is necessary to understand the nature of man.

Why study the nature of human nature? For a variety of reasons: Because (1) When we understand the nature of man it becomes possible to distinguish those of his functions which are inborn from those which are acquired. It then becomes possible to answer such questions as: Are the achievements of different peoples due to innate differences, or to differences in the history of experience to which they have been exposed? What makes one people aggressive and another submissive? Are social differences within the same people based on natural or acquired conditions? Is war inevitable because war is an instinctive urge of man? (2) In the light of such understanding it becomes possible to eliminate misconceptions relating to the nature of human nature which give rise to false ideologies, international rivalries and conflicts, and political and social policies which are unsound, socially harmful, and personally disintegrating. (3) A correct view of human nature enables us to view the history of man in all his complex variety in deeper perspective, or dimensionally. At the present day the false views of human nature which are pretty universally held cause us to evaluate historical as well as contemporary developments in terms of our own narrow cultural bias rather than in the light of the dimensions of human nature. These dimensions are man's organic nature, the socialization provided by his human cultivators, and the history of experience undergone by his cultural group.

Up to the very recent present and the advent of modern anthropology the belief had grown that human nature differs racially, ethnically, nationally, and even among social classes of the same people. Hence, it became a simple matter to account for the differences in human nature. Since it was generally believed that "You can't change human nature," it became quite obvious that the peoples who had conquered others during the history of the world were "superior" to those whom they had defeated, and world history could be regarded as a continuation of natural history. This conception of human nature gained ascendancy in the nineteenth century with the rise—in the midst of the Industrial Revolution and a rampant imperialism—of the Darwinian theory of evolution and its doctrines of natural selection, "The Struggle for Existence," and "The Survival of the Fittest." Intellectually honest men and distinguished scientists could persuade themselves and others that the virtual enslavement of "the lower classes," the exploitation of the lands of "inferior peoples" and their eventual supplantation by the "white race," were not only biologically justifiable but the clear judgment of Nature, with a capital "N." In recent years we have witnessed the culmination of this belief in the tragic events which followed the rise of Hitler.

It is seen, then, that ideas concerning the nature of human nature are not of purely theoretical interest but that they have the most important bearing upon the actual lives and welfare of human beings everywhere. They determine public and national policies and the fate of millions of human beings.

Hence, let us consider briefly what the anthropologist has to say about human nature. Man is born with certain basic needs or physiological urges which must be satisfied if the organism is to survive. These needs are oxygen hunger, food hunger, thirst, sleep, bowel and bladder emptying, rest, activity, and the avoidance of pain. The way in which these needs are satisfied differs substantially in different cultures. In socializing the child each culture serves to organize the child's needs in such a way as to cause it to expect its satisfactions in a particular style and to fulfill its duties to others in the manner expected of it.

In the past the approach to the problem of the nature of man has been unsound. The question asked usually took the simple form, "What is the nature of man?" Instead, the correct phrasing of the question should be, "What is it that has been organized or built into man?" Man is the animal beyond all others that has been freed from biologically predetermined responses, and therefore must learn those responses which have so often been miscalled "human nature." Human nature is the pattern of responses which is inculcated in the organism by the tradition of the group through the agency of its parents and teachers. Allowing for the fact that organically the potentialities of no two individuals are ever quite the same, the basic pattern of responses which all individuals learn within any culture is recognizably similar and different from that which exists in all other cultural groups.

It is this variety in cultural conditioning which accounts for the different forms which human nature assumes in different cultures. Basically there are no significant differences in the organic potentialities of different groups of mankind. We must therefore conclude that so-called differences in human nature are in fact differences in second nature, the nature which is artificially developed in response to the stimulation of a particular kind of cultural experience. It will depend entirely upon the kind of socialization the child has undergone whether his human nature will be that of a Congo Pygmy or that of a Norwegian fisherman. Children of one ethnic group who are socialized in the milieu of another develop the nature peculiar to the group in which they have been socialized. There are many records of white children who were captured by American Indians and raised as Indians who became so completely Indianized that it was only by being informed of their origin that others even learned their real extraction. In the United States we observe Japanese-Americans becoming completely Americanized within a few generations, while Negroes have lost almost every bit of their African cultural heritage.

It should always be remembered that so far as human behavior is concerned the one thing natural to man is to be artificial—artificial in the sense that man's behavior is made up of learned acquired abstractions and motor activities intended to make him comfortable in the world in which he finds himself. Human nature, in short, is what man makes of man or, perhaps more accurately, what he makes of his children.

Many anthropological studies of nonliterate peoples—a phrase to be preferred to "primitive peoples," who are in fact not really primitive—are now available which are calculated to show how great differences in so-called human

nature are produced in adjacent cultures. There are two fundamental source books on this phase of the subject: Ruth Benedict's *Patterns of Culture* and Margaret Mead's *From the
South Seas*. Material from these two books could, perhaps, be
incorporated early in the course in the unit on prehistoric and
nonliterate peoples.

A second phase of the subject, which might be placed in
the same unit, should deal with the fact that certain basic
institutions are found among all human groups. Here two
books are indispensable, namely, Bronislaw Malinowski's
A Scientific Theory of Culture and George Murdock's *Social
Structure*. These works answer the questions: (1) What are
basic needs of man and how does culture arise out of their
satisfactions? and (2) What determines the nature of certain
basic human institutions, and what institutions are most often
found in clusters and why?

See bibliography at end of chapter for further reading on
the nature of man.

Why study the subject of race? Largely to clear up the
misconceptions which have mushroomed about the most dangerous myth of the twentieth century. Something called
"race" is generally conceived to be the prime determiner of
all the important traits of body and mind, of the character
and personality of human beings and nations. This something
called "race" is further believed to be a fixed and unchange-
able part of the germ plasm which, transmitted from generation to generation, unfolds in each people as a typical
expression of personality and culture. Since the creators of this
view of "race" belonged to the white branch of mankind, they
claimed that the white "race" was superior to all others. In
recent years, in pre-Hitlerian and in Hitler's Germany, it was
claimed that the German people belonged to an exceptionally
pure branch of the white race which had been largely responsible for most of the achievements of Western civilization. All of these claims are utterly false.

What should be put into our world history courses to clear
up these misconceptions? Three phases of this subject should
be considered, as follows:

1. All mankind is derived from a common ancestry and all

belong to the same single species *Homo sapiens*. There are four major groups of mankind: the Negroid, the Mongoloid, the Archaic Caucasoid, and the Caucasoid. These major groups number a large variety of different physical types which are better called "ethnic groups" rather than "races." The differentiation of these ethnic groups has been brought about by such factors as isolation, mutation of genes, random fixation of genes or genetic drift (i.e., the Sewall Wright effect), natural selection, hybridization, and possibly sexual selection.

Every ethnic group is much mixed. There never were and there are not now any "pure races." The history of man has, from the earliest times, been one of migration and intermingling. If we would understand what has happened in the ethnic history of mankind all we have to do is to look about us in the present. Every nation of the modern world is made up of a large number of intermingled ethnic elements. The most recent and possibly outstanding example of such a nation is the United States, wherein, with few exceptions, every ethnic group in the world is represented. The newly added state of Hawaii is a vivid contemporary example. Ancient Greece, Britain, France, Germany, Italy, and the modern countries of Latin America are well-documented examples of extensive ethnic intermingling.[1] From the standpoint of the biologist and the student of civilization, "race mixture" has had nothing but good effects upon man as an organism and as a civilized being.[2]

2. The differences between the varieties of mankind are minor, the likenesses major. The differences, for the most part if not entirely, represent adaptive changes which have been favored by natural selection. The likenesses are due to common ancestry. The evidence, as set out by Dobzhansky and myself, indicates that the one factor which has had the highest survival value in the evolution of man has been the general trait of plasticity or the ability to make more or less

[1] See the works of Romanzo C. Adams, Carleton S. Coon, Caroline B. Day, Aubrey Diller, Harry L. Shapiro, and Ashley Montagu for studies of "race mixture" both in the past and present.
[2] See the writings of William E. Castle and John L. Angel.

rapid adjustment to changing conditions, that is, to profit from experience and education. The effect of natural selection in man has probably been to render genotypic (hereditary) differences in personality traits in different ethnic groups relatively unimportant compared to their phenotypic (expressed or visible) plasticity.

In spite of innumerable investigations calculated to discover whether there exist any innate mental differences between the ethnic groups of man, all the evidence indicates that there are no such significant differences. Such differences as are found can usually be explained by differences in such conditions as culture, socio-economic environment, and the kind of schooling experience. For example, American Negroes living in the North generally rate significantly higher on intelligence tests than do Negroes living in the South. Army intelligence tests of World War I showed that the Negroes from certain Northern states did better on intelligence tests than the whites from many Southern states.

3. All ethnic groups have made contributions, of which any people could be justly proud, to the great common stock of human knowledge. Each ethnic group has made social discoveries and invented devices which through diffusion have spread to many other peoples and thus benefited them. Civilization is the product of innumerable different peoples. No one has a monopoly, for though a contribution may be originally the invention or discovery of one group, when it is adopted by other peoples it is usually improved and modified by the adopters. Important works giving much data on the origin and diffusion of inventions and discoveries by non-literate and other peoples are those of Herskovits, Linton, and Lips.

Those who wish to read further about race will find a bibliography at the end of the chapter.

Why study cultural mutations? Largely in order to clear up the misconception that modern man has made the great discoveries of history, and that only modern man (and particularly modern man from Western civilization) has been bright enough to make such discoveries or inventions. Emphasis should be placed on prehistoric times and on the two great cultural revolutions of those times: (1) the discovery of agriculture and the domestication of animals and (2) the urban revolution.

The planting, cultivation, and improvement by selection of edible grasses, roots, and trees, and the domestication of animals constituted the first great change in man's way of life since the beginning of his history. These discoveries made possible the increase of population which is still continuing today. It is obvious that a food-producing economy could support a much larger population than a food-gathering and hunting economy such as existed throughout the vast eras of the ice ages. The food-gatherer and hunter was a nomad. Food production and domestication of animals necessitated permanent settlement and thus the growth of villages. Greater leisure and new needs produced craftsmen who could make new and better tools such as the hoe, the plow, the loom, the spinning wheel, the wheeled cart, the sailing boat, and, finally, copper and bronze tools. "In no period in history," remarks Childe, "till the days of Galileo was progress in knowledge so rapid or far-reaching discoveries so frequent."

The second revolution in man's way of life followed naturally upon the development of the food-producing economy—namely, urbanization. Urbanization first developed in Egypt and Mesopotamia where the rainfall is low and the need for water therefore high. It was discovered that the flood waters of the Nile and of the Tigris and Euphrates rivers could be controlled and put to work. Irrigation canals and ditches could be dug and dikes and reservoirs built. Such projects required the co-operative labor of many people working together. Greater organization was soon required for control over the use of water. Population increased, and the city developed to accommodate the needs of an increasing population. Craftsmen and artisans were encouraged to specialize. Administrators, technicians, judges, priests, and many new officers were created in order to take care of the increased complexity of living in this new kind of world. Geometry, arithmetic, writing, astronomy, and the calendar gradually developed to meet the demands of the new economy. In brief, the fundamental discoveries and inventions upon which modern civilization is based were made by the peoples of the Near East several millennia before the dawn of the Christian era.

Invention and discovery depend upon the demands of an economy which is developing and which therefore requires new ideas and new instruments for dealing with new problems. Where there is no need, inventions and discoveries will either not be made or, if they are, they will not be used. Ancient Greece is a good example. The Greeks were superlatively good at almost everything but mechanical devices. Their lack of interest in machines was due to the fact that the Greek economy was based on slavery, the slaves supplying all the necessary energy for the requirements of that economy. Hence, while some ingenious machines were invented, they were treated rather as curiosities or playthings than as economically important contributions.

See the bibliography at the end of the chapter for further reading on the great cultural mutations of history.

Why study the nature of the barriers to our understanding of other civilizations? Because of the need to evaluate our own ideas in an objective manner in order to secure greater progress in satisfying the needs of mankind. Our minds are not open and we are unable to understand the viewpoints of other peoples. As a result we are unable to work out sound relations with them.

Mankind can be rescued from the effects of closed-mindedness by training in open-mindedness. The criteria of the open mind are alertness, interest in the ways in which people make up their minds, skill in analyzing the influence of one's personal interests, prejudices, and allegiances, and skill in the processes of critical thinking. The history teacher is in a strategic position to teach the methods and the advantages of open-mindedness by exemplification through his teaching.

One of the greatest barriers to our understanding of other peoples and civilizations is our own cultural bias or ethnocentrism. This is a fault which we share with every other people, and probably with every people that has ever existed. Every human group tends to regard itself, at least in some way, as superior to all others. This is not a natural or inborn trait but the result of group conditioning. The function of a truly civilized community should be to de-condition its members of such tendencies and to condition them to be interested in other peoples and to understand their values. What should be put into our world history courses to help students see cultural bias? Emphasis should be placed upon the history of our own values, their sources, and their development. The evidence should be given for the fact that our own system of values is based upon, and largely derived from, Assyrian, Hebraic, and Greco-Roman moral and secular codes, plus the modifications introduced by our own way of life. The interaction of these ways of life to form our own could be traced through ethical codes, legal systems, religions, and principles of government. The discovery, settlement, and conquest of America may serve as an excellent illustration of the way in which values become modified and substantially changed by the necessities involved in the pioneering of a new country and the development of a "frontier spirit," in this case "rugged American individualism." The emphasis upon "success" in our culture may be traced as an outgrowth of the immigrant pioneering spirit which causes parents to socialize their children "to do better" than their parents. Equality of opportunity for oneself becomes a dominant overt value, though covertly we believe in the inequality of opportunity and of men. The historical sources of these and other of our values should be fully explored.

Values are attitudes of mind. Values represent judgments as to the manner in which the best adjustment may be made to certain conditions. All peoples obviously must have values. It should be made clear that since the conditions of life—the history of each people—have differed, the value system of each people will therefore differ accordingly. Once this concept of historical or cultural relativity is grasped it becomes possible to understand *why* the values of other peoples differ from ours. This can best be demonstrated by showing how some other peoples got their values. Ruth Benedict's *Patterns of Culture* is invaluable here. Study of the great cultures outside Western civilization, those of China and India in particular, should most efficiently serve to develop a more balanced view of the quality and value of value systems other than our own.

All through the course the history teacher should emphasize the historically relativistic viewpoint, which causes one to look at things from other viewpoints and to examine them in the light of what we know about man's needs and the adaptations which under different conditions he makes to them.

The teacher can include some of the practical applications of anthropology during the last war as an example of ways in which cultural relativity can be of value in promoting understanding between peoples. Immediately prior to and during World War II the United States government called into its service many anthropologists for advice on our relations with other peoples. By placing in the hands of the army and the government written analyses of the value systems and the basic patterns of culture and personality of all the peoples with whom we were likely to have any relations, anthropologists greatly facilitated the handling of situations which would otherwise have been difficult. Anthropologists enabled our government officials, our intelligence service, and our armed men to understand and get along with people upon whom they had never previously set eyes and of whom they had no other experience than what they had read in their anthropological briefs.[3]

The following references will be of value for those who wish to read further:

THE NATURE OF MAN

Benedict, Ruth. *Patterns of Culture*. New York: New American Library, 1950.

Childe, V. Gordon. *Man Makes Himself*. New York: Oxford University Press, 1936.

Childe, V. Gordon. *What Happened in History*. New York: New American Library, 1946.

Gillin, John. *The Ways of Men*. New York: Appleton-Century, 1948.

Kardiner, Abram. *The Individual and His Society*. New York: Columbia University Press, 1939.

[3] Clyde Kluckhohn has a detailed description of these services.

Kluckhohn, Clyde. *Mirror for Man.* New York: Fawcett World Library, 1957.

Kluckhohn, Clyde, Murray, Henry A., and Schneider, D. M., editors. *Personality in Nature, Society, and Culture.* 2nd ed. New York: Knopf, 1953.

Linton, Ralph. *The Cultural Background of Personality.* New York: Appleton-Century, 1945.

Linton, Ralph, editor. *The Science of Man in the World Crisis.* New York: Columbia University Press, 1944.

Malinowski, Bronislaw. *A Scientific Theory of Culture.* Chapel Hill: University of North Carolina Press, 1944.

Mead, Margaret. *From the South Seas.* New York: Morrow, 1939.

Montagu, Ashley. *The Direction of Human Development.* New York: Harper, 1955.

Murdock, George P. *Social Structure.* New York: Macmillan, 1949.

Peckham, H. H. *Captured by the Indians.* New Brunswick: Rutgers University Press, 1954.

RACE

Adams, Romanzo C. *Interracial Marriage in Hawaii.* New York: Macmillan, 1937.

Angel, John L. "Social Biology of Greek Culture Growth," *American Anthropologist,* 48:493-533, 1946.

Castle, William E. "Biological and Social Consequences of Race Crossing," *American Journal of Physical Anthropology,* 9:145-146, 1926.

Castle, William E. "Race Mixture and Physical Disharmonics," *Science,* 71:603-606, 1930.

Coon, Carleton S. *The Races of Europe.* New York: Macmillan, 1939.

Day, Caroline B. *A Study of Some Negro-White Families in the United States.* Cambridge: Peabody Museum, Harvard University, 1932.

Diller, Aubrey. *Race Mixture Among the Greeks Before Alexander.* (Illinois Studies in Language and Literature, Vol. XX) Urbana: University of Illinois, 1937.

Dobzhansky, Th., and Montagu, Ashley. "Natural Selection and the Mental Capacities of Mankind," *Science,* 105: 587-590, 1947.

Herskovits, Melville J. *Man and His Works.* New York: Knopf, 1948.

Linton, Ralph. *The Study of Man.* New York: Appleton-Century, 1936.

Lips, Julius. *The Origin of Things*. New York: Wyn, 1947.

Montagu, Ashley. "The Intelligence of Northern Negroes and Southern Whites in the First World War," *American Journal of Psychology*, 68:161-188, 1945.

Montagu, Ashley. *An Introduction to Physical Anthropology*. 3rd ed. Springfield, Ill.: Thomas, 1960.

Montagu, Ashley. *Man's Most Dangerous Myth: The Fallacy of Race*. New York: 3rd ed. Harper, 1952.

Shapiro, Harry L. *Descendants of the Mutineers of the Bounty*. Memoirs of the Bernice P. Bishop Museum (Honolulu), Vol. IX, 1929.

CULTURAL MUTATIONS

Braidwood, Robert J. *Prehistoric Men*. 3rd ed. Chicago Natural History Museum, Popular Series, Anthropology Number 37, 1957.

Childe, V. Gordon. *The Dawn of European Civilization*. New York: Knopf, 1948.

Childe, V. Gordon. *Man Makes Himself*. New York: Oxford University Press, 1936.

Childe V. Gordon. *What Happened in History*. New York: New American Library, 1946.

Turner, Ralph. *The Great Cultural Traditions*. 2 vols. New York: McGraw-Hill, 1941.

CULTURE, CULTURE BIAS, AND PRACTICAL APPLICATIONS OF ANTHROPOLOGY

Benedict, Ruth. *The Chrysanthemum and the Sword*. Boston: Houghton Mifflin, 1946.

Benedict, Ruth. *Patterns of Culture*. New York: New American Library, 1950.

Gorer, Geoffrey. *The American People*. New York: Norton, 1948.

Kluckhohn, Clyde. *Mirror for Man*. New York: Fawcett World Library, 1957.

Mead, Margaret. *And Keep Your Powder Dry*. New York: Morrow, 1942.

Open-Mindedness Can Be Taught. Curriculum Office, Philadelphia Public Schools, 1949.

4

The Origin and Nature of
Social Life

T HE FINDINGS and ideas which I discuss in this chapter
have emerged from an inquiry calculated to throw some
light upon the manner in which the organism is turned
into a social human being. For the purposes of this study it was
necessary to inquire into the nature of social life in unicellular
as well as in multicellular organisms. At the outset of the
inquiry I had no idea where it would lead me, and the somewhat dramatic and altogether unexpected results have helped
me, as I hope they may help the reader, to a new understanding of the meaning of life, of man, and of religion. These findings provide us with a biological basis for religion and the
living of the good life. Their consequences for personal, group,
national, and international relations can hardly be exaggerated.

While definitions are meaningful at the end rather than at
the beginning of an inquiry, it may be of assistance at this
point to say that by "social" we generally mean all those
interactions between persons or groups in which needs are
satisfied, a need being understood as any desire of the organism. By "cultural" is meant the particular form or way

From *The Journal of Social Psychology*, vol. 29, 1949, 267-282.

of life which characterizes the social activities of a group. By "life" is meant that condition in which a body exhibits the functions of irritability (response to stimuli), motility (movement), and reproductivity (multiplication). An "organism" is that organization of interactive elements which displays the functions of life in a self-consistent manner.

It is a fairly well-established view that in the early stages of life upon this earth the only forms of life were represented by single-celled plant and animal organisms. In all these forms the single cell is a complete and self-supporting organism which performs all the necessary vital functions for itself by means of the differentiated parts of its protoplasmic body. The amoeba and paramecium are the most familiar examples of such unicellular organisms. These organisms always originate from a parent cell. In this fact, at this early stage, may be perceived the fundamental ground of social life in the origin of one cell from another, in the relation of a daughter cell to the parent cell in the process of budding-off or cleavage.

In amoeba reproduction is effected by simple fission of the parent body into another single cell; the plant cell haematococcus, which occurs in temporary pools of stagnant rain water or in the resting condition in dried-up mud or dust, multiplies itself by simple fission within the old cell wall, this process almost immediately resulting in the production of four new individuals (the same thing may happen in amoeba). Sometimes, however, another method of multiplication occurs in haematococcus. Instead of dividing into four relatively large zoospores, a restive individual may divide into thirty-two or sixty-four much smaller microzooids which differ from the ordinary active form in the absence of the characteristic cell wall and its underlying vacuole.

The microzooids freely swim about by means of their flagella and sooner or later come together in pairs, the members of each pair fusing with one another to form a single individual. This is an excellent illustration of sexual reproduction, the essential feature of which is the union or conjunction of two sexual cells or gametes (in this case the microzooids) to form a single cell, the zygote, which is the starting point of a fresh series of cell generations.

Whether reproduction or multiplication is secured by fission or by conjugation of gametes, the process is always an interacting one between the parent and the developing new organism. The parent organism supplies the vital tissues to the new organism and in the process of fission metabolic and other physiological exchanges occur before parent and daughter cells become organically independent of each other. This type of relationship in varying degrees is characteristic of all plant and animal life.

It is here suggested that the fundamentally social nature of all living things has its origin in this physiological relationship between parent and offspring, in the fact that the two are for a time bound together in an interactive association, in the fact that the life of either one or the other is at some time dependent upon the potential or actual being of the other. Thus, for example, when the amoeba has reached a certain size it can avoid death only by dividing, and this it does. The new organism is, at least during the period of division, entirely dependent upon the proper functioning of its parent. In this dependency, brief as it may appear to our senses, we may perceive the origins of infant dependency in the higher animals and the very obvious social and, particularly in man, cultural consequences of that dependent relationship. In short, the universal fact of reproduction and all that it implies is the foundation of the social relationship which characterizes all living organisms. Where the offspring are born in a helpless condition and their postnatal care is more or less extended we have a setting for the development of more complex forms of social life. As we have said, it is in the nature of the reproductive process that we see the basis for the development of social life, and the suggestion is that social life represents the response to organic drives, the expression of functions which are inextricably a part of the life of the organism. The universality of social life would seem to indicate as much.

No living organism is either solitary in its origin or solitary in its life. Every organism from the lowest to the highest is normally engaged in some sort of social life. The solitary animal is, in any species, an abnormal creature.

If the origin of social life owes its existence to the organic drives arising from and determined by the reproductive relationship, it is of more than passing interest to note that physically the multicellular organisms owe their origin to the same processes; that originally separate cells developed the habit of remaining attached together after division, as the spores in the encysted envelope of the parent amoeba might do to form a multicellular organism. Such an aggregation of cells would provide the means for the development of the multicellular higher animals. Such interactive cells would, by their increasing ability to co-operate, develop specialized functions and increasingly complex relations. The multicellular organism is therefore to be regarded as the expression of increasing intercellular co-operation in which the interdependent co-operating activities of its cellular masses function together so that at all times the organism is able to function as a unit and as a whole.

With the development of this interpretation of the facts we reach the view, not that society is an organism, which it is not, but that the organism is, in fact, a species of society. The organismal conception of society is today very generally discarded; yet, while the notion of society as an organism cannot be justified, a strong case can be made for the organism as a form of society. Every word in Cooley's definition of society,[1] for example, can be applied to the definition of an organism:

> Society is a complex of forms or processes each of which is living and growing by interaction with the others, the whole being so unified that what takes place in one part affects all the rest. It is a vast tissue of reciprocal activity, differentiated into innumerable systems, some of them quite distinct, others not readily traceable, and all interwoven to such a degree that you see different systems according to the point of view you take.

The system which a multicellular organism constitutes can also be so defined. But there is much more to human society

[1] Cooley, C. H. *The Social Process*. New York: Scribners, 1918 (p. 28).

than is stated in Cooley's definition, though that definition will do as a description of society in general. It will not do as a definition of human society in particular because it omits any explicit reference to the fact that human society represents a development of mind, of interactive consciousnesses and the complex of relationships to which these give rise, in a sense quite different from that which might be conceived as possessed by the individual or masses of cells which are the interactive elements which constitute the organism. The units constituting human society are free, those constituting the organism are, for the most part, fixed. The greater part of a society can be destroyed without causing the death of its remaining units, whereas under similar conditions death would generally follow in organisms. A person in human society exercises his will and his independent being in thought, feeling, and action. This is not the case with regard to the cells which make up the organism. All this is not to say that there is no relation between the society of the organism and human society, but simply that there is a very real difference between the two forms of society and that one must not be identified or confused with the other. The organismal analogy as applied to human society is quite false, but the relationship of the behavior of the cells which in interaction constitute the organism and human society is a phylogenetic one, and this is far from being false.

Whatever the nature of the factors involved in the co-operation of cells cohering to form functioning many-celled organisms, such co-operation does exhibit the elements of a social act. It would seem clear that such acts originally represent the expression of a drive which has its origin in the reproductive-dependency relationship of parent cell and daughter cell, and that the tendency of living things to form societies is coeval with life itself. Finally, it is clear that human society represents the culmination of this tendency and that in virtue of what seems to be the accident of the development of man's remarkable mental powers, his great plasticity, and freedom from biologically predetermined forms of behavior, human society has assumed a unique form; it has become highly culturalized.

The fact that such diverse groups as insects and mammals have developed social life indicates beyond any reasonable doubt the existence in organic life of deep-seated potentialities toward socialization or, rather, what might be more properly called "societization," the process of forming society.

Allee has presented the evidence which shows that among the simpler plants and animals there exists a sort of unconscious co-operation of automatic mutualism.[2] This is primarily reflected in their tendency to aggregate together, while the biological benefits which follow from their activities are exhibited in the significantly greater survival rate of organisms living in fairly dense populations than those living in sparse populations or in an environment in which they are isolated. Varying with the nature of the environment the isolated animal will, in general, be retarded in growth or irremediably damaged or suffer death, whereas the animal living in association with others will increase in size and in the speed of its physiological reactions, tend to recover quickly from wounds, and survive more often. Thus, planarian worms which have been exposed to ultraviolet radiation disintegrate more rapidly when isolated than when they are together with other worms. They survive exposure to ultraviolet radiation better when crowded while being radiated, and there is a much higher death rate among those which are isolated a few minutes after irradiation than among those which are left together. Goldfish placed together in groups of ten in a suspension of colloidal silver survive much longer than those which are placed in similar suspensions alone. Allee writes: [3]

> When exposed to the toxic colloidal silver the grouped fish shared between them a dose easily fatal for any one of them; the slime they secreted changed much of the silver into a less toxic form. In the experiment as set up the suspension was somewhat too strong for any to survive; with a weaker suspension some or all of the grouped animals would have lived; as it was, the group gained for its members a longer life. In nature they could have had many more minutes for rain to

[2] Allee, W. C. *Animal Aggregations*. Chicago: University of Chicago Press, 1931; and *The Social Life of Animals*. New York: Norton, 1935.
[3] Allee, *The Social Life of Animals* (pp. 56-57).

have diluted the water or some other disturbance to have cleared up the poison and given the fish a chance for complete recovery.

This experiment illustrates in the case of these goldfish, and presumably holds true for all other aquatic organisms, the physicochemical basis of the advantage which lies in numbers. Allee's studies on the rate of cleavage of the fertilized egg of the common sea urchin *Arbacia* show that, with few exceptions, the rate is more rapid in the denser clusters of eggs than in isolated fellow eggs. Protozoans, it has been experimentally shown, grow more rapidly when they are introduced in large numbers into a sterile medium of relatively simple salts than if the cultures are started with only a few organisms. The biological advantages are all in the crowding, not overcrowding, while separation or isolation would appear to be so lethal to the organism that we can be fairly certain that it never occurs in nature. What an optimal population size for different groups in nature is will depend upon the group and its environment, but thus far the evidence strongly indicates that optimal numbers present in a given situation have certain positive survival values and positively exert stimulating effects on the growth of individuals and the increase of populations. Thus, for example, Darling [4] has found that among herring gulls the members of larger colonies stimulate each other to commence sexual activities earlier than when the colonies are smaller and, furthermore, there tends to be a speeding-up of egg-laying, so that breeding activities are more intense while they last. The survival value of the short spread of time between laying and hatching lies in the fact that a greater number of young gulls survive under such conditions than do so where the colony is small and the spread of hatching time therefore longer.

The unconscious kind of mutualism or co-operation which universally exists among lower animals not commonly regarded as social or viewed only as partially social undoubtedly represents an earlier stage in the development of social life among the higher animals. It is important to understand in

[4] Darling, E. F. *Bird Flocks and the Breeding Cycle.* Cambridge: University Press, 1938.

its full implications the fact that this principle of mutualism, of co-operation, is the fundamental principle which appears to have governed the relations of organisms from the very first. The organic basis for this, the explanation which best fits the facts, would appear to lie in the nature of the reproductive relationship, with the accompanying mutual interrelations which are for a time maintained between parent and developing organism. Whatever truth there may be in this, it is certain that the conception of nature "red in tooth and claw," in which animals are conceived to be in a constant state of warfare with one another, in which the "struggle for existence" and "the survival of the fittest" are the two cardinal principles of "natural selection," is grossly one-sided and false. Activities which may collectively be called the struggle for existence do characterize the behavior of most animals, but such activities are not all that characterizes their behavior, the two forms of behavior complementing rather than being in opposition to one another. In what might be called the tough Darwinian period of the last century the concept of natural selection in its crude form so completely dominated the thought of biologists and Spencerian sociologists—and practically every sociologist was a Spencerian in those days— that the existence of co-operative behavior on a large scale, though known to some biologists and certainly well understood by Darwin, was virtually completely neglected in favor of the quite properly regarded important principle of natural selection.

Darwin's great book, published in November, 1859, was entitled *On the Origin of Species by Means of Natural Selection, or The Preservation of Favoured Races in the Struggle for Life*. And that essentially is what throughout the last forty years of the nineteenth century most biologists were engaged in proving. The voices which were raised in defense of co-operation were drowned out in the din created by the one-sided proponents of natural selection. It was not that the natural selectionists denied the existence of co-operation but that they passed it by and neglected it in favor of natural selection. The extreme viewpoint of the natural selectionists was stated by that great man, T. H. Huxley, in 1888 in his "struggle for life" manifesto, *The Struggle for Existence and Its Bearing Upon Man* (*Nineteenth Century*, February, 1888). The reply made by Prince Petr Kropotkin in eight articles published between the years 1890 and 1896 in the pages of the *Nineteenth Century*, and in 1902 published in book form as *Mutual Aid, a Factor of Evolution*, made, and has steadily continued to make, a deep impression upon all who read it. It succeeded in drawing attention to substantial works which had already dealt with the subject and in focusing attention upon an important and much underrated factor in evolution. Giddings, in *The Principles of Sociology*, was the first sociologist to emphasize the importance of co-operation in evolution. Among English publicists Henry Drummond, for example, chose for his Boston Lowell Lectures, published in 1894 as *The Ascent of Man*, the exposition of the thesis that while in nature there was a struggle for life there was also such a thing as the struggle for the life of others. A goodly number of works having the same theme for their subject have been published since the beginning of the century.

At the present time the principle of co-operation is in a fair way to becoming established as the most important factor in the survival of animal groups. Summing up the modern point of view Allee says: [5]

> After much consideration, it is my mature conclusion, contrary to Herbert Spencer, that the coöperative forces are biologically the more important and vital. The balance between the coöperative and altruistic tendencies and those which are disoperative and egoistic is relatively close. Under many conditions the coöperative forces lose. In the long run, however, the group-centered, more altruistic drives are slightly stronger.
>
> If coöperation had not been the stronger force, the more complicated animals, whether arthropods or vertebrates, could not have evolved from simpler ones, and there would have been no men to worry each other with their distressing and biologically foolish wars. While I know of no laboratory experiences that make a direct test of this problem, I have come to this conclusion by studying the implications of many experiments which bear on both sides of the problem and

[5] Allee, W. C. "Where Angels Fear to Tread; a Contribution from General Sociology to Human Ethics." *Science*, 97, 1943 (pp. 518-525).

from considering the trends of organic evolution in nature. Despite many known appearances to the contrary, human altruistic drives are as firmly based on an animal ancestry as is man himself. Our tendencies toward goodness, such as they are, are as innate as our tendencies toward intelligence; we could do well with more of both.

The tendentious habit of thinking of evolution in terms of the struggle for existence, by means of which, it is believed, the fittest are alone selected for survival while the weakest are ruthlessly condemned to extinction, is not only an incorrect view of the facts but is a habit of thought which has done a considerable amount of harm. Only by omitting any reference to such an important evolutionary force as the principle of co-operation and by viewing evolution as a process of continuous conflict between all living things can men be led to conclude that survival or development depends on successful aggression. Omitting important facts and basing their arguments on false premises the tough Darwinians could only arrive at false conclusions. As Allee says, "Today, as in Darwin's time, the average biologist apparently still thinks of a natural selection which acts primarily on egoistic principles, and intelligent fellow thinkers in other disciplines, together with the much-cited man-in-the-street, cannot be blamed for taking the same point of view."

Certainly aggressiveness exists in nature, but there is also a healthy nonruthless competition, as well as very strong drives toward social and co-operative behavior. These forces do not operate independently but together as a whole, and the evidence strongly indicates that of all these drives the principle of co-operation is the most dominant and biologically the most important. The coexistence of so many different species of animals throughout the world is a sufficient testimony to the importance of that principle. It is probable that man owes more to the operation of this principle than to any other in his own biological and social evolution. Indeed, without this principle of co-operation, of sociability and mutual aid, the progress of organic life, the improvement of the organism, and the strengthening of the species become utterly incomprehensible.

We may, by induction from the facts, arrive at a generalization or law to the effect that the greater the co-operative behavior exhibited by the members of any group the more thoroughly socially organized is that group likely to be. The social ants constitute an interesting example of this law, for in them the principle of co-operation has been developed to the limit of fixity. But, as Schneirla [6] has suggested, it is perhaps more accurate to speak of *biosocial facilitation* rather than of co-operation here because of the psychological limitations of social ants. The distinction is, however, simply one of organization at qualitatively different levels. The principle of co-operation has been resumed by a group of distinguished biologists [7] in the statement that the probability of survival of individual or living things increases with the degree in which they harmoniously adjust themselves to each other and to their environment. A. E. Emerson [8] has concluded that the dominant directional trend in evolution is toward a controlled balance of the important factors within the system. "Human society co-operatively brings the social environment under control for the better survival of the species."

If we would seek for one word which describes society, or the social, better than any other, that word is co-operation. The important point to grasp here is that contrary to the beliefs of the struggle-for-survival school of thought man does not have to create a co-operative mood for himself to erect over the tufa of his savage strivings to be otherwise; not at all. The impulses toward co-operative behavior are already present in him at birth and all they require is cultivation. As for any other kind of strivings, the infant of most vertebrates is equipped with the ability to compete with the universe for attention, and it generally succeeds in eliciting co-operative behavior, usually from one or both parents. In the process of socialization a certain quantity of the energies of aggressiveness are transformed into co-operative processes.

[6] Schneirla, T. C. "Problems in the Biopsychology of Social Organization." *Journal of Abnormal and Social Psychology*, 41, 1946.

[7] Leake, Chauncey. "Ethicogenesis." *Proceedings of the Philosophical Society of Texas*, 10, 1944.

[8] Emerson, A. E. "The Biological Basis of Social Cooperation." *Illinois Academy of Sciences Transactions*, 39, 1946 (pp. 9-18).

The reproductive process is a co-operative one and, in addition, development as one of a litter or group of siblings represents another early experience in the development of co-operation. Development within a family represents a still further experience in the learning and practice of co-operation.

To summarize briefly the points thus far: (1) some sort of social life is present in even the lowest organisms and such a thing as a completely asocial variety of animal probably does not exist; (2) social life confers distinct advantages, biological and social, upon the animals participating in it; (3) the dominant principle of social life is probably coeval with life itself, otherwise it could not have become established; and (4) the organic basis of social behavior is to be found in the nature of the reproductive relationship between parent and offspring.

Consider the reproductive process and all that it implies. Reproduction is based on interaction and interrelationships of an interdependent kind, and these determine the pattern of dependency of one organism upon another. Furthermore, continuity of substance and physiological function is thus established between parent and offspring, and this implies the continuity of all living things. Our kinship is with the whole world of life. That kinship demands that we fulfill our natural obligations to our more lowly relations in sympathy and understanding, recognizing that we are all of the same remote origin, merely different forms of the same world-stuff.

Is it not a remarkable fact that the reproductive process which is concerned with the creation of life itself should constitute the fundamental social relationship? Yet nothing could be more appropriate. The pattern is determined by the fact that the maternal and fetal organisms are for a time bound together in interacting association, and the fetus is entirely *dependent* upon the maternal organism for its sustenance, for the satisfaction of its needs. In the uterus the process proceeds largely upon the vegetative level. But at birth the dependent relationship becomes more active and complex, both on the part of the newborn and the maternal organism or its substitute. The dependency of the newborn is a continuation of the dependency of the fetus; the dependency of the child and adult is a continuation of the dependency of the infant, a dependency which has its origin in the once inseparable connection between the organism and that other organism out of which it developed.

Dependency may be defined as the relation of the organism to the conditions which support it. In the newborn it is doubtful whether dependency is experienced as anything more than a generalized, diffused tonal state related to its more specific urges, satisfactions, and dissatisfactions. The generalized dependency state never assumes a definite form in the absence of socializing agents, as is testified by the complete failure of development of personality in isolated children. To be dependent means to rely upon some other organism or organisms for the satisfaction of one's needs. The consciousness of a distinct feeling of dependency cannot be developed in the absence of factors which produce a growing awareness in the infant that practically all his satisfactions are obtained through the responses made to his basic needs by other persons. Such an awareness is, as it were, a precipitate of recurring experiences of unsatisfied cravings which have eventually been satisfied by others but for whose intervention those cravings would never have been satisfied. The child learns that it is dependent and the whole of its social training teaches it, in effect, to become more and more dependent. Interdependency is the social state. Nondependent individuality is the nonsocial state.

The need for love simply represents the growth of a condition originating in the impulses of the dependency state. These impulses are developed by those who help to give greater form to the dependent state by satisfying the infant's needs. The infant loves those who satisfy its needs. It hates those who fail to satisfy or who frustrate the satisfaction of its needs. In this latter sense one may readily see that hatred is but love frustrated.

The process of caring for the infant consists principally in satisfying its needs. This process represents the commencement of the socialization of the person, the preparation of the person for participation in the social group. To telescope much into a few words, as the child matures and the socializing process continues, with its frustrations as well as its satisfactions, the child becomes more and more firmly bound to the socializing agent, more and more dependent rather than more free, and this social binding continues throughout life. This view of the development of the person cannot be too strongly emphasized, particularly in a land in which the myth of rugged American individualism still prevails. The conventional view of the person in the socializing process as developing to greater and greater individuality is a seriously misleading one.

Of course, every person has a unique personality in the sense that it is never identically like that of any other person, and the differences between personalities are important and valuable and tend to become more distinct with age. This is something very much to be thankful for. But it must be realized that every one of these differences has developed under the influence of socializing factors and that, were it not for the creative action of those socializing factors, those functional-structural differences, the pattern of psychic differences which characterizes each person would not exist. The "individual" is a myth. A creature apart from a social group is nothing but an organic being. The member of a social group is a *person*, a personality developed under the molding influence of social interstimulation. The person is a set of social relationships.

The "rugged American individualist" is no more an individualist than is a soldier sniping at the enemy. Both behave as they do because they have been subordinated to imperatives which in each case represent functions of their social conditioning. They act as they do because they are the results of certain historically conditioned social processes. They act as they do, not because they are independent individuals, but because they are dependent persons bound to their social group by ties which cause them to desire to maintain their relationships in that group in the manner, in each case, allowed and encouraged by the group. Free will the person has and is constantly exercising, but it is a freedom and a will which acts strictly within the limits determined by the pattern of the social group. In short, the person is an interdependent system of social relationships which may by abstraction alone be recognized as a unit, as an individual. As Leo Loeb [9] has remarked in a masterly work, "In consequence of the more and more intricate interaction between environment and psychical-social individuality, a separation between individuality and environment, especially the social environment, becomes impossible."

That is the truth which must forever shatter what I insist on calling the pathetic fallacy, the organismal fallacy which maintains that man is essentially a function of his genes. The biologically exclusive sacredness of the individual is a chimera not only for man but for all other animal groups. The biology of an earlier day may have cried "the individual for itself." To this the most distinguished of living physiologists, Sir Charles Sherrington, has made the proper reply in one of the great books of our time: [10]

> The individual? What are the most successful individuals which Life has to show? The multi-cellular. And what has gone to their making? The multi-cellular organism is in itself a variant from the perennial antagonism of cell and cell. Instead of that eternal antagonism it is a making use of relatedness to bind cell to cell for co-operation. The multi-cellular organism stood for a change, in so far, from conflict between cell and cell to harmony between cell and cell. Its coming was, we know now, pregnant with an immense advance for the whole future of life upon the globe. It was potential of the present success of living forms upon the planet. Implicit in it was for one thing the emergence of recognizable mind. It was among the many-celled organisms that recognizable mind first appeared. It is surely more than mere analogy to liken to those small beginnings of multi-cellular life of millions of years ago the slender beginnings of altruism today. Evolution has constantly dealt with the relation between physical and mental as more than mere analogy. The bond of cohesion now arising instead of being as then one of material contact and interchange between related cell-lives is in its nature mental. It is a projection of the self by sympathy with other life into organismal situations besides its immediate own.

[9] Loeb, L. *The Biological Basis of Individuality.* Springfield, Ill.: Thomas.
[10] Sherrington, C. *Man on His Nature.* New York: Macmillan, 1941.

It is altruism as passion. It marks, we may think, at the present time the climax of mind.

To bind cell to cell for co-operation, that is the essence of social life. No cell is more intimately bound to another than man is to his fellows and his social group. The binding of the individual to his group represents, in fact, a loss of individual freedom and a gain in personal freedom through more or less complete identification with the social group—an identification in which the wholeness of the person is preserved only because it is a functioning part of a greater whole, society. In this process the consciousness of self may actually increase, the sense of personal identity may become even more vivid, and one's bondage to one's society more firmly established than ever. "Individuation" as the development of personal identity is neither the contrary nor the contradictory of social identification. It *is* social identification.

As Robert Frost has written:

> "Men work together," I told him from the heart,
> "Whether they work together or apart."

The organism becomes a person with a definite identity only through the process of socialization, the process of becoming identified with a social group. The physiological dependency of the fetus and the newborn becomes, in society, a socially organized dependency, a social dependency in which the interacting person finds the meaning of his life in his relations with other persons and their thoughts and activities. Unheeded, the physiologically dependent infant would die. Unheeded, the socially dependent adult falls into an apathy which may lead to death.

The prolonged period of infant dependency in man produces interactive behavior of a kind which within the first two years of the child's life determines the primary pattern of his subsequent social development. It is within this period that he learns to love others: the mother who has so consistently, intimately, and lovingly attended to his needs; the father, his brothers and sisters, and whoever else has participated in the process of satisfying his needs. Certain persons become to him the symbols of satisfaction, for they are always the objects which provide him with the means of satisfaction. The first conditioning which the child undergoes is this: persons who have fairly consistently been the objects which have provided the infant with the means of satisfying its needs now become satisfying objects in themselves. The satisfaction of its basic needs become indissolubly associated in the infant's mind with persons who have become linked with those satisfactions. The mother is, of course, normally the principal producer of satisfactions and she becomes the first love object of the child. In this sequence of events can be seen the determinants, as it were in high relief, of the pattern of life which every person everywhere seeks to secure, namely, a state of dependency in which one's needs are satisfied by persons whom one (therefore) loves. What human beings desire most of all is to have their needs satisfied, that is, security. They also want to feel dependent, either upon some mother-ideal, a deity, or other persons, or narcissistically upon themselves, but dependent they must feel. Man does not want to be independent, to be free in the sense of functioning independently of the interests of his fellows, free and detached. This kind of negative independence leads to lonesomeness, isolation, and fear. What man wants is that positive freedom which follows the pattern of his life as an infant within the family, dependent security, the feeling that one is part of a group, accepted, wanted, loved, and loving, the positive freedom which makes the development of the person emphatically a matter of personal realization in terms of his membership in the social group in the mutual interest of the person and of society, the opportunity to develop interdependently, not as an "individual," but as a person.

It is when men erroneously begin to think that they can be independent of one another, the "social isolationists," that they begin to frustrate and hate each other, that they do violence to all that they are and create much psychological and social havoc. When men learn to understand how dependent they are upon one another, that they are interdependent beings in a great co-operative enterprise, that it is their nature to be affectionate, co-operative persons, when they understand that being anything else is to be in conflict with themselves and therefore with society, mankind will be a great deal healthier and happier than it is today.

We now know that if a child is inadequately loved it will develop as an inadequate social being. Not only this, we know that the organism is born with an innate need for love, with a need to respond to love, to be good and co-operative. Were the infant's needs adequately satisfied he could not help but be good, that is, loving. All of man's natural inclinations are toward the development of goodness, toward the continuance of states of goodness and the discontinuance of unpleasant states.

The biological basis of love consists in the organism's drive to satisfy its basic needs in a manner which causes it to feel secure. Love *is* security. Mere satisfaction of basic needs is not enough. Needs must be satisfied in a particular manner, in a manner which is emotionally as well as physically satisfying. Babies as well as adults cannot live by bread alone.

It is in the organism's ever-present urge to feel secure that social life has its roots, and the only way in which this need can be satisfied is by love. It is a discovery of the greatest possible significance for mankind that the ethical conception of love independently arrived at by almost all existing peoples is no mere creation of man but is grounded in the biological structure of man as a functioning organism. The implications of this discovery are of the very greatest importance, for it means that man's organic potentialities are so organized as to demand but one kind of satisfaction, a satisfaction which ministers to man's need for love, which registers love, which is given in terms of love, a satisfaction which is defined by one word—*security*. This is what the person seeks all his life, and society, culture, and man's institutions, however inefficient some of them may be, all exist to secure that one fundamental satisfaction. The emotional need for love is as definite and compelling as the need for food. The basic needs of man must be satisfied in order that he may function on the organic level. But in order that he may function satisfactorily on the social plane, the most fundamental of the basic needs must be satisfied in an emotionally adequate manner for personal security or equilibrium.

To conclude, then, we see that the biological basis of co-operation has its origins in the same sources as social behavior, namely in the process of reproduction, and that social, co-operative behavior is simply the continuation of the maternal-offspring relationship. Co-operative, social behavior is therefore as old as life itself, and the direction of evolution has, in man, been increasingly directed toward the fuller development of co-operative behavior. When social behavior is not co-operative it is diseased behavior. The dominant principle which informs all behavior which is biologically healthy is love. Love, social behavior, co-operation, and security mean very much the same thing. Without love there can be no healthy social behavior, co-operation, or security. To love thy neighbor as thyself is not simply a good text for Sunday morning sermons but perfectly sound biology.

At a period in the history of the world in which men have turned their faces against each other, instead of turning the other cheek, these truths need to be cried aloud from every citadel of learning. Men who do not love one another are sick. They are sick, not from any sickness arising within themselves, but from a sickness which the malorganization of their societies has thrust upon them. The belief in false values, in competition instead of co-operation, in class and race and national prejudice instead of love, in narrow selfish interests instead of altruism, in atomism (especially atom-bombism) instead of universalism, in the value of the dollar instead of the value of man, represents social man turning upon all that is biologically good in him.

Science shows us that the way to survival and happiness for all mankind is through love and co-operation, that do what we will our drives toward goodness are as biologically determined as are our drives toward breathing. Our highly endowed potentialities for social life have been used to pervert and deny their very nature, and this has led us close to the brink of disaster, a disaster which spells doom unless we realize what we have done and take the proper steps to undo it before it is too late. For we cannot deny the power of the world forces which we share with all life and which have reached their highest development in our potentialities as human beings without destroying ourselves.

Our world at the present time is still imperiled by criminally irresponsible adventurers and cynical and complacent men who have grown old in the ways of self-interest and ultranationalism. Unless they are replaced by men of understanding and humility whose guiding principle is love, the world will remain precariously poised upon the very edge of doom.

The life of every human being is a part of our own, for we are involved in mankind and each one of us in the Western world has become a problem in search of a solution. We now know the answer to the problem. It is up to us to make it known and to apply it. In the immortal words of John Donne, a minister of the gospel of the first recorded discoverer of these truths:

> No man is an *Island,* entire of itself; every man is a piece of the *Continent,* a part of the *main;* if a *Clod* be washed away by the *Sea, Europe* is the less, as well as if a *Promontory* were, as well as if a *Manor* of thy *friends* or of *thine own* were; any man's *death* diminishes *me,* because I am involved in *Mankind;* And therefore never send to know for whom the *bell* tolls; It tolls for thee.

5

"Wolf Children"

I N 1941 PROFESSOR ARNOLD GESELL of the Clinic of Child
Development, Yale University, published a book entitled
Wolf Child and Human Child, Being a Narrative Inter-
pretation of the Life History of Kamala, the Wolf Girl. A few
months later, in 1942, Professor Robert M. Zingg, then of the
University of Colorado, published a book entitled *Wolf-*
Children and Feral Man, his coauthor being J. A. L. Singh.

These two books at once brought to the attention of the
public the existence of the first "authenticated wolf children,"
children who had been, so it was claimed, raised by wolves.
During the twenty years since the advent of the wolf children
was announced to the world, these children have steadily crept
into the literature on all fours as genuine examples of human
beings raised by animals.

The story of Kamala and Amala, the wolf children of Godamuri or of Midnapore, constitutes an interesting study in
scientific credulity. Very briefly, two children were claimed
to have been repeatedly seen by natives and other villagers
emerging together with several wolves from the ant-hill den
of the said wolves. The Reverend J. A. L. Singh states that,
while traveling in the company of two Anglo-Indians who
were witnesses to the event, he captured or liberated the two

From the *American Anthropologist,* n.s., vol. 45, 1943, 468-472.

children from the wolves' den at Godamuri on October 17,
1920. At the time of their rescue, or liberation, the younger
child was guessed to be about eighteen months old. She was
given the name Amala. The older child was estimated to be
about eight years of age, and was named Kamala. It is assumed that both children were about six months of age when
taken by the wolves, and that they were stolen from different
families. Amala died on September 21, 1921, while Kamala
died November 14, 1929. Thus Amala was observed for almost a year and Kamala for nine years.

When first observed, Kamala and Amala were unable to
stand in the erect position but habitually progressed on all
fours. They ate raw meat and entrails in what is alleged to
have been wolf fashion, were without sphincter control,
howled like wolves, preferred the society of dogs to that
of human beings, and exhibited other feral traits. They were
entirely without speech and all those other attributes which
we have come to regard as specifically human.

In *Wolf-Children and Feral Man* Dr. Robert Zingg makes
available an account of the history of these children written
by the Reverend J. A. L. Singh based upon the records which
the latter kept while the children were under his own and
his wife's observation in their orphanage at Midnapore. In the
second part of the work Dr. Zingg discusses the subject of
feral man in general and records a number of cases of extreme isolation of children in particular, the latter for their
own interest and also in order to serve as checks against the
description of the behavior of the "wolf children." There are
forewords by Professors R. Ruggles Gates, Arnold Gesell,
Francis N. Maxfield, and Kingsley Davis, each attesting his
belief in the genuineness of the discovery and the account
of the children as given by the Reverend Singh. A preface
by Bishop H. Pakenham-Walsh, together with an affidavit by
the District Judge of Midnapore, E. Waight, to both of whom
the Reverend Singh was well known, testifies to his good
character and reliability and their belief in the truth of his
account of the discovery of the "wolf children."

Let me say that having read the volume very critically I
find that despite certain difficulties, the Reverend Singh's

account of his discovery and observations has an impressive ring of authenticity about it. The writer impresses me as a naive but honest person who records his observations frankly, while even those which seem to belong to the realm of folk-lore, rather than to that of sober fact, read quite as convincingly as those which do not seem to be either a little east or a little west of the truth.

But when all this has been said, it must regretfully be added that this account of the "wolf children" cannot be accepted as true. I say "regretfully" for several reasons. Firstly, because I should very much like to believe the greater part of this story since it appears to fit into the general theory of personal social development fairly well, and we should at long last have at least one authentic case of children reared by animals with which to support our theories. Secondly, because I have a private Franciscan belief in the fellowship of man with all nature which I should like to have seen supported by so striking an instance. But as Mr. Peck-sniff would have said, "Facts is facts." And the facts in this book, alas, rest on the completely unsupported testimony of one person, the Reverend Singh. Now, however much and however sympathetically we might be inclined to put our trust in his word, no scientist can accept as true any statement of a fellow scientist or the statement of anyone else until it has been independently confirmed by others. Such confirmation is altogether wanting in the present case, and that being so, with all the good will in the world and in spite of all the prefaces and forewords by learned professors, bishops, and magistrates, we cannot accept as true the story of the discovery of the "wolf children" and their presumed rearing by wolves.

The process of verification and confirmation is a cardinal principle of scientific method, the method of arriving at scientifically supportable results. Whether or not children have been reared by animals can be determined only by observation not necessarily premeditated and carried out under conditions which provide the means of verification. Hundreds of stories and legends say that they have been so reared, and the investigation of these stories constitutes a legitimate and scientific activity. Dr. Zingg has been interested in examining such stories for some time, with not altogether happy results. It seems to me that in the present volume he is not so much concerned with an impartial examination of the evidence as with insisting upon one interpretation of it. I regret to have to say this because I have every sympathy for the enthusiast, and it is quite understandable that once having become enamored of a story one might be carried away by it. But this is just the sort of thing against which even the best of scientists must continually be on his guard. Even scientific structures are sometimes erected on emotional foundations. Emotionally I am in favor of the Singh-Zingg & Co. story; as a scientist I cannot accept it.

Even if the whole story were better authenticated, here are a few points which would cause me to make some reservations:

Two Anglo-Indians, a Mr. P. Rose and a Mr. Henry Richards, are said by the Reverend Singh to have witnessed the rescue of the children from the wolves' den, but unfortunately the former is now untraceable and the latter is dead. Why, during all the years that the Reverend Singh was studying the children, did he make no attempt to obtain statements from these and other men who were present at the alleged rescue? Neither Mr. Rose nor Mr. Richards ever came forward to avow or disavow the Reverend Singh's story.

Kamala is presumed to have been kept in the wolves' den for about seven and a half years. But wolves do not keep their young for anything like so long a period under normal conditions. Is it likely that they would have departed from the universal practice of wolves in the case of Kamala?

Could a six-month-old child be suckled by a wolf? It is, no doubt, possible, but it is difficult to imagine why a wolf should want to do such a troublesome thing.

Even if the statement were fully corroborated that the children were found together with the wolves in their den, that in itself would not constitute evidence that they were brought there by wolves nor that they had been suckled and reared by them.

The Reverend Singh states that Kamala and Amala used

to howl regularly almost every night at about ten o'clock, and at one and three o'clock in the morning. The fact is that the idea that wolves howl at regular hours every night is a widespread folk belief not borne out by the observation of wolves' habits. So that what was obviously intended as an irrefutable indication of the children's lupine nature serves, rather, to arouse further doubts as to the accuracy of the narrative.

The statement that the children were not observed to sweat is yet another example of the obvious influence of folkloristic belief upon the Reverend Singh's narrative. The widespread notion that dogs do not sweat except through the tongue is quite untrue; dogs possess numerous sweat glands on every part of the body. But for the purposes of the Reverend Singh's narrative, since dogs and wolves are closely related—and since the wolf children were alleged to have adopted the habits of wolves—it must follow that the wolf children did not sweat.

The eyes of the children are said to have emitted a blue light at night. "Night glare" is a phenomenon not unknown in human beings, but it is a condition of such great rarity that the chances against its ever occurring in two individuals living together are so astronomically high that we are forced to give up all attempt at normal explanation. The necessary extreme myopia or hypermetropia may have been present, but there is very definitely no evidence of any such condition in the Reverend Singh's account. I have been unable to find any record of children who were brought up in darkness exhibiting a like phenomenon. It is difficult to conceive of the special structure necessary, the tapetum (the iridescent layer of the choroid coat of the eye of certain carnivorous animals), developing as a special adaptation to the conditions of life of Kamala and Amala. But what is even more difficult to conceive is the emission of "a peculiar blue glare, like that of a cat or a dog, in the dark" without the presence, as far as one can gather, of any external source of light. This is, in fact, quite impossible, for the light must always be of external origin and is only reflected back by the eye. It was an old Arab belief that the eye itself emitted light! As for the "blue" glare itself, this would appear to be impossible in the case of human beings for the simple reason that the only possible source of such "glaring" is the fundus (the posterior portion or base of the eye), and this normally reflects either a dark red, or an orange-yellow color. The blue eye glare of cats and dogs, and many other animals, is due to the refraction of particles in the tapetum similar to those which in the human iris produce the appearance of the normal blue eye, but which have no connection in the latter case with "night glare." In the offspring of Malayan-Negro crosses, the fundus, through the ophthalmoscope, may appear somewhat bluish, or even gray, depending upon the presence of certain pigment particles, but it is doubtful whether in such cases one could obtain a bluish or grayish glare from the eyes. It is of significance to note that all the supporting cases cited by Dr. Zingg gave either a dark red or, as in the case referred to by Parsons, "a yellow reflex from the pupil." But the latter case refers specifically to the presence of glioma of the retina.

There are other difficulties which could be similarly discussed. But let us come to the point. The Reverend Singh claimed that Amala and Kamala were reared by wolves. What evidence exists in support of his claim? The answer is *none*. The grounds upon which this answer is based have already been briefly stated.

Were Amala and Kamala abandoned by their parents? No one knows. Were these children congenitally defective in any way? It is impossible to say. If they were not congenitally defective, then it would be a reasonable inference to make that their retardation, or rather nondevelopment as human beings, was due to the fact that during the critical period of their development they were practically entirely isolated from the conditioning influences of human contacts. It is during this conditioning period that it is assumed they spent their lives with wolves, living the life of wolves, so that behaviorally they became what they were assumed to have been exposed to—wolves.

On that point we must suspend judgment, but taking the matter from the general standpoint of the development of behavior one thing is certain: Given all the necessary normal potentialities an individual does not become a functioning human being simply by virtue of being born into the species *Homo sapiens;* indeed, he cannot become a functioning human being until he is exposed to the humanizing influences of other human beings. The attributes of humanity are a function of human society, of human socializing factors acting upon potentialities capable of being humanized.

Dr. Zingg writes that "radicals" who believe that "environment completely molds the human mind and mentality . . . overlook the fact that mentality is a bioneurological mechanism, and mind, the environmentally conditioned content organized by that mechanism. Though here we see a well-attested case of human beings reduced to wolf-conditioning, the radical case still needs a case of a wolf raised to human behavior."

Dr. Zingg may be allowed a distinction between "mind" and "mentality," though I do not know what that distinction may be, but he certainly entertains some strange notions on the nature of what "radicals" are supposed to believe. Dr. Zingg disagrees with the straw men of his own making that a wolf or other animal could be "educated into the behavior of a man." But surely, whatever Rousseau or the ingenious Monboddo may have thought, no one today, not even the "radicals," believes anything else than that it is utterly impossible to make a human mind out of the cellular characters of the nervous system of any nonhominid animal. The characters or potentialities of such animals do not possess the necessary qualities.

As for Dr. Zingg's statement that mentality may be regarded as the environmentally conditioned content organized by the bioneurological mechanism, I am not sure that he is not right. But is it not perhaps more in accord with the evidence to say that mind represents the environmental organization—or, better, integration—of the bioneurological mechanism? Does behavior represent the bioneurological organization of environmentally conditioned contents or do the environmentally conditioned contents acting upon a relatively undifferentiated variety of nervous tissues serve to differentiate and organize those tissues into a bioneurological system which then functions as mind? The truth, perhaps, lies somewhere between the two views.

I believe that the work of cultural anthropologists, and of experimental biologists and psychologists, would favor the second view. As Coghill has remarked in the final sentence of that most fundamental of all works on the subject, *Anatomy and the Problem of Behaviour*, "Man is, indeed, a mechanism, but he is a mechanism which, within his limitations of life, sensitivity, and growth, is creating and operating himself."

6

The Nature of War and the
Myth of Nature

I T IS NOW EIGHTY-NINE YEARS since that fatal morning
when a dust-laden young Prussian officer galloped into
Paris at the head of a small advance party of Uhlans,
thus signalizing the capitulation of the French and the unequivocal victory of the Prussians. Forty years later this
self-same Prussian officer, now a general, descended upon
Europe with a book which at once attained a universal notoriety. That book was entitled *Germany and the Next War*.[1]
It is hardly an exaggeration to say that no book of a similar
nature had before, nor has any book since, been so fervidly
and widely discussed. In England, at any rate, the book
passed through more than a score of impressions in as many
weeks. As a child, then living in London, I well remember
the sensation it caused, and how often I saw it in the most
unexpected places. Since those days I have learned that the
volume used to be kept on tap in the precincts of those lesser
parliaments, the pubs, where those who "talked politics"
could freely consult it over a tumbler of beer or a pipe.

From *The Scientific Monthly*, vol. 54, 1942, 342-353.
[1] Bernhardi, Friedrich von. *Germany and the Next War*. Popular Edition,
16th Impression, 1912.

In this book the author, General von Bernhardi, boldly threw down the gauntlet to the world and virtually with saber in hand called upon the German people to protest against "the aspirations for peace which seem to dominate our age and threaten to poison the soul of the German people." It is understandably rather hard for an iron-headed soldier, after some forty years of comparative inactivity, to recall an event so stirring as the entry at the head of a victorious army into a defeated enemy's capital without feeling that if things were not actually going to the dogs it was, at least, high time that something were done to prevent the possibility. And so in order to convince the German people of the "unnaturalness" of that "inactivity which saps the blood from a nation's sinews," Bernhardi did something that he had never done before; he wrote and published a book, making the pen, as it were, temporarily do service for the sword, and ink for blood.

"War," declared Bernhardi, "is a biological necessity"; it "is as necessary as the struggle of the elements in Nature"; it "gives a biologically just decision, since its decisions rest on the very nature of things." "The whole idea of arbitration represents a presumptuous encroachment on the natural laws of development," for "what is right is decided by the arbitrament of war." In proof whereof such notions of Darwin's as "The Struggle for Existence," "Natural Selection," and the "Survival of the Fittest" are invoked with a sententiousness quite military both in logic and in sense. According to Bernhardi, it is plainly evident to anyone who makes a study of plant and animal life that "war is a universal law of Nature."

This declaration and fortification of Germany's will to war —for it had the highest official sanction and approval—was published in 1911. Three years later the greatest holocaust the world had ever known was launched upon its ghastly way by those

> vultures sick for battle,
> Those bloodless wolves whose dry throats rattle,
> Those crows perched on the murrained cattle,
> Those vipers tangled into one,

the inhuman militaristic Bernhardis, the legislators of a victimized Europe.

The Great War came to an end forty-three years ago, having cost the lives of thirteen million men, eight million of whom were slaughtered upon the field of battle, and ten million civilians who died either directly or indirectly as a result of the war. As for the maimed and wounded combatants, these amounted to a mere twenty million more. The cost of running this fracas amounted to $125,000,000 a day during the first three years, and $224,000,000 during 1918—the total cost of the killing amounting to some $400,000,000,000.

World War II is a horrible memory. There is today hardly a human being, with the exception of the militarists, who can see either sense, good, or anything but misery in war— yet for many years my revered friend and teacher, Sir Arthur Keith, continued to aver in articles [2] that war has its biological justification. Keith maintained that the impulses which lead men to aggressive and defensive wars are "Nature's mechanisms for preserving the individual and the tribe or nation . . . which make individuals and nations willing to risk life itself to further the means and opportunities of life."

Sir Arthur Keith's opinions upon this subject first came into prominence with the publication of his Rectorial Address to the students of Aberdeen University in 1931, published in the same year under the title *The Place of Prejudice in Modern Civilization*. These opinions he continued to reaffirm. I propose to take Keith's views of the nature of war and, treating them as representative of the views of the biological-nature-of-war school, subject them to a brief critical examination.

Keith began by declaring his firm conviction that "prejudices are inborn; are part of the birthright of every child." These prejudices "have been grafted in our natures for a

[2] *The Truth Seeker*. New York: March 1939; *Sunday Express*. London: August 27, 1939; *Man*. London: April 1940; *Essays on Human Evolution*. New York: 1947; *A New Theory of Human Evolution*. New York: 1948.

special purpose—an evolutionary purpose. . . . They are essential parts of the evolutionary machinery which Nature
employed throughout eons of time to secure the separation
of man into permanent groups and thus to attain production
of new and improved races of Mankind. . . . Nature endowed
her tribal teams with this spirit of antagonism for her own
purposes. It has come down to us and creeps out from our
modern life in many shapes, as national rivalries and jealousies and as racial hatreds. The modern name for this spirit
of antagonism is race-prejudice." "Race-prejudice, I believe,"
continues Sir Arthur Keith, "works for the ultimate good of
Mankind and must be given a recognized place in all our
efforts to obtain natural justice for the world." And now for
the passage which has gained such widespread notoriety:

> Without competition Mankind can never progress; the price
> of progress is competition. Nay, race-prejudice and, what is
> the same thing, national antagonism, have to be purchased,
> not with gold, but with life. Nature throughout the past has
> demanded that a people who seeks independence as well as
> peace can obtain these privileges only in one way—by being
> prepared to sacrifice their blood to secure them. Nature keeps
> her orchard healthy by pruning; war is her pruning-hook. We
> can not dispense with her services. This harsh and repugnant
> forecast of man's future is wrung from me. The future of my
> dreams is a warless world.

Essentially similar views were expressed by Keith in his
Robert Boyle Lecture, "Nationality and Race" (1919).

Now, unlike Bernhardi, Keith is a physical anthropologist
of the first rank and, as I well know, a man of the noblest
and most generous nature. Nevertheless, in his treatment of
the subject of prejudice and war the fact is unfortunately
betrayed that he has overstepped the frontiers of his own
particular field, to which he has made such lasting and classical contributions, with results that, to say the least, are not
altogether happy. Charles Singer has well said that "Even
professional men of science, when they pass beyond the
frontiers of their own special studies, usually exhibit no more
balanced judgment or unprejudiced outlook than do non-
scientific men of comparable social and educational stand-

ing." Keith's Rectorial Address may be taken as a case in point.

What, we may ask to begin with, is this "Nature," always, it is to be observed, spelled with a capital "N"? Keith's "Nature" is apparently a very intelligent affair, working things out purposefully and with much premeditated thought. I use the term "intelligent" here in a general sense to cover the operations of what is conventionally known as the intellect. It would seem, however, that an intellect which can conceive of no better device to improve its breed than warfare must be a very poor intellect indeed. For surely the biological vitality of a species can be preserved and improved by a large variety of immeasurably more effective means than this, means which do not necessitate or require the annihilation of a single individudal.

But what, indeed *is* this "Nature" of Bernhardi and Keith which makes war a biological necessity? Apparently it is anthropomorphism akin to the *élan vital* of Bergson or the "life force" of Shaw. In other words, it is God with the capital "G" in very much the old form, divested here and there of a few sacraments, and perfectly clean-shaven, but otherwise much the same. Voltaire's jibe that if God had made men after his own image they had returned the compliment is as appropriate a truth today as it ever was. Nature or God today is an anthropologist as well as a mathematical physicist, sometimes an entelechist, and, often enough, merely a set of differential equations, unlimitedly limited and with an infinite number of functions at one and the same time— but if the truth were really known, merely a set of conditioned reflexes!

In fact "Nature" may mean anything according to the whim of the user. Nature, says Aristotle, makes some men slaves and others free. By Nature, retorts Cicero, all men are free. In Nature, says Hobbes, "the life of man is solitary, poor, nasty, brutish, and short"; it is a condition of "war of every man against every man" in which "the notions of right and wrong, justice and injustice have no place" and "force and fraud are the two cardinal virtues." "The state all men are naturally in," replies Locke, is "a state of perfect free-

dom to order their actions . . . as they think fit, within the
bounds of the law of nature . . . a state of equality." "Nature," writes Wordsworth, "to me was all in all, she never
did betray the heart that loved her." "Nature," rejoins Tennyson, "red in tooth and claw, shrieks against the creed of
man." And as Professor Pollard has remarked of these anti-
nomies, "Some see red, others see God, it all depends upon
the kingdom that is within them."

In effect, "Nature" is the name we give to the projection
of the totality of our ignorance concerning the forces which
are conceived to be responsible for the generation of life
and its maintenance. Nature is not a "thing in itself" which
operates upon other things; the term denotes rather, if it denotes anything at all, an artificial construct, the purpose of
which is to serve as a general stereotype for our ignorance,
in addition to serving as a *deus ex machina* to which, in a
quandary, we may appeal in order to be comfortably relieved of our perplexities.

For most people to say that a thing is "natural" explains
it. But does it? What do we mean by "natural"? Prejudices are
natural according to Sir Arthur Keith and others, prose according to M. Jourdain, warfare according to Bernhardi, and the
golden lie according to Plato and some of his modern suc-
cessors. Nature, it is said, is the universe of things as made
or produced. Nature, it is added further, operates according
to definite laws. All, in fact, is determined by law. The movements of the planets are determined by laws as immutable
as those which determine the behavior of a dog or a man.

But all this is mythical.

The universe, as far as we know, is composed of a system
of ever-changing *relations* in the form, for example, of gases,
stresses, forces, strains, velocities, dimensions, substances, and
so on, truly ad infinitum. Nothing in it is fixed; all is flux.
Between certain limits of infinity—that is, in a given space-
time continuum—the relations of certain planetary velocities,
for example, may remain (relatively) constant; the recurring
averages in which these relations manifest themselves may
be calculated to a high degree of probability and when so
calculated may be stated as laws. These laws are always

probability laws and are valid only as long as the relations of the planetary velocities, as well as numerous other factors, remain (relatively) constant. Should, however, any of these relations change, the old law will have to undergo modification, or an entirely new one will have to be elaborated.

With this in mind we may proceed further. A unicellular organism living at the bottom of a stagnant pool and environed by a stable universe of stimuli will tend to undergo little change as long as the constancy of those stimuli persist. But modify its relations, the form and nature of the stimuli acting upon it, alter its environment, and if you go on long enough, say for a few thousand million years, sufficiently and adequately varying the nature of the environmental stimuli, not to mention the inherent tendency of the organism to vary, you will, let us suppose, produce a man. And your man, as an organism, will obviously represent the sum of the effects of the responses to the environment organically made by his ancestors. Organically your man will be the product of an innumerable variety of conditions—the changing relations collectively termed "heredity" and "environment." So will, and so indeed is, any plant or any other form of animal life. Thus, all plant and animal life is not *produced* according to definite laws but in response to a series of arbitrary or *chance* alterations in the relations of the factors affecting it.

Nature is thus not an intelligent teleologically directed process which acts according to predetermined law but is a composite of chance relations which may be arbitrarily observed as unit groups of recurring averages of relations. The behavior of the independent variables, or the quanta, are both indeterminable and unpredictable, whence the *principle of indeterminacy*. Man, indeed, owes his present supremacy to just such a series of indetermined chance relations, which may more briefly be described as an accident of accidents; the accident referred to having been initiated in the early Miocene epoch approximately some thirty million years ago when, owing, most probably, to the denudation of the forests due to causes which at present remain speculative, a number of unspecialized apelike creatures, resembling the extinct ape known to paleontologists as *Sivapithecus sivalensis*, were forced to adapt themselves to a life on the sparsely treed plains, the savannas. This revolutionary change in their immediate environment led ultimately to the development of all those physical characteristics which we have learned to recognize as distinctive of man. Those apes who lived in the unaffected regions stayed in the forests and therefore still remain apes.

Was there any directive, telic, intelligent natural force at work here? Not at all. Changes in climate affecting rainfall, extending over a long period of time, may have been the responsible factor. The colossal number of varied forms of life, extinct and living, that are to be found upon this earth today have arisen owing to very similar causes. Every form of life with which we are acquainted is due, or rather owes its peculiar form, to the infinite number of changes that have been and are taking place in the environment peculiar to each—the internal as well as the external environment. These changes are not regulated by law but by chance. The processes of the universe of life are discontinuous and infinitely variable. The universe consists of an infinitely changing series of relations. Action and reaction, stimulus and response, occur always *relatively*, never *absolutely*. Nature, in short, in the determined immutable sense of the traditionalists does not exist, save as a Procrustean fiction.

The law and order that man sees in Nature he introduces there, a fact of which he seems to have grown quite unconscious. Natural systems of classification work so well that, following an unconscious pragmatic principle, they are assumed to be true, or at least representative of the truth— the latter being conventionally defined as correspondence with the reality of whatsoever it may be. In this way the tacit assumption is made that one has but to seek and one will find the law and order that is undoubtedly there in Nature. This process is termed discovery.

Now, while systems of classification are of incalculable value in aiding the processes of understanding and discovery, such systems are none the less quite artificial and do not in any way reflect a law and order which characterizes the operations of the processes we commonly ascribe to Nature itself. Nature is a fiction which uses neither measuring rod nor timetable. It is man alone who uses such instruments in order that he may the more fittingly orient himself in relation to this self-created fiction. The classificatory systems of man are fictional devices and represent merely the attempt—and it is a grand attempt—to unravel the tangled skein of some of the relations of the various forms of life and substance to one another, but no more.

But of this man loses sight and confuses himself with the belief that the law and order which he has worked into an arbitrary scheme is that law and order according to which Nature works. *Homo additus Naturae,* remarked Bacon long ago. Nature, if it consists of anything, represents a series of discontinuous processes, a complex of entangled gossamer strands, which man attempts to gather together and spin into a web which he naively imagines is the real thing; the real thing being merely as he sees it, and he sees it in an infinite number of ways according to the kingdom that is within him. Nature comes in this way to mean anything. And what may mean anything, in fact, means nothing. Nature is a term without definite meaning. Logically the conception of it is without the slightest value. Psychologically, perhaps, the term may not be without some significance in the sense of Nietzsche's words in *The Joyful Wisdom:* "Laws and laws of nature are the remains of mythological dreaming."

With respect to the "war of Nature" which is alleged to be a "universal law of Nature," that, it must be said, is pure fancy. We are told that even trees and flowers "fight." Do they? There is not the slightest evidence that they do. And if they do, what connection has this "fighting" with the warfare practiced by men? Some flowers digest insects; some plants "strangle" others. Does this constitute war between the flowers and the insects concerned? Do the plants that strangle others have to plead guilty to murder? Are these "warlike" actions of plants and flowers advance or rear guard actions? It would be extremely helpful to know whether it is defensive or offensive war that is "natural."

Sir Arthur Keith believed that both are. The illegitimate use of such terms as "struggle," "fighting," "force," and so on, when applied to plant and animal life, and the deliberate confusion of these terms with war, is too often made and far too often allowed to pass unchallenged. I cannot resist quoting Professor Pollard in this connection, who entertainingly remarked of this confusion: [3]

> The sun and the moon, we suppose, declare war with great regularity because they get into opposition every month. Parties in the House of Commons are perpetually at war because they are opposed. The police wage war because they are a force; for *naturally* if we use force against a criminal, we must needs make war upon other communities. War, indeed, will last for ever, because men will never "cease to struggle." So the League of Nations has obviously failed whenever a stern parent is caught chastising a peccant child; and "fighting" will go on without end because drowning men will fight for life, doctors will fight disease, and women will fight for places at drapery sales. And this is war.

The case could not be put more neatly.

Man, like other creatures, kills a large number of animals for food and various other uses. Does the process of killing and consuming these animals constitute war? In any case, is the killing of those animals either necessary or natural? It is neither innate in the psychophysical structure of man, nor necessary in order that he may live to kill any animal whatsoever, or plant for that matter—at least not for men living in the highly civilized centers of the Western world. Man's taste in food is culturally determined, like his taste in cigarettes or alcohol. In primitive conditions of life he is forced to kill animals for food and apparel, just as it was "natural" a short time ago to kill prisoners of war in order that the food supply might not be unnecessarily depleted. Animals in the wild state kill large numbers and varieties of other animals, where they are available, for the satisfaction of their hunger, for the very good reason that they have no

[3] A. F. Pollard. "The War of Nature and a Peace of Mind." *Vincula* (University of London Student Journal), 14, December 1925 (pp. 60-61).

other means of remaining alive. But man has. Man has improved upon the wild ways of life of the beasts of the jungle, and there is not the slightest reason why he should revert to them.

In medieval England it was considered natural and perfectly legal for all claims to real property to be settled and tried by battle. Since then man has developed more peaceful means of settling such claims, not by blood but by reason, by virtue of an understanding made possible by a more enlightened form of culture. For culture, if it means anything, represents the fact of man's ability to elaborate and improve upon the normal processes of the universe, commonly called Nature, in a very real sense to elaborate and improve upon his original endowment. And indeed today, through means purely cultural, man is in a position to control and regulate, in every possible respect, his own future evolution. He holds the power within himself of total self-extermination or more complete development, and it is by the weakness or strength of his intellect alone that either the one or the other will eventually be brought about.

Fundamentally, man is quite an intelligent animal, but he is a victim, alas, of the two-handed engine of his culture which distorts his mind and renders him unintelligent. Outworn traditional teachings have made of Western man a shockingly unintelligent creature who lives under the continuous and unrelieved domination of a chaos of ideas more degrading, more stupid, more idiotic, and more saddening than it may ever be possible to describe. This confused morality has, without question, been substantially responsible for his present deplorable state. For the reflexes and patterns of thought of every child born into the Western world today have been conditioned according to the prescriptions of these teachings, so that culturally Western man has come to be a function almost entirely of the reigning spirit of confusion and prejudice. And since in his conduct he functions without effort as a victim of confusion and prejudice, he arrives at the belief that it is thus "natural" to act and to think. In this way is produced the mentally and spiritually bludgeoned individual who gropes his way confusedly through life—and whose number is legion. It is in his world alone that today war still remains a legitimate and defensible means of settling a dispute or forcing an issue.

With respect to Keith's "race-prejudice," that, of course, is a purely acquired sentiment, a constellation of socially manufactured emotions, as he would undoubtedly have known had he made as deep a study of cultural as he did of physical anthropology. Nature, according to him, secures the separation of man into permanent groups by means of the operation of race prejudices, which express themselves as natural rivalries and jealousies in order to produce "new and improved races of mankind." This, we suppose, is a form of natural selection operating upon psychological bases, a form of selection peculiar to man alone, for no other animal, as far as we know, exhibits the slightest symptom of anything akin to what Keith calls "race-prejudice."

So-called race prejudice among lower animals, like their so-called natural fears and terrors, are acquired, not inborn. Experiments on young animals first carried out by Benjamin Kidd many years ago, and by numerous investigators since, have conclusively proved that the "instinctive" fear and terror of their allegedly natural enemies exhibited by the adult members of the species are emotions which are generally completely absent in the young, and are acquired only by learning from other members of the species or by individual experience. A lamb or any other animal, for example, which has had no long association with members of its own species from whom it could have acquired fear—or past experience with lions—will exhibit not the slightest fear of a lion when confronted with one.

No animal or human is born with any fear or prejudice whatsoever, of snakes, mice, or the dark, to cite but a few of the most familiar common fears usually considered of "instinctive" origin. All such fears or prejudices are acquired by learning and may, and usually do, act as conditioned reflexes, simulating physical reflexes which are innate but which in the former cases are conditioned to react culturally —not biologically or instinctively.

Upon the innate prejudice theory how are we to account

for the well-authenticated fact, familiar to most people of experience, that children of one nation brought up in the milieu of a "foreign" nation feel no prejudices whatsoever, in wartime or out of it, against the nation of their adoption, but on the other hand are generally to be found in the ranks of their adopted land fighting against the motherland of their ancestors whether it be in ideas or in powder? The most notorious example of this is the case of Houston Stewart Chamberlain, the egregious author of that stupendous miracle of nonsense, *The Foundations of the Nineteenth Century*, in which we witness the spectacle of an apostate Englishman glorifying the Teutonic spirit, and the German brand of it in particular, at the expense, among others, of his ancestral land and heritage. One may well wonder what happened to Chamberlain's "birthright" of prejudice when, as an adult, he became a champion of German prejudices? Possibly William James's law of transitoriness of instinct may be invoked here! And what shall we say of the author of *Religio Medici*, who wrote: "I am of a constitution so general, that it consorts and sympathiseth with all things; I have no antipathy, or rather idiosyncrasy, in anything. Those national repugnances do not touch me, nor do I behold with prejudice the French, Italian, Spaniard, or Dutch"?

As a matter of fact, there is every reason to believe that race sentiment and antipathies are comparatively recent developments in the societies of Western man. Lord Bryce in his Creighton Lecture, "Race Sentiment as a Factor in History" (1915), after surveying conditions in the ancient world, in the Middle Ages, and in modern times up to the French Revolution, arrives at the following conclusions which he regards as broadly true. The survey of the facts, he says:

> has shown us that down till the days of the French Revolution there had been very little in any country, or at any time, of self-conscious race feeling. . . . However much men of different races may have striven with one another, it was seldom any sense of racial opposition that caused their strife. They fought for land. They plundered one another. They sought glory by conquest. They tried to force their religion

on one another. . . . But strong as patriotism and national feeling might be, they did not think of themselves in terms of ethnology, and in making war for every other sort of reason never made it for the sake of imposing their own type of civilization. . . . In none of such cases did the thought of racial distinctions come to the front.

In America, where white and black populations frequently live side by side, it is an indisputable fact that white children do not learn to consider themselves superior to Negro children until they are told that they are so, a fact which is beautifully illustrated by the words of a white American farmer from the South who, in answer to the query as to what he thought of the Negro, replied, "I ain't got anything against niggers; I was fourteen years old before I know'd I was better than a nigger."

Numerous other examples could be cited of the cultural acquisition of prejudices, but to enter into a fully satisfactory discussion of the mechanism of race prejudice here would be quite impossible. It need only be said that it has been abundantly proven that race prejudices, or ideas of any kind, are inherited in just the same way as our clothes are, not innately but culturally. The statement so often made that "war is a universal and everlasting law of Nature" is at best a shallow judgment, for it seems never to occur to those who make it that the "conflicts" which they are pleased to term "war" and which are alleged to take place between animals in the wild state are pertinent only when they refer to the conflicts between animals of widely separated species, orders, and, almost universally, classes. Thus, mammals prey upon reptiles, reptiles upon birds, and birds upon insects. Lions will attack almost anything that moves, so will, to a lesser extent, wolves and hyenas. Domestic cats will kill small rodents and birds; monkeys will kill and eat birds and insects. But in all these examples chosen at random not a single animal will "fight" with a member of its own species in the sense that it will fight with members of other species, orders, or classes of animals. In the wild state it is not the practice of animals to prey upon or fight with each other but rather with animals of widely separated species. When they do fight with each other the results are rarely fatal and approximate more often than not to play. Of course, very hungry animals will devour, upon occasion, members of their own species, but this is a form of conduct which is normally resorted to only in extreme necessity. In serious conflicts between wild or domesticated animals of the same species the fight is rarely between more than two individuals, and is usually provoked by the same causes and is fought from motives similar to those which cause men to fight with one another; namely, the possession of a sexually desirable mate or an object of physical value such as food. But this sort of fighting is a very different thing from the fighting which we know as war. War is an organized attack of one community upon another community, and as such is never fought by animals other than those of the "human" variety. It is impossible to produce a single instance from the animal kingdom, outside of man, in which it is shown that within a definite species a form of behavior resembling warfare is waged by one group upon another, or for that matter upon any other order or class of animals—as a means of improving the species or what not. If one thing is certain it is that it is *not* natural for members either of the same species or of any other to wage war upon one another. War, let it be said at once, is the most unnatural, the most artificial, of all animal activities, for it originates in artificial causes, is waged by highly artificial entities called states, is fought from artificial motives, with artificial weapons, for artificial ends. Like our civilization war is an artificial product of that civilization itself, the civilization that has been achieved by the repeal and the repudiation of those very processes of so-called "Nature" which the Bernhardis are pleased to regard as an everlasting universal law.

We have already seen that there is good reason to believe that aggressive race sentiment and prejudice are comparatively recent acquisitions of man. So, too, there is very good reason to believe that warfare is but a recent development resulting from the artificial and perverted activities of men living in highly civilized groups. Among the extinct races of men of whom we have any knowledge no evidence of anything remotely resembling warfare has ever been found. Plenty of weapons of a rather simple nature have been discovered in association with the remains of ancient man but these were clearly for use against animals and not against his fellow men. Adam Smith long ago pointed out that a hunting population is always thinly spread over a large area and possesses but little accumulated property. Primitive man was, and in many cases still is, a hunter and no doubt, as is the case among most existing nonliterate peoples, his hunting grounds were marked off by definite boundaries—boundaries separating different communities—"but these boundaries were sacred and, as no one would think of violating them, they could not form a cause of war." Wars for conquest among nonliterate peoples are completely unknown.

> Savages [writes Ellis] are on the whole not warlike, although they often try to make out that they are terribly bloodthirsty fellows; it is only with difficulty that they work themselves up to fighting pitch and even then all sorts of religious beliefs and magical practices restrain warfare and limit its effects. Even among the fiercest peoples of East Africa the bloodshed is usually small. Speke mentions a war that lasted three years; the total losses were three men on each side. In all parts of the world there are people who rarely or never fight; and if the old notion that primitive people are in a state of chronic warfare of the most ferocious character were really correct, humanity could not have survived. Primitive man had far more formidable enemies than his own to contend with, and it was in protection against these, and not against his fellows, that the beginnings of cooperation and the foundations of the State were laid.

War came into being only after men had taken to the cultivation of the land upon which it was necessary for them to settle permanently. Such an agricultural stage of development we know first appeared among men about ten thousand years ago in Neolithic times. The agricultural life results in the accumulation of property, the accumulation of property results in more or less organized industry, industry in wealth, wealth in power, power in expansive ambitions and the desire to acquire additional property necessary to gratify those ambitions, and thus, by no very complicated process, in war. Such conditions as are peculiar to the industrial civilizations of today are, of course, highly artificial, as are the prejudices and race sentiment which they serve to generate.

In the modern world undoubtedly the most potent cause of war is economic rivalry—a purely cultural phenomenon having no biological basis whatsoever. The desire for foreign concessions and foreign markets, the increase in population, *lebensraum*—such things will upon little provocation set nations in opposition and at each other's throats. It is from such economic causes that patriotism, chauvinism, and the widespread fear of aggression, which more than anything else serves to consolidate the group and is responsible for the generation of race sentiment and prejudice, are born.

If all this is true, then it is apparent that war arises not as the result of natural or biological conditions but from purely artificial social conditions created by highly "civilized" modes of living.

There remains to be examined the statement given expression by Sir Arthur Keith, and implied in the writings of many before him, that war is Nature's "pruning-hook," Nature's method of keeping her orchard healthy. This, of course, means that war acts as a process of natural selection—an idea which on the face of it is preposterously absurd. For, as everyone knows, the manner in which modern war acts is to kill off the very best members of the race while jealously preserving the worst, such as the mentally and bodily diseased and the generally unfit.

In any case, as World War I fully proved, the nation superior to all others in the techniques of waging war, the most ingenious and fertile in the invention and use of the instruments of destruction, may in spite of this lose the war by the selectively irrelevant fact of being overwhelmingly outnumbered. In writing of World War I Professor Pollard aptly remarked that "if the result had depended on scientific invention the Germans would have won. As it was, they neutralized enormous odds in numbers to such an extent that for four years the principal front hardly shifted on an average more than half a dozen miles in either direction. The

Allied victory was due not to scientific superiority but to the economic exhaustion of the foe, and to the fact that in Foch's decisive campaign America was pouring more fresh troops into the line of battle in a month than the Germans could raise in a year." From the standpoint of natural selection it is apparent to all those who lived through it that the Germans, who proved themselves the most intelligent and certainly not the least valorous of all the combatants, should have won World War I. Instead, they lost it. Something clearly had gone wrong with natural selection, or rather with war as an agency of it.

As a matter of fact the whole concept of war as an agency of natural selection in the case of man completely breaks down when we consider that throughout the historic period there were numerous instances of victories in war gained by nations who were culturally far inferior to the peoples whom they conquered. It must, however, be freely acknowledged that on the whole up to the modern era the nations victorious in war were generally superior to the people whom they conquered—superior in the strict sense of the military superiority of the combatant individuals. In former wars men actually fought with one another, the superior warrior generally killing the inferior in hand-to-hand combat. But in modern warfare the combatants scarcely ever see each other and when they do it is not military skill or native superiority which decides who shall die but a shell fired from a battery some five to ten miles away, or a machine gun hundreds of yards distant, or a bomb dropped from an airplane a mile or more up. In actual battle the superior men are the first to go over the top; in dangerous and generally useless raids they are the first to be chosen—and killed. Where in all this slaughter is there to be detected any evidence of natural selection? There is selection, certainly, in that the superior are selected for death and the inferior are protected against it. In this way does modern warfare act as an agency of natural selection, for the worse.

Man has reached his present supremacy of reason through the inhibitive and integrative powers of his mind, the ability to reject and suppress what he considers to be undesirable, the ability to *control*. Human society depends upon the maintenance of that ability of the mind to control, not so much the brute in man, for there is really little that is brutal in him that is not forced upon him, but those elements which under miseducation are capable of making a brute of him. All that is fine, noble, beautiful, and desirable in our civilization has been achieved by the supercession of mind over Nature, and much of this has been achieved through the resolute determination of individual minds not so much to conquer and to vanquish what is customarily called "Nature," red in tooth and claw, but to enlist the aid of "Nature" in the service of man and to control it effectively. All that is so ugly and inhuman and so destructive in our civilization is due to the activities of those who are anxious to exploit their fellow men to their own advantage and who use measures of control only toward this end. To them war is a profitable activity, for it increases their fortunes and thus their power. It is individuals of this order, in all countries, and from the earliest historical times, who make wars, not "Nature." "The fault, dear Brutus, lies not in our stars, but in ourselves."

Let those who are wise enough awaken to the fact that too long have they been deceived by a chaos of ideas for which there is not the slightest basis in fact but which represent, as Spinoza said, the errors of the ages grown hoary. Let men realize that such flowers as bloom in the verbal spring of thinkers like Bernhardi and Sir Arthur Keith have nothing whatsoever to do either with the logical case or the factual reality. Nay, in spite of Kant et al., there is no instinct toward peace in man just as there is none toward war. The early Egyptians, the Cretans, and the people of Mohenjo-Daro in India did not wage war simply because it was totally unnecessary for them to do so; socially and economically they were entirely sufficient unto themselves. Aboriginal Australians, however, have fought with one another, because for economic reasons, such as a dog or a wife, it was necessary for them to do so. Men, it seems, fight only when and if they want to. There is nothing within their native structure, no *primum mobile,* no innate prejudice, save for such prejudices as have been cultivated in them by education, that originally forces them to fight.

The tradition of thought which renders possible such glib talk of war and its supposed natural causes as I have here surveyed represents the bequest to us from the remote past of obsolete modes of thought which are conspicuous for their profound irrationality. So powerful is this traditional detritus that it has not failed to influence many of the most respected minds of our day to the extent of making mathemagicians of our mathematicians, casuists of our philosophers, and an apologist for war of the gentlest and kindest anthropologists. This tradition constitutes a Gordian knot that one must sever completely, since it resists being untied. At present this tradition of thought constitutes the sole constrictive force operating upon the mind of man as well as being the main impediment in the way of its rational functioning, coercing the good in him toward evil and, in short, representing a tyranny of the strongest and subtlest power. If man is to be saved from himself before it is too late his tyranny must be broken. This can be achieved only by the unequivocal action that must follow the reasoned dissolution of such errors of belief and thought that form so great a part of our traditional social heritage today.

7

A Brief Excursion Into Cannibalism

QUALITIES are often attributed to fossil men which, upon the evidence offered, would in any primate court of justice be considered actionable. It is time that a protest was entered against a practice which is altogether indefensible, more particularly since those to whom such qualities are attributed are unable to defend themselves.

When the charred remains of human bones are found on some Pleistocene hearth it is generally at once assumed that those who were responsible for their condition were cannibals. Is such a find evidence of cannibalism? Possibly not. But when it is added that the bones so found are cracked in such a manner as to indicate that the marrow was extracted by some human agency, who can deny that these fossil humans must have been cannibals? I submit that denial or affirmation is here a matter of scientific impossibility, but I would also point out that under conditions of scarcity modern nonliterate peoples, who by any standard could hardly be called cannibals, have been known to kill their young and feed them to those who were left. Is it not also true that under similar conditions highly civilized men have been

From *Science*, vol. 86, 1937, 56-57

known to do the same? And are they therefore to be characterized as cannibals?

The point need not, I think, be pressed. The consumption for occasional ritual purposes of certain parts of the human body is a practice which is to be found among many nonliterate peoples today, but no people of whom we have any knowledge makes a habit of cannibalism. In fact, cannibalism as more than an occasional practice is a pure traveler's myth.

My friend Dr. G. H. R. von Koenigswald has endowed the fossil Pleistocene men of East Java discovered by him with the quality of being brain-eaters. The evidence for this he finds in the fact that in each of these skulls the facial bones were completely broken away by some human agency. He assumes, therefore, that the human agents were desirous of securing the brain for gastronomical purposes. This is certainly a possible inference, but is it a probable one?

Reading recently in Herbert Basedow's delightful *The Australian Aboriginal*,[1] I came across the following paragraph:

> The Narrinyerri and other tribes south of Adelaide used human calvaria as drinking vessels. *The facial skeleton of a complete skull was broken away so as only to leave the brainbox; and this held the water.* [Italics mine]

I leave the eduction of the proper relation to others.

Java is, of course, very near Australia. Let the ethnologist who will whoop with delight at what he may take to be the persistence in Australia today of a culture trait which was already in existence in Pleistocene Java. Or shall we say that we have here a case of independent invention?

[1] Adelaide, 1929 (p. 95).

8

Problems and Methods Relating to the Study of Race

I T MAY BE logically deduced from an analysis of the title
of this chapter that problems and methods are related
to the study of race. It is implied in this title that race
constitutes a subject offering certain problems the solution
of which may be attempted by certain methods. It is not
indicated in this title why problems relating to race exist or
why methods relating to their study are necessary. Yet these
are extremely important questions, since any study which
neglects to answer them cannot possibly succeed in accurately defining the meaning of the subject of our discussion and its principal term, that is, "race."

No function of man, whether it be the contraction of a
muscle, the manufacture of a brick, the expression of an
idea, or the writing of a book such as this, can be fully
understood without a knowledge of the history of that function in so far as it has been socially determined. For, obviously, any neglect to take into consideration the relations
of the social parameter can only lead to a defective understanding of such events, since it should be clear that man
develops in and through a continuum which is social as well
as physical. There is perhaps no subject and no event of

From *Psychiatry*, vol. 3, 1941, 493-506.

which this is more conspicuously true than "race." I say "event" because in a very definite sense it would be preferable to think of race as an event rather than as a term, for, apart from the cells of a dead lexicographer's brain or the taxonomist's judgment, "race" in reality hardly ever functions as a term but almost always as an event.

In our society—and it is within the universe of our society that I am speaking—"race" is not merely a word which one utters but it is an event which one experiences. The word itself merely represents a series of sounds which usually serves as a stimulus to set in motion a host of feelings and thoughts which, together, form an emotional experience which, for most people, is what "race" is. It seems to me of the greatest importance that this fact be clearly understood, for an attempt will here be made, among other things, to inquire into the development of those psychological factors which tend to make this event possible. That such psychological factors or tendencies exist is indisputably clear.

"Race" in our society is not a term which clearly and dispassionately defines certain real conditions which can be demonstrated to exist, but, as I have already said, the word acts rather as a stimulus which sets off a series of emotional changes that usually bear as much relation to the facts as bees do to bonnets. Feelings and thoughts concerning such a concept as "race" are real enough and so, it may be pointed out, are feelings and thoughts concerning the existence of unicorns, pixies, goblins, ghosts, satyrs, and "Aryans." Endowing a feeling or a thought about something with a name and thereby imputing to that something a real existence is one of the oldest occupations of mankind. Pixies, ghosts, satyrs, Aryans, and the popular conception of "race" represent real enough notions, but these have their origin in erroneous interpretations of simple facts. Error, imagination, and rationalization are among the chief components of these notions.

It is not my purpose here to show that concepts denoted by such terms as "ghost" or "race" do not, in the sense in which they are commonly used and understood, correspond to anything scientifically demonstrable as having a real existence. Madame de Staël once remarked, "I do not believe in ghosts, but I am afraid of them." Intellectually convinced of the nonexistence of ghosts, Madame de Staël none the less reacted emotionally to the notion of ghosts for all the world as if they had a real existence. Most of us are familiar with this kind of situation, and it is evident that in her childhood Madame de Staël must have been emotionally conditioned to the idea of the existence of ghosts to such an extent that as an adult she was quite unable to throw off the effects of that conditioning.

It is probable that in some parts of the world some children early become emotionally conditioned to a belief in the existence of race differences.[1] In many parts of Europe, for example, where the larger number of the troubles of state and individual have traditionally been attributed to the Jews, such attributions can hardly have failed to escape the attention of many children. And such children would grow up to accept the existence of imputed race differences as real and act upon such beliefs in all sincerity. But just as Madame de Staël became intellectually convinced that ghosts do not exist in spite of the acknowledged strength of the emotion attached to the notion, so too, is it quite possible to produce an intellectual appreciation of the nature of their error among those who have been emotionally conditioned to accept the mythology of race as real. Indeed, nearly all of us have been so emotionally conditioned, and many of us have been more or less able to emancipate ourselves from such conditioning by becoming acquainted with the facts relating to these matters. Hence, one of the first requirements necessary for the production of an intelligent understanding of race problems in the individual must be the existence of a readily available body of scientific facts relating to every aspect of the race problem for use in the education, or re-education, of the individual. But such facts must be used, and they must be made available in a form for use. Science and knowledge are meaningless unless they can be applied in a practical way to the increase of human happiness. The

[1] On this subject see Lasker, Bruno. *Race Attitudes in Children.* New York: Henry Holt, 1929.

dispassionate scientific collection and analysis of facts is of the first importance, but the end of such activities should not rest with their publication in learned journals. The ultimate purpose of such activities must be recognized as having been defeated unless the most pertinent results so obtained and published are disseminated in such a way as to increase the understanding and sympathy for such matters in every human being.

I am not among those who consider that all who at present appear to be hopelessly confused upon the subject of race are beyond redemption. This seems to me an altogether gratuitous assumption. I believe that methods can be developed by means of which many who now harbor myths and delusions concerning race may be reached and redeemed. Through the press, periodicals, popular lectures, books, the film, the church, and a thousand and one other agencies, millions of misguided individuals can have the truth made available to them.

But far more important than these are the growing generations. It is through the lower and upper grade schools that the most significant work can be done in clarifying the minds of individuals concerning the facts of race and in educating them in the proper attitudes of mind toward that subject. Let us teach geography, but instead of presenting the arid facts of that subject let us humanize its teaching and furnish its field with the living peoples who inhabit this earth. Or else let us teach our children simply what we know about the peoples of the earth and about their respective values for one another and for civilization as a whole. Relations between other human beings and ourselves form the most important of all the experiences and situations of our lives. Would it not be incredible, did we not know it to be a fact, that in our society human beings are permitted to enter into such relations without being equipped with the most elementary understanding of what they mean? Certainly, scarcely any attempt is made to supply them with the facts relating to race as demonstrated by science, but we do, on the other hand, supply them with the kind of information which makes fertile ground for the development of race prejudices.[2] Here, then, is a most important field in which a great and valuable pioneer work remains to be done. Academic discussions will not carry us very far unless we are willing to roll up our sleeves and set to work on such untilled fields.[3]

One of the first points to be grasped before much progress in this subject can be made is that as far as human beings, and as far as society and social development are concerned, race is not a biological problem at all. Furthermore, it does not even present any biological problems which society needs in the least to consider. "Race" is a term for a problem which is created by social factors, and by social factors alone; it is, therefore, entirely a social problem. The problem of the origin and development of different physical types is part of the larger problem of discovering how we all came to be the way we are. But that, too, is a social problem, and only arbitrarily, and in a very limited technical sense is it a biological problem. Man is outstandingly the one animal species in which "biological" development has, from the very earliest times, been very substantially influenced by the operation of social factors, and this, ever increasingly, continues to be the case. The biological development of man cannot be considered apart from his social development, for man is a domesticated, a self-domesticated animal,[4] and domestication

[2] See Baker, Emily V. "Do We Teach Racial Intolerance?" *The Historical Outlook,* 24, 1933 (pp. 86-89).

[3] The type of teaching which can be carried out in the schools is very efficiently discussed at some length in *The Teaching Biologist,* 9, 1939 (pp. 17-47).

[4] Upon this important subject, in which far too little original work has yet been done, reference is made to the following: Hahn, Eduard. *Die Haustiere,* Leipzig: Duncker and Humbolt, 1896; Fischer, Eugen. *Rasse und Rassenentstehung beim Menschen, Wege zum Wissen.* Berlin: Ulstein, 62, 1927 (pp. 1-137); Laufer, Berthold. "Methods in the Study of Domestications." *Scientific Monthly,* 25, 1927 (pp. 251-255); Friedenthal, H. *Die Sonderstellung des Menschen in der Natur, Wege zum Wissen.* Berlin: Ulstein, 8, 1925; Herskovits, M. J. "Social Selection and the Formation of Human Types." *Human Biology,* 1, 1929 (pp. 250-262); Klatt, B. "Mendelismus, Domestikation und Kraniologie." *Archiv für Anthropologie,* 18, 1921 (pp. 225-250); Renard, Georges. *Life and Work in Prehistoric Times.* New York: Knopf, 1929; Boas, Franz, editor. *General Anthropology.* Boston: Heath, 1938 (p. 108); Fortuyn, A. B. Droogleever. "The Origin of Human Races." *Science,* 80, 1939 (pp. 352-353).

is a social process by means of which biological changes are produced in animals. Such changes, to a certain extent, represent the socially preferred expression of genetic rearrangements of characters common to the whole of mankind. The chief agency in the production of such changes is social, yet the scientific study of such social agencies has hardly been attempted. Thus far the emphasis has for the most part been upon the biological aspects of such changes, the socially induced origin of which has not been recognized.

While the biological aspects of the subject are important, they are only so insofar as they render possible an understanding of the physiological and genetic mechanisms underlying the actual processes of change. As R. A. Fisher has remarked, "While genetic knowledge is essential for the clarity it introduces into the subject, the causes of the evolutionary changes in progress can only be resolved by an appeal to sociological, and even historical facts. These should at least be sufficiently available to reveal the more powerful agencies at work in the modification of mankind." [5]

When the mechanism of such physiological and genetic changes is understood, it is then fully realized that race is no more than a process, a series of temporary genetic conditions always in process of change. It then becomes clear that the stage at which one catches this process depends upon the segment of time which one arbitrarily selects from the space-time continuum in which the process is occurring. Neither "races" of men nor "races" of lower animals are immutable. They become so, and then only conceptually, when an anthropologist or taxonomist follows the traditional practice of pinning his specimens down for study and classification according to some socially determined method of classification. But it is wrong to conceive of any animal group, and particularly any human group, as static and immutable. It is wrong to do so in the case of man because the facts of prehistory and those of recent times indicate that new "races" of man have been and are being synthesized very rapidly. In this process social factors play a very important role.

[5] Fisher, R. A. *The Genetical Theory of Natural Selection.* Oxford: Clarendon Press, 1930 (p. 174).

Recognizing this fact, we must further recognize that in our own society the problem of race is essentially a problem of race relations, and that it is, of course, fundamentally a social problem. In our own society explanations of the race problem have been offered in terms of economic forces, social stratification, and biological differences—or all three, but such explanations have never been altogether convincing. The causes motivating human behavior are complex, and human behavior is hardly ever to be explained in terms of single processes such as the economic, the biological, or the purely sociological. In any case, in order to understand the nature of the cause of any event it is necessary to discover and to relate all the conditions entering into its production. In short, what is required is a specification of all the necessary conditions which together form the sufficient cause of the event into the nature of which we are inquiring.

The second question which we have to answer leads naturally from the first and is inseparably linked with it. It is: Why are methods relating to the study of "race" necessary? This question is actually neither as obvious nor perhaps as stupid as it may at first appear. For while it may be true, for instance, that certain conditions arising out of our present economic organization of society are responsible for maintaining and exacerbating the problem of race, it is certainly not true that a reorganization of our economic system would automatically result in a solution of that problem. It is quite conceivable that race problems may exist under ideal economic conditions. These problems, indeed, are by no means simple, and it is therefore necessary to approach them by the use of such methods as are most calculated to clarify them. It would obviously be an egregious error to approach the study of race from the standpoint of the economic determinant alone, precisely as it would be an error to approach its study from the viewpoint solely of biology or of sociology, as is to a large extent customary today.

This brings us to what I consider to be an extremely important methodological aspect of this whole question. It is the matter of the individual who discusses the subject of "race." Hitherto, practically anyone with the ability to develop a hoarse throat has been able to set himself up as an authority on race. We need only recall the names of Gobineau, Lathrop Stoddard, Houston Stewart Chamberlain, Madison Grant, and others to discover that the principal equipment necessary to qualify as an authority on race consists in a well-rounded ignorance and an unshakable confidence! To listen to such "authorities" has been to suffer a positive increase in one's ignorance.

In the universe of science the situation, though incomparably better, is not by any means all that could be desired. Until recently very little progress has been made in the scientific study of race. This has been chiefly due to the fact that the subject has been dealt with in piecemeal manner and by specialists with an insufficient grasp of the complexities of the subject. Thus, psychologists have failed to take into account the sociological and biological factors, while sociologists have failed to give adequate consideration to the psychological and biological factors. Finally, and worst of all, until recently the physical anthropologists restricted their studies almost entirely to the morphological aspects of the subject. Actually what we need are more students who will combine the best qualities of the psychologist, the sociologist, and the biologist, and who will focus their attention upon the problems of race. Such a combination of qualities is scarcely realized in the modern anthropologist who treats of man as if he were constituted of two distinct and separate universes, a social and a physical, each of which is considered to be the proper field of study of one who qualifies by agreeing to know nothing about the other.

In the modern world racial problems, as I have already pointed out, are essentially social problems. No sociologist can ever hope to assist in the solution of these problems without acquiring an adequate understanding of what the biologist, the psychologist, and the psychoanalyst can alone supply, namely, an appreciation of the nature of the fundamental facts of physical and mental development. Obviously, what we need are more human ecologists, more liaison officers between the sciences of man.[6] Such human ecologists are at present pitifully few, and until their numbers increase the study of the race problem must become a co-operative task in which representatives of all the sciences relating to the study of man must participate.

Meanwhile let us endeavor to place the problem of race in some sort of operational framework. No one will deny that our society is a stratified one, and there are few students of society who would deny that the social stratification is determined principally by the way in which our society works economically. The proof of this lies in the fact that it is usually possible to migrate from one social stratum to another only by means of the economic process. By the acquisition of economic power one rises in the social hierarchy; by the loss of economic power one falls. Groups and individuals who are denied effective participation in the economic process clearly cannot rise above the lower social strata, while the only way to exclude groups and individuals who have not been so denied from rising and maintaining their places socially is by erecting barriers against them, by depriving them of their economic rights. We need hardly go farther back than our own time in search of the evidence with which to prove the truth of this statement.

In Europe, under Nazi rule, we witnessed the deliberate creation of such a barrier in the form of a mythological racial dogma which was imposed upon whole peoples, a dogma which, in operation as a barrier, deprived all those who were not mythical "Aryans" of the right to earn a living and subsequently of their lives. No more patent or painful example could be cited than this of the blatant economic motivation underlying the creation and practice of this mythology which so effectively led to the social and economic disfranchisement of helpless groups.

In the United States there are several perfect examples which may be cited as illustrating the relationship between the economic factor and the presence of racial barriers. Along

[6] For a detailed discussion of this aspect of the subject see my "A Cursory Examination of the Relations Between Physical and Social Anthropology." *American Journal of Physical Anthropology,* 26, 1940 (pp. 41-61).

the Pacific Coast, where the Japanese and Chinese constitute an appreciable economic threat, there is considerable race prejudice against them. Along the Atlantic Coast, where the numbers of these "races" are comparatively small and they do not constitute an economic threat, there is relatively little prejudice against them. Similarly, in California, where American Indians are numerous, there is a great deal of prejudice against the Indian. In the Midwest, where Indians are relatively few and under control, there is very little prejudice against them, while in the East a little Indian blood definitely constitutes a prestige point, for Indians are so rare that they are almost worth their weight in genes! In areas such as the South, where the social status of the Negro is changing and he emerges as an economic competitor, the prejudice against the large population of Negroes constitutes a serious problem. In the North, where the economic situation is much better, the Negro has always enjoyed a much greater degree of social and economic freedom.

In England, when Negroes or Indians were few there was no prejudice against these peoples. But when their numbers increased in various localities, they began to be regarded with a quizzical eye. As an economic threat they began to elicit the kind of racial behavior that many had thought impossible in so civilized a country as England.

In reality there is no necessary or sufficient relationship between economic conditions and racial problems, and just as it is possible to conceive of difficult racial problems existing under ideal economic conditions, so it is quite possible to conceive of perfect race relations and mutual appreciation under the most difficult economic conditions. It simply happens to be the case that in our own society the regrettable discovery has been made that, by utilizing the physical and cultural differences which exist between groups and individuals, it is a relatively simple matter to evade the consequences of one's own conduct by attributing them to the conduct of some other group.

The discovery is actually a very old one and as a device for moving people is extremely well grounded in that it caters to a deep-seated tendency in man to find some cause outside himself upon which to blame his troubles or release his feelings. Tertullian, for example, in pagan Rome, was fully aware of the fact that the persecution of the Christian minority was merely being used as a device to sidetrack the attention of the people from the real causes of corruption in the Roman state. Said he, "If the Tiber rose to the walls of the city, if the inundation of the Nile failed to give the fields enough water, if the heavens did not send rain, if an earthquake occurred, if famine threatened, if pestilence raged, the cry resounded: 'Throw the Christians to the lions!'" In this manner the Roman populace was provided, as later peoples have been, with a socially sanctioned outlet for their pent-up feelings. The scapegoat is as old as man.

Race prejudice is easily generated in our society because our society is socially and economically so organized as to be continually productive of frustrations in the individual, which in turn produce an aggressiveness within him which must find expression in some way. But the aggressiveness for which the individual must find release is not entirely, or even for the most part, produced by economic factors. This, however, is a matter to which we shall return later. It should be obvious that the frustrative situations called into being by economic and social factors, while producing some aggressiveness in the individual, do not in themselves, and need not necessarily, lead to race prejudice. That the aggressiveness produced by such factors may lead to race prejudice is entirely to be explained by the fact that race prejudice constitutes a socially sanctioned, and a socially directed, means of releasing that aggressiveness. The aggressiveness may in part be produced by socioeconomic factors, but the form of the response which that aggressiveness takes is not necessarily linked with such factors. Alternative responses are available, but race prejudice is among the easiest and, psychologically, the most satisfying.

Merton has described the frustrative situation very effectively. He writes: [7]

> It is only when a system of cultural values extols, virtually above all else, certain *common* symbols of success *for the popu-*

[7] Merton, Robert K. "Social Structure and Anomie." *American Sociology Review,* 3, 1938 (p. 680).

lation at large while its social structure rigorously restricts or completely eliminates access to approved modes of acquiring these symbols *for a considerable part of the same population,* that antisocial behavior ensues on a considerable scale. In other words, our egalitarian ideology denies by implication the existence of noncompeting groups and individuals in the pursuit of pecuniary success. The same body of success-symbols is held to be desirable for all. These goals are held to *transcend class lines,* not to be bounded by them, yet the actual social organization is such that there exist class differentials in the accessibility of these *common* success-symbols. Frustration and thwarted aspiration lead to the search for avenues of escape from a culturally induced intolerable situation; or unrelieved ambition may eventuate in illicit attempts to acquire the dominant values. The American stress on pecuniary success and ambitiousness for all thus invites exaggerated anxieties, hostilities, neuroses and antisocial behavior.

The avenue of escape from such frustrative conditions is almost always the same, namely, through aggressiveness. The object to which that aggressiveness may attach itself is culturally determined by what is rendered culturally available. "Race" represents a cultural misunderstanding of certain facts, but from the point of view of the psyche of the individual it presents a most satisfactory solution to a particular problem, affording, as it does, both a convenient and a suitable release-object for aggressiveness. It should, however, be clearly understood that the misunderstanding is cultural in origin and not economic. The conception of "race" is a cultural artifact and does not in itself lead to race prejudice. What leads to race prejudice is the cultural manipulation of those psychophysical energies which in most individuals overtly find expression in some form of aggressiveness, no matter what the nature of the underlying motivation for that manipulation may be.

Economic factors represent but one group of conditions— and those of the greatest importance—by means of which such aggressiveness may be called forth under conditions and in situations in which it may be easily attached to "race." Economic factors, in our society, are certainly among the most important of the factors leading to situations in which race prejudice may develop, but that such factors are virtually entirely dependent upon cultural factors for the direction which they will be made to give to individual aggressiveness is proven by the fact that the aggressiveness arising under those same economic conditions can be directed toward the production of good fellowship and mutual aid between different groups. Such fellowship and co-operation between different groups has been repeatedly witnessed in times of war when, for example, an alien nation has become the socially sanctioned scapegoat for one's aggressiveness. In peacetime the repair of some natural disaster, affecting the lives of all, frequently produces the same effect by providing a wholesale outlet for such aggressiveness. The attack upon some social problem requiring solution is in every way a far more satisfactory outlet for aggressiveness than an attack upon other human beings.

Clearly, then, it is what is culturally offered as the most suitable object for the release of these aggressive tendencies that is the primarily important fact, while the economic factor is only of secondary importance. Economic conditions are culturally utilizable, for good or for evil purposes, as each culture, or segment thereof, sees fit. If in some cultures the aggressiveness which arises under such conditions is made to release itself in hostile behavior toward some group, that can hardly be said to be due to economic conditions but must clearly be held to be due to those factors which render possible the cultural manipulation of the situation to which such conditions give rise. In short, economic factors may provide some of the conditions in which race hostility may be generated, but unless those conditions are directed into channels leading to race hostility there will be no race hostility, and the aggressiveness which must be released will have to find some other object.

It is at this point that I wish to focus attention upon the one general factor which seems to have been consistently overlooked in discussions of the racial problem. This is the factor of the normal psychophysical and psychological traits of the individual—traits which are utilized in the generation of racial enmities and which have already been touched upon in the preceding section.[8]

The one thing clear concerning racial hostility and prejudice is the ease with which individuals are led to exhibit it. There are very few people in our society who have not at some time or another exhibited evidences of racial prejudice, and it would seem clear that most individuals are capable of being brought to a state of mind in which they are really glad of the opportunity of freely releasing their feelings against some group or individual representing such a group. When society as a whole lends its sanction to the attachment of such feelings to any group, the free exercise of racial intolerance is enjoyed as a happy release for feelings which are ever ready to find expression in relation to some suitable object.

Now, it is in the nature of such feelings—the character of which we shall presently discuss—that they can be suitably directed against some individual or particular group of individuals, and it is for this reason that they can be so easily directed to the support and maintenance of race prejudices. The individual exhibits race prejudice because it affords him a means of easing certain tensions within himself, because he is happiest when he is most freely able to release those tensions by giving vent to his feelings. As far as the individual is concerned the prejudice itself is unimportant, it merely provides the channel through which his feelings are allowed their necessary expression. What is important is that his feelings do gain expression. Such feelings must, and for the health of the individual should, find expression. As I have already said, such feelings will attach themselves to the most suitable object offered, whatever it may be. Such feelings are not feelings of race preju-

[8] I find that this factor has not been so consistently overlooked as I had thought. After this was originally written the following works in which this factor is either discussed or referred to came to my attention: Dollard, John, and others. *Frustration and Aggression.* New Haven: Yale University Press, 1939 (pp. 151-156); Durbin, Evan F. M., and Bowlby, John. *Personal Aggressiveness and War.* New York: Columbia University Press, 1939; Fremont-Smith, Frank. "The Physiological Basis of Aggression." *Child Study,* 15, 1938 (pp. 1-8).

dice, or any other kind of prejudice, and they are not inborn. On the contrary, such feelings are to the largest extent generated during the postnatal development of almost every individual during early childhood. There can, however, be little doubt that the elementary forms of these affective states in their undifferentiated condition are physiologically determined.[9] The manner in which such feelings are generated has been discussed in great detail by psychoanalysts and others, and I shall here briefly resume the processes involved in the production of these dynamisms.

The aggressiveness which adults exhibit in the form of race hatred would universally appear to have the same origin. By this I mean that the aggressiveness, and not the race hatred, has the same origin universally and is later merely arbitrarily directed, in some societies, against certain groups. This same aggressiveness under other conditions could be directed against numerous different objects, either real or imagined. The object against which aggressiveness is directed is determined by particular conditions, and these we shall later briefly consider.

If it be agreed that in racial intolerance and prejudice a certain amount of aggressiveness is always displayed, we must ask and answer two questions: Where does this aggressiveness come from? and, Why is it exhibited?

Briefly, it is here suggested that the aggressiveness which adults exhibit is originally produced during childhood by parents, nurses, teachers, or whoever else participates in the process of socializing the child. By depriving the infant, and later the child, of all those means of satisfaction which it seeks—the nipple, the mother's body, uncontrolled freedom to excrete, to suck, to cry at will, to scream and shout, to stay up as late as it wishes, to do the thousand and one things that are forbidden—frustration upon frustration is piled up within the child.[10] Such frustrations lead to resentment, fear, hatred, and aggression. In childhood this aggres-

[9] Fremont-Smith, Frank. op. cit.; and "The Influence of Emotional Factors upon Physiological and Pathological Processes." Bulletin of the New York Academy of Medicine, 15, 1939 (pp. 560-569).
[10] Frustration may here be defined as the thwarting of an expected satisfaction.

siveness or resentment is displayed in "bad temper" and in general "naughtiness." Such conduct almost invariably results in further frustration, in punishment. At this stage of its development the child finds itself in a state of severe conflict. Either he must control the expression of his aggressiveness or else suffer the punishment and the loss of love which his aggressiveness provokes. Such conflicts are usually resolved by excluding the painful situation from consciousness and from direct motor expression—in short, by the repression of one's aggressive energies. These are rarely ever completely repressed but only insofar as they permit a resolution of the original conflict situation; and the more the original derivatives of what was primarily repressed become further removed from the latter, the more freely do these energies gain access to consciousness, and the more available for use do they become.[11] The evidence renders it overwhelmingly certain that these energies are never to any extent destroyed. Being a part of the total organism they must, in one way or another, find expression, and the ways in which they can find expression are innumerable. Race hatred and prejudice is merely one of the ways in which, under certain conditions, aggressiveness may express itself.

Fear of those who, in childhood, have frustrated one, and anxiety concerning the outcome of the situation thus produced, lead to the repression of aggression against the original frustrators, and thereby to the *conditioning* of an emotional association between certain kinds of frustrative, or fear, situations and aggressive feelings. As a result of such conditioning any object even remotely suggesting such fear or frustrative situations provokes the aggressive behavior with which such fears and frustrations have become associated.

It must again be repeated that the aggressiveness which is more or less common to all human beings is not a cause of race prejudice but merely represents a motive force, or affective energy, which can be attached, among other things, to the notion that other groups or "races" are hateful, and

[11] Will someone please oblige by noticing how fitly the second law of thermodynamics and the concept of entropy apply here?

which may thus serve to keep such ideas supplied with the emotional force necessary to keep them going.

Since the infliction of mental, and even physical, pain, as well as the frustration and depreciation of others, is involved in the process of race prejudice, and since much of the aggressiveness of the individual owes its existence to early experiences of a similar sort, it is perhaps not difficult to understand why it is that most people are so ready to participate in the exercise of race prejudice. By so doing they are able to find an object for their aggressiveness which most satisfactorily permits its free expression in ways almost identically resembling those which in childhood were indulged in against them and which led to the production of aggressiveness, namely, by punishment, frustration, and checks to one's positive self-feeling. Thus is the frustrated child enabled, as an adult, to pay off—quite unconsciously—an old score. The later frustrations of adolescent and adult life suffered by the individual naturally add to the store and complexity of aggressiveness, and require no discussion here. We can do no more than refer to such important psychological mechanisms as displacement, which defines the process whereby aggression is displaced from one object to another, and projection, the process of attributing to others feelings and impulses originating in ourselves which have been refused conscious recognition.

Briefly, then, the factor which has been most consistently overlooked in the discussion of race problems is the psychological factor, the deep motive forces represented by the aggressiveness which is present in all human beings. It is this aggressiveness which renders so easily possible the usual emotional and irrational development of race prejudice. A rational society must reckon with this factor, for since a certain amount of frustration is inevitable in the development of the individual, and since a certain amount of latent aggressiveness is an ineradicable and necessary part of the equipment of most human beings,[12] the task of an intelligent society is clear. Society must provide outlets for the aggressiveness

[12] "In this world it is very important to be aggressive, but it is fatal to appear so"—Benjamin Jowett.

of the individual which will result in benefits both to the individual and to society. Outlets for aggressiveness which result in social friction and in the destruction of good relations between human beings must be avoided. Frustrations in the early and subsequent development of the individual must be reduced to a minimum, and aggressiveness must always be directed toward ends of constructive value.

It has already been pointed out that the problem of "race" in our society is a social problem and not a biological one in any but the narrow technical sense. Racial tolerance is a matter of simple human decency, and decency is an attitude of mind which is, for the most part, culturally produced. Whether "races" are biologically equal or not is an utterly irrelevant consideration where tolerance is concerned. Where differences exist between peoples it is surely obvious that tolerance ought to increase in proportion to the magnitude of the differences which are believed to exist. Until such an attitude of mind becomes part of the equipment of every individual, no amount of instruction in the biological facts concerning race will ever succeed in eliminating race prejudices. Race prejudice is ultimately merely an effect of a poorly or incompletely developed personality. If race prejudice is ever to be eliminated, society must assume the task of educating the individual, not so much in the facts of race as in the processes which lead to the development of an adequately integrated human being. The solution here, as in so much else, lies in education. Education for humanity first and in the facts afterward. For of what use are facts unless they are intelligently understood and humanely used?

Supposing, for a moment, that significant differences did exist between different peoples which rendered one, in general, superior to the other. An adequately developed human being would hardly consider such differences a sufficient reason for withholding any opportunities for social and cultural development from such groups. On the contrary, he would be the more anxious to provide them with such opportunities. Undeveloped personalities operate in the opposite way and, creating most of the differences they condemn, proceed to intensify those differences by making it more and more difficult for the groups thus treated to avoid or overcome them. Both the form of the mind and the form of the body are so dependent upon social conditions that when the latter are unequal for different groups little or no inference can be made as to the mental and physical potentialities of the groups not enjoying equal social opportunities.

Until we have succeeded, by means of the proper educational methods, in producing that cultivation of the mind which renders nothing which is human alien to it, the "race" problem will never be completely solved. The means by which that problem may to some extent be ameliorated have already been indicated. Meanwhile, in order that we may be quite clear concerning the real nature of the "race" problem as a social problem, it would be well to have some acquaintance with such biological facts relating to race as have been scientifically established.

Concerning the origin of living human races we can say little more than that there is every reason to believe that it was a single stock which gave rise to all the "races" of man. All the "races" of man belong to the same species and have the same remote common human ancestry. This is a conclusion to which all the relevant evidence of comparative anatomy, paleontology, serology, and genetics points. On genetic grounds alone it is virtually impossible to conceive of the varieties of man as having originated separately as distinct lines from different anthropoid ancestors. Genetically, the chances against such a process ever having occurred are in terms of probability of such an order as to render such a suggestion inadmissible.

Up to the present time no satisfactory classification of human races has been devised, and it is much to be doubted whether such classification is possible in any manner resembling the procedure of the botanical or zoological taxonomist. The reason for this is that all human races are very much more mixed than are plant or animal forms, and hence there is a greater dispersion, or scattering, of characters, which has the effect of producing a considerable amount of overlapping between ethnic groups. The more or less great variability of all ethnic groups constitutes a genetic proof of their mixed origins. From the biological standpoint the physical differences which exist between the ethnic groups of mankind are so insignificant that when properly evaluated they can only be described in terms of a particular expression of an assortment of genes which are common to mankind as a whole. At most, ethnic groups can differ from one another only in the distribution of a comparatively few genes. This one may say very much more definitely than one may say it of the differences exhibited by any of our domesticated varieties of cats, dogs, or horses. There are numerous varieties of cats, dogs, and horses, and these represent highly selected strains of animals which have been bred as more or less pure breeds and domesticated by man.

Man, too, is a domesticated, a self-domesticated, animal, but, unlike our domestic animals, the ethnic groups of man are much mixed and are very far from representing pure breeds. The range of variation in all human varieties for any character is very much more considerable than that which is exhibited by any group of animals belonging to a pure breed. All the evidence indicates that the differences between the so-called "races" of man merely represent a random combination of variations derived from a common source which, by inbreeding in isolated groups, have become scattered and more or less stabilized and hereditary in a large number of the members of such groups. Furthermore, the evidence indicates that such selection of variations as has occurred in different groups has been primarily restricted to physical characters. There is no evidence among the races or varieties of mankind that any process of mental selection has ever been operative. The conception of selection for mental qualities seems to be a peculiarly modern one adapted to modern prejudices. We shall presently refer to the nature of the mental differences which are alleged to exist between different races.

Whether the races of mankind have a common origin or not is a matter which need concern us little in view of the fact that structurally they are all now so very much alike. No one physical trait is limited to any particular race although different races show higher frequencies in the possession of certain physical traits than others. Such differences in the distribution of the frequencies of physical characters in different human races simply means that at some time in the past individuals of different heredity interbred, and in isolation continued to do so, with the result that a new combination of characters became more or less evenly distributed throughout the group. In this way a new human variety or genogroup was produced. A genogroup may be defined as a breeding population which differs from other breeding populations in the frequency of one or more genes. The fact that all human genogroups are generated in this way is suggested not only by what we know of human crosses today or the behavior of other animal groups but by the presence in all human beings of a large number of the characters most frequently found in any one genogroup. The fundamental genetic kinship of all the ethnic groups of man would, therefore, seem to be clear.

With respect to the nature of those physical characters in the frequency distributions of which ethnic or geno-groups differ from one another, it requires to be said that not one can be classed as either "higher" or "lower" in the scale of development than another. Every normal physical character must be appraised as equally valuable for the respective functions which it is called upon to perform. Such a character, for example, as black skin color probably represents the original skin color of man, while white skin is probably due to the effects of several mutant genes. Whatever its origin, a black skin is undoubtedly a character of adaptive value since it enables the individual to withstand the dangerous actinic rays of the sun. Hence, for groups living in areas of intense sunlight a black skin would, in terms of natural selection, be superior to a white skin. There would seem to be some evidence that a broad nose is associated with breathing air at high temperatures and a narrow nose with breathing air at low temperatures,[13] but whether such characters are due to adaptation or to natural or social selection, or to a combina-

---

[13] Thomson, A., and Buxton, L. H. D. "Man's Nasal Index in Relation to Certain Climatic Conditions." *Journal of the Royal Anthropological Institute*, 53, 1923 (pp. 92-122).

tion of such factors, is uncertain. What is certain is that such characters do enable the individuals possessing them to meet the demands which their environments have made upon them and upon their ancestors. And this may be said for all the normal characters of all the races of man. There would appear to be no grounds, therefore, for the notion that there exist any physical or biological inequalities between the races of man—in the sense of a physical superiority or inferiority to one another.

Let us now briefly turn our attention to the nature of the mental differences which exist between different races. The material basis of those structures which are eventually organized to function as mind are to a large extent inherited precisely as are all other structures of the body. This is an assumption, but it seems a perfectly legitimate one to make. The qualification, "to a large extent," is introduced for the reason that it is necessary, since in man the nervous system continues to develop long after birth and is therefore appreciably influenced by the experience of the individual. There is every reason to believe, as Edinger has pointed out, "that in certain parts of the nervous mechanism new connections can always be established through education." [14] And as Ranson, a leading neuroanatomist, has added, "The neurons which make up the nervous system of an adult man are therefore arranged in a system the larger outlines of which follow an hereditary pattern, but many of the details of which have been shaped by the experiences of the individual." [15] It is evident that experience must play a considerable role in the development of the structure of the nervous system,[16] and

[14] Edinger, Ludwig. *Vorlesungen über den Bau der nervösen Zentralorgane des Menschen und der Tiere.* Leipzig: Vogel, 1911.

[15] Ranson, S. W. *The Anatomy of the Nervous System.* Philadelphia: Saunders, 1939 (p. 56).

[16] See the fundamental work of Coghill, G. E. *Anatomy and the Problem of Behaviour.* New York: Macmillan, 1929 (pp. 105-107): "It is possible also that conditioning processes are registered in structural counterparts in the sense that neural mechanisms acquire functional specificity with reference to the experience. In the counterpart of the form of the pattern . . . the specificity of function is fixed by the relations into which the elements grow. In the counterpart of experience, on the other hand, specificity of function is established by interaction of growth and excitation; that is to say, the excitation fixes upon the growing terminals of

it is also clear that the form of the nervous system which we know as mind is dependent upon the interaction of several factors; these are primarily the inherited, incompletely developed structure of the nervous system and the character of the external developing influences.

There can be no doubt that the material bases of mind are inherited in much the same way as are the remaining structures of the body and, while the organization of the structures of the body is appreciably influenced by external factors, the resulting effects are incomparably less complex and fewer than are those which are capable of being produced through the organization of those nervous structures which function as mind.

While it is possible, though this has never been demonstrated, that in different human ethnic groups the nervous system differs in some of its structural characters, *it is certain that, if such differences exist, then they are of the most insignificant kind.* The measurable mental characters of different human groups strongly suggest that no significant mental differences exist between such groups which may be attributed to the characters of the nervous system alone. Furthermore, the mental differences which exist between human groups would appear to be much less than those which are found to exist between individuals of the same group. In the light of our present knowledge the evidence shows that within the limits of the normal, brain weight, cranial capacity, head size, or the gross stature and form of the brain bear no relation whatever to the characters of the mind, as between

---

neurones its own mode of activation. . . . cortical cells, beginning their function with the beginning of experience, grow as experience progresses till all of the essential behavior and conditioning processes are registered in them. Every pyramidal cell as a growing unit may be conceived as blending, so to speak, the experience of the individual from the beginning to the end of stimulation and response. . . . As a result of this, although the behavior at any moment may be dominated by some particular phase of experience, it cannot be disconnected from any part of the whole. Only with the retrogressive changes of senescence or with arrested development in pathological cases does experience cease to register in a progressive manner."

individuals of the same or different races.[17] Nor is there any necessary association between certain racial characters and certain kinds of mentality. Since mental functions are so largely dependent upon experience, upon cultural conditions, it is impossible to make any inferences as to the equivalence or nonequivalence of mental potentialities as between races or peoples among whom the cultural conditions are not strictly comparable.

In short, no statement concerning the mentality of an individual, a group, or a race is of any value without a specification of the environment in which that mentality has developed. No discussion of "racial" mental characters can be countenanced which neglects a full consideration of the associated cultural variables. For it is evident that it is precisely these cultural variables which play the most significant part in producing mental differences between different cultural and racial groups. As I have already indicated, there can be little doubt that genetically determined mental differences do exist between individuals of the same and of different ethnic groups, but there is absolutely no evidence that significant mental differences which are determined by the genetic characters of the nervous system exist between any two such groups. It would appear to be chiefly, if not entirely, because of differences in cultural experience that individuals and groups differ from one another culturally, and it is for this reason that where the cultural experience has appreciably dif-

[17] On these subjects see the following: Pearson, Karl. "Relationship of Intelligence to Size and Shape of the Head and Other Mental and Physical Characters." *Biometrika*, 5, 1906 (pp. 105-146); Pearl, R. "On the Correlation between Intelligence and the Size of the Head." *Journal of Comparative Neurology and Psychology*, 16, 1906 (pp. 189-199); Murdock, K., and Sullivan, L. R. "A Contribution to the Study of Mental and Physical Measurements in Normal Children." *American Physical Education Review*, 28, 1923 (pp. 209-215, 278-288, 328); Reid, R. R., and Mulligan, J. H. "Relation of Cranial Capacity to Intelligence." *Journal of the Royal Anthropological Institute*, 53, 1923 (pp. 322-332); Bonin, Gerhardt von. "On the Size of Man's Brain, as Indicated by Skull Capacity." *Journal of Comparative Neurology*, 59, 1934 (pp. 1-28); Pickering, S. P. "Correlation of Brain and Head Measurements, and Relation of Brain Shape and Size to Shape and Size of the Head." *American Journal of Physical Anthropology*, 15, 1931 (pp. 1-52); Levin, G. "Racial and 'Inferiority' Characters in the Human Brain." *American Journal of Physical Anthropology*, 22, 1937 (pp. 345-380).

fered cultural achievement is an exceedingly poor measure of the mental value of an individual or of a group. For all practical purposes, therefore, and until evidence to the contrary is forthcoming, we can safely take cultural achievement to represent the expression chiefly of cultural experience and not of biological potentiality.

The average individual in our society observes that certain "races" possess physical and mental traits which differ from his own. He concludes that these physical and mental traits are somehow linked together, that they are inborn, and that they are immutable. Vague notions about a unilinear "evolution" assist him to believe that such "races" are "lower" in the "scale" of evolution than is the group to which he belongs. From some such starting point as *Pithecanthropus erectus* he envisages a continuous progression upwards culminating in the development of his own "race." Between *Pithecanthropus* and himself stand, in an intermediate position, all the other "races" of mankind. "Race" is a very definite entity to him, and all the intellectual supports for his conception of it are there ready to his hand. The significance of "race" for him emotionally is, as we have already seen, of considerable importance. Race exists. Such is the conception of race with which we have to reckon. That there are no scientific grounds for such a conception of race has already been shown. In fact, the prevailing conception of "race" probably represents the greatest delusion of our time. I hope that some of the facts which have been set down in this chapter will be instrumental in suggesting the methods by means of which this great common error may be corrected.

The great error that most anthropologists have committed in their approach to the problem of "race" has been to think of "race" in terms of statistical averages which could be converted into "racial" standards for the purposes of comparison. This has in turn led to the fatal error of taking such standards to represent static "racial" entities, somehow existing by a special act of evolutionary creation.[18] The mechanism of this

[18] For a most pertinent discussion of this subject and of the whole question of species and race from the standpoint of the geneticist, see Dobzhansky, Theodosius. *Genetics and the Origin of Species*. 3rd ed. New York: Columbia University Press, 1951.

special act of evolutionary creation has hardly interested them at all; all that they seem to have been interested in has been to describe its end effects. But even here their efforts have been defeated by the incorrigible habit of "races" to vary so much.

With the rise of modern genetics the biological mechanism of race production has been rendered, in its main principles, perfectly clear. Race is simply a more or less temporary genetic stage in a process, and any race at the present time is merely the stage in which we observe that process at our own time level. At an earlier time level it was undoubtedly in a different stage of that process; at a later period it will probably be at still another stage. Each stage in the process is determined by the way in which the individual genes which are contributed to the "race"—that is, the process—by the individuals comprising it are combined. The factors influencing the ways in which the genes are combined are many, but perhaps among the most important is the inherent tendency of the genetic materials to vary in themselves. Time, isolation, environment, miscegenation, natural, social, and sexual selection are important additional factors either in themselves or together.

What genetics teaches us is that the "race" problem before the world today is not a biological problem at all. What the facts presented here have taught us is that the "race" problem is essentially a social problem and that when we have succeeded in approaching it with that full understanding for which it calls we may eventually succeed in releasing our fellows from the miserable effects of the delusion of "race."

9

Racism and Social Action

T HE REACTION of scientists to the propaganda of those who sought to convince the world of the truth of racism has had an interesting history. At first the errors and spurious arguments of the racists were duly exposed by the simple appeal to the facts of science. Facts after all, it was felt, speak for themselves. With the monstrous unfolding of the Nazi racist policy of extermination of the Jews in Europe, and mounting racial tensions in this country, the very real seriousness of the problem at last broke in on many scientists. As a result we have witnessed a considerable increase in the literature devoted to the examination of the causes of race tensions and prejudice and the refutation of racist ideas and dogmas. By these means scientists have hoped to arrest, at least, the spread of the infection of racism. Ideally they would have liked to render immune those who stood in danger of acquiring it and to cure those who had already been infected with the virus of racism.

The attempt has been a noble one and it has enjoyed something of a rewarding success. But that success, in the face of a growing intensification of "race" feeling, has been a strictly limited one. Many persons and groups have, gratifyingly, been influenced to think and behave more intelligently with respect

From *Psychiatry*, vol. 9, 1945, 143-150.

to race relations, but the population in many parts of this country—not to mention others—has made no such progress. It has, instead, become more race conscious than at any previous time in the history of the United States. Little Rock is but one example. It has become evident that to make the truth readily available is not enough. Facts, it appears, do not speak for themselves nor, it seems, are they necessarily understood when they do. And when they are understood, it far from follows that they will be accepted and acted upon.

These are by no means new discoveries, but the responses which they define have come to most workers in the field of race relations with something of the shock of a new discovery, and this because the seriousness of the issues at stake has given so much greater force to the errors and perversions of thought and conduct of which so many persons and groups are guilty. The silly stereotypes, absurd beliefs, vulgar errors, and unfortunate attitudes, when multiplied several million times, actually add up to a tremendous amount of social pathology. Western society, and our society in particular, is very sick indeed.

We have spent a fair amount of time inquiring into and investigating the causes of the social disease which is racism, and we have yet a great deal of work to do before we shall have brought such studies to completion. Investigations of this kind are invaluable and they must be encouraged to continue upon an even larger scale than hitherto, but it should be quite obvious that investigation and the clearest analysis and description of causes will never succeed in curing the disease of racism. The better, however, we understand the causes of the disease, the more efficiently it will be possible to prescribe the remedy for it. Hence, research into every aspect of the problem of prejudice and racism must continue on an ever-widening front. But it is now coming to be more and more widely understood that the prosecution of such researches and their publication in technical journals, periodicals, and books is not an end in itself but a means to an end. The theoretical phase of the attack on racism has now reached the stage which renders it clear that not much more can be achieved by this means. What we now need is to enter upon the second, the applied, phase of the attack in which, using our theoretical knowledge gained from the actual investigation of the necessary [1] conditions, we embark upon the practical application of that knowledge.

We now know something of the nature of the causes of racism and we know how spurious are the arguments which are brought to its support, and of this we have heard a great deal. What we want to know now is what we can do about racism in a practical way in the form of social action in the attack upon this most critical of social problems.

One of the first things to be realized is that partial measures and measures which we know to have no more than a palliative effect are not going to accomplish very much. Education, full employment, and good housing will help, but they will not solve the racial problem. Such measures are doomed to failure for the simple reason that race prejudice stems from sources which these remedies, for the most part, fail to reach. These sources are the internalized basic structures which determine the social functioning of the personality—the basic structures which are erected as the framework of the personality by the process of socialization, by the manner in which the socially undifferentiated human organism is turned into a socially differentiated human being. The basic personality structure of every human being is determined by the forms of social response which have been institutionalized in each society.

An analysis of the institutions determining such responses in American society renders it perfectly clear that in order to change any of those responses it will be necessary to change the character of some of our institutions. For example, perhaps the one ideal beyond all others which has become predominantly institutionalized in the United States is the ideal of success—success measured in terms of how many dollars a man possesses or how much he can "make" in a year. The emphasis is almost entirely upon material success in the open competitive market. Margaret Mead has discussed this trait

[1] The term "necessary" is here used in its logical sense as an indispensable condition entering into the group of conditions which together determine a cause.

of American culture at length in her book *And Keep Your Powder Dry*. The spirit of aggressive competition is inculcated in the young American almost as soon as he is capable of understanding what is required of him. He soon learns that his parents' love is conditional upon how he compares—measures up—with others; he must compete and be successful.

The hunt for status and the impetus to obtain prestige by the achievement of substantial quantities of dollars represents a very powerful drive indeed. All potential competing persons and groups, as a consequence of such a process of socialization, therefore come to be regarded as rivals, and inevitably they will be regarded with varying degrees of hostility and fear. The frustrations of infancy, childhood, adolescence, and adult life, which have been either wholly or partially repressed, find a very ready outlet in the sanctioned aggressiveness which the American competitive system of living encourages. Under such conditions racial prejudice and discrimination is inevitable, for in a society such as ours, in which there are definitely recognized "in-groups" and "out-groups" which are regarded as in competition with each other, hostility will always be directed toward the "out-group," since by its very presence it constitutes a threat to the security of the person whose personality is structured in terms of competition and the drive to succeed. In view of the fact that such persons spend a great part of their anxious lives in a state of actual or anticipated insecurity, it is not surprising that they should give their fears substantial form in the shape of some minority or ethnic—so-called "racial"—group which may then serve as the object to which one may transfer—displace—aggressions which have been directed to other frustrating objects, and thus serves as a convenient scapegoat.

The insecurities incident to life in highly industrialized societies are continually productive of frustrations, and race prejudice constitutes a socially sanctioned outlet for the resulting accumulated aggressiveness; this at once serves to explain the person's failure to himself and at the same time enables him to revenge himself upon the imagined cause of it.

As long as we maintain the kind of emphasis we do in this country upon competitive success, and as long as we continue to produce the kind of frustrations and insecurities which we do in infants, children, adolescents, and adults, active feelings of hostility toward members of "out-groups" will continue to plague our society, no matter how well we succeed in restraining their expression by means of external constraints. This is not to say that such external constraints are useless. On the contrary, I am going to suggest that they can be of the first importance, and that they must be applied much more rigorously than any have yet been. But this *is* to say that in order to eliminate the sickness of group hostility we must eliminate the conditions which give rise to it, and, as I have indicated, a number of the most important of those conditions are to be found in the character of some of our institutions.

In the first place we must change our ideal of success in terms of material achievement to one which will have as its goal success in terms of the perfection of the human spirit, *humanitas*. We must change from the disoperative ideal of the rugged American individualist to the ideal of the co-operative citizen who is passionately devoted to something other than himself, to his fellow men, and to the good of his society. In other words, we must concentrate our energies on making humane beings out of men. When we have achieved this we shall have solved not only the problem of group hostility but most of the social problems arising out of interpersonal relations. Obviously this is an ideal to be aimed at. But how is such an ideal to be practically achieved?

The answer is, By social reform and by education. The two processes must proceed together; the development of one without the other will not be good enough. The person educated in certain ideals of behavior toward his fellows must be given an opportunity to practice them. If the society in which he lives makes it difficult for him to do so he will find himself at odds with far too many people for his conduct to make itself appreciably felt upon the masses. And if he makes any progress at all it will be slow, partial, and unsatisfying, and it is doubtful whether what little he may achieve at so great a cost will endure. This is the lot of most would-be social reformers today. On the other hand, where conditions are such as to make it possible for the socially educated person with some assurance of support and approval, or at least the absence of determined and widespread opposition to his ideals, to live his life humanely and co-operatively, there can be little doubt of the great social progress that could be made within a single generation. If conditions could be made easier for the average man to co-operate in this way—even if, as in most cases, he would have to be directed by the imperatives of the law—we shall have made a very great advance in the right direction. And this brings me to the one great agency of social regulation which has thus far not been adequately utilized in the attack upon the problem of group hostility. I mean the law. It has been said that one cannot legislate race prejudice out of existence. This may be true, but no more true than to say that one cannot legislate libel and slander out of existence.[2] The fact is that our laws of libel and slander exercise a most effective control over the publication, written or spoken, of malicious statements calculated to bring a person into contempt or expose him to public hatred and derision. Virtual anarchy would reign were there no such laws. Imagine the orgy of defamatory vituperation in which certain elements of our press would indulge, a state in which no man's personality would be respected and every man could be threatened with the blackmail of public ridicule and contempt. From such vicious conduct the law of the land protects the individual when the defamatory remarks are specifically directed at him as a person, but it does not protect him when these remarks are directed at any religious, ethnic, or minority group of which he is a member. Thus, it is possible to defame a whole ethnic group and therefore every person belonging to it without either the group as a whole or any member of it being able to defend themselves against such attacks by an appeal to the law which should protect every person from attacks upon his character, no matter whether they are made directly or indirectly. The rights of the group should be no less inviolable than the rights of the person, for

[2] Let us remember that there were men in the seventeenth and eighteenth centuries who held that it would be impossible to legislate slavery out of existence.

the group derives its being from the collectivity of interacting persons so that when the group as a group is defamed every one of its constituent members is similarly defamed. Those who defame Jews as a group defame every single Jew on earth, and those who claim the exception of "some of my best friends" prove the rule that this is indeed so.

It is surely perfectly clear that it is a far more harmful thing to libel a whole group than it is to libel an individual. The very law of libel which exists in all civilized societies is, in the Western world at least, based on the recognition of and respect for the intrinsic worth of the person as such. The individual is valued as a person, not as an undifferentiated spoke in the wheel of society. This is admirable, but when defamation of the individual is secured through the device of defaming the group of which he is a member, the purpose for which the law of libel was instituted—the protection of the rights of the person—is defeated. Yet our legislators have never recognized this fact. The law up to the present time has been concerned, for the most part, with the relations between individuals rather than with the relations between individuals and groups within the same society. But the law cannot much longer remain out of touch with the realities of the situation. Now that the whole world has witnessed the frightful crimes which have been committed against millions of persons not as individuals but as members of a group, the dangers of group libel require no further demonstration. When we observe that the course of a person's whole life may be made to depend on the group to which he belongs rather than upon his own individual qualities, and that one of the chief mechanisms by means of which such a condition of affairs is maintained is the group-sanctioned device of group libel, it should be apparent that we need to outlaw this category of libel at the very least as forcibly as we have outlawed all other forms of malicious defamation.

Because it is morally reprehensible, socially disruptive, and the cause of gross injustice and unhappiness to the individual, group libel must be recognized for what it is, as a crime against both the individual and society. The institution by the state of a law making the defamation of any religious, ethnic, or minority group a crime will not only have the deterrent effect of reducing the expression of group hostility to a minimum but will have the more positive moral effect of causing men to recognize the evil for what it is and to condemn it. It will then become unequivocally clear that race prejudice and race discrimination are evils punishable as offenses against society. With the removal of the permissive negative sanctions which they formerly enjoyed and the substitution of positive sanctions against such forms of prejudiced behavior, one of the worst causes of racism would be brought under effective control and virtually eliminated.

Mr. Carey McWilliams has very ably presented the lawyer's case for legislation against race discrimination. Here I am attempting to make out a case for legislation against race prejudice and group hostility of any kind based on race, religious, or ethnic prejudice. Race prejudice and race discrimination are not the same things. Race prejudice is essentially an attitude of mind but it does not always necessarily lead to race discrimination, though it usually does. Race discrimination is the active form of race prejudice as exhibited, for example, in exclusion laws against Jews, Negroes, and Italians in educational institutions, but more particularly as it functions in connection with business, housing, transportation, employment, voting, and so on. Race prejudice gives rise to race discrimination, and race discrimination serves to maintain and continually add fuel to race prejudice, and, in this viciously circular manner, to intensify and extend discriminative practices.

A law against group libel would obviously not necessarily affect the practice of race discrimination, while a law against race discrimination would not of itself eliminate race prejudice. The question arises whether both forms of group hostility should be attacked together or separately. This is ultimately a matter of strategy and the answer will vary for different areas. In the South, for example, legislation calculated to reduce discrimination would stand a better chance than any attempt to enact a law against group libel. In the North, I suspect that there would be no more difficulty in securing legislation against group libel than there has been in securing the passage of the Ives-Quinn bill in New York State. The strategy is a matter for those to determine who know their localities best.

The case against group libel is clear. It should and must be enacted as a law by every state in the Union, while at the same time legislation should be passed against every form of discrimination on the basis of ethnic, religious, or minority association. A concerted attack of this kind upon group hostility will do more for the improvement of group relations than any other practical measures of which I can think. Coordinated with educational measures such a program will begin to produce results immediately.

Here, then, is something we can do in a practical way, here and now. We can not only begin thinking and working for state and federal legislation against group hostility and discrimination, but the ground can be prepared for it and local situations improved by working up sufficient interest to secure the passage of such legislation in one's own particular town.

We must press for the permanent establishment of a Federal Fair Employment Practices Commission as a first step, since this is an issue of which Congress has already been made aware, and our energies in this direction must be unflagging. As supplementary, or perhaps as part of the task of securing this and allied legislation, we can, as has already been suggested, interest the proper people in our own particular localities in such legislation. But beyond all else it is legislation on a national scale that must be our objective.

With the passage of such antidiscriminatory legislation the issue of group hostility, whether ethnic, religious, or minority, would be squarely before the people. Let us then be prepared to meet the issue in the best possible manner by paving the way now for the immediate passage of the bill making group libel a crime against society, a crime against the expressed ideal of this society, *e pluribus unum*, "out of many, one."

From the viewpoint of the worker interested in the elimination of race prejudice, the early years of the developing person must receive far greater attention than has yet been bestowed upon this capitally important period. The mind of the preschool child—the first five years—is to a very large extent molded by its parents, particularly by the mother. Since within the first five years of life the foundations of many later attitudes are laid—and the antecedents of race prejudice can in most cases be clearly traced to this early period in the life of the person in our society—the knowledge must be put into the hands of all who are concerned with the process of socializing the child, which will enable them to help the child grow into a well-balanced, co-operative human being.

The growth of the nursery school movement in this country provides an educational complement to education in the home, the potential importance of which cannot be overemphasized. It is through the nursery school that parents can be reached and educated in the co-operative task of educating their children. Because of the importance of the issues involved the state should provide free nursery schools to accommodate the population of children between the ages of two and five years, and in this area of public instruction special stress should be placed upon the parents' obligation to co-operate with the nursery school. Parent-teacher relationships should be an integral part of the educational program and the nursery school should be conducted as an integral part of the community, the child being a member of a community as well as of a family.

It should be a prerequisite required of all teachers in such nursery schools that they be adequately trained to guide young children in laying the foundations of good habits in interpersonal and intergroup relationships. Such teachers should come to the school in the full awareness of the structure and problems of their society and of the particular community in which they are to serve. Especially must they be aware of their particular function in assisting the child to avoid all those developments which are later easily turned into group hostility. More positively, the teacher must help the child to a sense of security within his family and the community, and must help him to lay the foundations of that feeling of fellowship with people of all kinds which is the true basis of cultural democracy. In this task the co-operation of the parents is indispensable, and parents can, in most cases, be made to see the advantages of such co-operation.

Before we proceed to consider some of the practical steps which can be taken in this area of the educational program, let us briefly consider some of the antecedents of race prejudice encountered in preschool children. In the first place it should be said that while most preschool children do not show any developed form of race prejudice they can and do show potentialities which may develop into socially destructive "race" attitudes, although these attitudes are not likely to materialize until later. They do, however, quite often show "race" discrimination. Such discrimination, as Ruth Horowitz has shown,[3] is frequently made in relation to "racial" self-identification. The differences discriminated mostly relate to skin color, language, clothes, customs such as eating different foods or in a different way, and absence from school on certain festivals.

The primary bases out of which group prejudices may easily grow if not properly handled are present in the predispositions which are to be found in all children. Among the fears, for example, which children exhibit are the fear of being left alone, fear of a strange person—which is really the same thing as the fear of being left alone—and fear of the dark. These fears may become the bases for insecurities of various sorts and aggressive feelings toward members of other groups unless they are properly handled and directed.

Crying when left alone as exhibited, for example, by infants of three or four months when physical contact ceases is perhaps the first social fear. The child is a highly dependent being and as it develops it draws its feeling of security from those persons upon whom it has learned to grow dependent. Unless his social development is properly handled he will tend to feel "alone" and insecure in the presence of strangers, he will be afraid, and he will dislike the object of his fear. Hence, an unreasoned prejudice against persons of all "out-groups" may easily develop from this kind of situation. Good early conditioning in interpersonal relationships and the in-

[3] Horowitz, Ruth. "Racial Aspects of Self-Identification in Nursery School Children." *Journal of Psychology*, 7, 1939 (pp. 91-99).

surance of the maximum of security for the child are the two primary generalizations which can be made here concerning the manner in which such fears may be handled. More particularly, where fears arise in the child as the result of the observation of striking differences in other people, such occasions must be converted into as pleasantly conditioning ones as possible.

As Jersild and Holmes have shown,[4] preschool children may not only be afraid of strangers and cling to mother when seeing a stranger on the street but they are often afraid of familiar people when they look temporarily different. Thus, one child showed extreme fright when she first saw her mother with a thick layer of cold cream on her face; another child showed fear when she first saw her grandmother with her hair down. Nuns in their usual habiliments are fearsome sights to young children upon their first experience of them. Anyone who has carefully observed young children in such situations will have been struck by the extreme sense of insecurity which they exhibit. The unfamiliar lacks the supportative quality of the familiar and hence induces a feeling of insecurity.

Such situations should be anticipated, as far as possible, by such devices as picture books and accompanying stories which are calculated to introduce the child to the as yet unencountered reality in a friendly and interested spirit. The natural curiosity of the child should be fully exploited. When the child inquires whether a Negro is black all over and whether the color will not rub off, correct conditioning at this time is a simple matter, and it is of the first importance. The child should be given a sensible explanation of the facts as we know them and afforded every opportunity to play with colored children.

Improperly handled, fear of the dark may bring about a generalized fear of whatever is dark. Hence, special attention should be paid to this aspect of the child's development.

Since the antedecents of "race" prejudice manifested by the

[4] Jersild, A. T., and Holmes, F. B. "Children's Fears." *Child Development Monographs,* No. 20. New York: Teachers College, Columbia University, 1935.

child at the preschool level have their roots primarily in parent-child and adult-child relationships, and are very definitely not something that grow autochthonously from within the child itself, we must see to it, whenever possible and principally through the medium of the school-parent relationships, that the necessary equipment for directing these antecedents into the proper sympathetic channels is made available.

We stand in need of a revaluation of the place of the schools in our society. If children are to be properly educated, their parents must be, too. The development of parent-teacher associations all over the country represents a spontaneous recognition of this need. Parents and teachers must become even more fully aware than they are at present of the need for cooperation between them. They can mutually be of the greatest help to one another in the process of socializing the child and thus, between them, be the principal contributors to a happy harmonious society.

Education for democratic living in a unified society should begin in the nursery school. The cultural, ethnic, and religious differences at that age level must be treated as of no less importance than at any other age. Such group differences should be made the basis for creating an understanding, enriching, and enduring interest in other persons not only as persons but as members of different groups. The differences should be utilized to interest and educate rather than to antagonize and prejudice. In this way the natural curiosity of the child will be constructively satisfied and the proper attitudes initiated. At the same time the essential likenesses must be fully stressed. Children must be made to feel unqualifiedly secure in the presence of what is too often left as the strange and unfamiliar. In this direction no pupils are so apt as the very young.

The great curiosity which all small children exhibit can be creatively utilized in getting them accustomed to and interested in others. At the nursery school level the foundations can thus be effectively laid for what may later be developed as the truly cultivated human point of view—the understanding of and appreciation for the other person's point of view.

By the calculated and judicious choice of toys, books, of

dolls representing a good selection of the peoples which have entered into the formation of this nation, group games with emphasis on co-operation, fair play, and respect for the other person, and similar means, we can hope to achieve much good in the conditioning and preconditioning of good interpersonal attitudes and relations. But again it must be emphasized that at this age level, as well as at the following age levels, the parents must be persuaded to co-operate with the schools; otherwise the best-laid plans of philosophers and teachers will go astray.

10

Racism, Religion, and
Anthropology

ODERN MAN in search of a soul stands a good chance
of finding it at the very brink of the pit in which
he is still in some danger of losing it. At the very edge
of this deadly chasm he stands with one foot solidly planted
on the terra firma of his common humanity, while the other
is perilously poised toward the disaster of annihilation in the
chasm of racism. He has for too long already breathed the
poisonous vapors of the pit to the detriment of his powers of
independent judgment and too long suffered the debilitating
effects of its infectious viruses—the viruses which are, to a
large extent, responsible for that most distressing of all forms
of social pathology which goes by the name of "racism." I
say "to a large extent" because alone these viruses could not
have produced so disastrous an effect had the social agencies
charged with the care of the public health, the public spiritual health, fulfilled their obligations to the people. Indeed, it
is these very social agencies which have often constituted the
worst vectors of infection.

It is difficult to think without despair of a church which,

From *Phylon*, vol. 8, 1947, 230-238.

drawing its life from the example and death of a great martyr to humanity, one of the greatest of all spiritual doctors, has not only departed so widely from his teaching but has, in effect, in several of its denominations negated it and left the message of Christ undelivered. It is more than a hundred years since Lessing remarked that "the Christian religion has been tried for nineteen centuries, but the religion of Christ remains yet to be tried." The statement, alas, is on the whole still quite true. Had the religion of Christ been faithfully brought to the people instead of the cults and dogmas, spiritual prevarication, bigotry, intolerance, and *autos-da-fé* which have to so large an extent served in its place, Western man could never have fallen into the spiritual uncleanliness in which he finds himself today.

I shall not say that the Church has failed, but I think it is evident that the Church has not succeeded in establishing as a ruling principle of man's social conduct the original and essential teaching of Jesus of Nazareth, the principle of altruism, to "love thy neighbor as thyself." Until the Church makes it its undeviatingly consistent purpose to establish this principle in the hearts of men as a compass to steer by on profane as well as on sacred days, it cannot claim to speak in the name of Christ or in the name of humanity.

As I read the evidence it seems to me that Christ conceived the true task of religion to be the perfection of human nature. William Temple, the late Archbishop of Canterbury, put this very clearly when he said that "the aim of a Christian social order is the fullest possible development of individual personality in the widest and deepest possible fellowship." That is the aim of good men everywhere, and whether they work toward the achievement of such an ideal within or without any particular church is, I think, of little import. It was the genius of Jesus to have perceived this ideal as a universally valid one for all people in all times, everywhere. He did not conceive of it as being achieved through the exclusive medium of any particular sect. The truth is one, but there are many different roads by which it may be reached. Man's common purpose is clearly to attain this goal through a great diversity of approaches, differently and freely. Every human being is a problem in search of a solution and so, too, is every society. Indeed, it is his society which creates most of his problems for the individual. And it is principally by utilizing those values in each society which represent the universal moral truths which each society, in its own way, has discovered that we shall effect the fellowship of man. These values, whatever form they may take, are all reducible to the universal principle of love.

In assisting to achieve the fellowship of man, the anthropologist, the student of the comparative science of man as a physical and cultural being, has, he believes, something to offer which is of value. Particularly to those who have the spiritual care of mankind in their hands he can bring the support of knowledge gleaned and tested in the laboratories of different times and various cultures. He can complement and support and reinforce those basic truths which have been independently arrived at by the great religious teachers of the world.

I am not sure that it is always true that there is no evil without some good coming of it, but, in any event, the great negative good which has come of racism is that it has brought to a head many of those fateful questions which have always confronted humanity and with which religion in all its forms has from the first been preoccupied.

Racism puts these questions squarely on the agenda of mankind. It declares that mankind is naturally divisible into races which have originated independently of each other and that these races are each characterized by the possession of inborn physical and mental traits which together serve to distinguish them from one another. These groups are always inferior to the racist's group and must therefore be carefully discriminated against so that no member of such inferior groups is allowed to migrate across the barriers into the ranks of the self-styled superior status group.

Are the races of mankind independent of each other in their origin? Are they differentiated from each other by inborn physical and mental traits? Are there any groups of mankind that are superior mentally and physically to any other? Has God made the nations of men each of a different blood?

The anthropologist, whose task it is as a scientist to investigate the facts which have a bearing in returning an answer to such questions, finds himself in the happy position of being able to give a scientific validation to those basic truths which have been arrived at by the great religious thinkers of all faiths.

In the first place, with respect to the unity of mankind, anthropologists are generally agreed that the evidence indicates that the existing varieties of mankind are derived from the same ancestral group and that all belong to a single species, possibly somewhat prematurely defined as *Homo sapiens*. The physical differences which serve to distinguish the members of the various divisions of mankind from one another represent the end effects of the operation of such factors as the inherent variability of the human organism, geographic and social isolation, inbreeding, outbreeding, and similar elements. But in spite of even the most marked physical differences, all human groups are more or less of mixed origin, and the biological materials of which they are composed, the carriers of their physical and spiritual potentialities, are demonstrably common to all mankind.

The genetic structure of the varieties of mankind is so like, that the conclusion would on this ground alone seem inescapable that all living men are truly brothers under the skin.

So far as the mental traits of the varieties of mankind are concerned, it is now quite certain that such traits are not linked with physical characters and it is reasonably certain that those behavioral traits which are alleged to be racial or inborn are acquired by social heredity and not by biological inheritance. The vast majority of investigators agree that the tests which have been made do not reveal any significant differences in the potentialities of mind between any of the groups of mankind. Indeed, in the evolution of man the one factor which seems to have been at a premium is plasticity, the ability to make rapid adjustments to changing conditions. The emphasis has not been placed on special abilities but on the general ability of plasticity, and in the evolution of man those individuals have tended to survive who were possessed of faculties sufficiently supple to allow themselves to be eclipsed by the selective quality of plasticity. On such grounds alone it is highly unlikely that any differential selection of special traits has been operative in the evolution of man, a probability which is supported even more strongly by the evidences of observation than it is on these theoretical grounds.

The evidence indicates that such mental and cultural differences as are observed to exist between different groups of mankind are traceable to differences in the history of their conditioning, to such influences as social and physical environmental differences, geographic and cultural isolation or otherwise, socioeconomic conditions, and opportunities for cultural development. It is the considered judgment of most anthropologists that these differences are due to differences in social experience and not to differences of a biological nature. The major triumphs of civilization have come from the mixture of cultural traditions, and peoples like individuals grow through the interaction of the stimulating influences to which they are exposed. In the absence of such influences development is slow and unspectacular.

Hence, in order to understand how it is that one people differs from another culturally it is necessary to obtain a specification of the conditions under which each has developed. When this, the accounting of their past history, has been obtained, it is invariably found that differences in cultural achievement by different groups, and to a large extent by persons, may be summed up as due to differences in opportunities for achievement.

If a social order is to be realized in which the fullest possible development of the individual personality may be achieved in the widest and deepest possible fellowship, anthropology is in a position to be able to tell the would-be makers of that social order that no biological barriers stand in the way, that, as E. L. Thorndike has put it, "to the real work of man—the increase of achievement through improvement of the environment—the influence of heredity offers no barrier"; in short, that the best and the surest way of insuring achievement of such a social order is by affording equal opportunities to all men everywhere.

Since the expression of heredity is a function of achievement, man's potentialities, to a certain extent, are subject to human control and guidance. Heredity, it has been well said, determines what we can do, and environment what we do do. It is, hence, the duty of those concerned in establishing the most humane and efficient social order to provide opportunities for all human beings wherever they can so that they may realize to the full the potentialities that are within them; that is, to do what they can.

Anthropology, in providing the facts, gives support to the aspirations of religion and enables it with full authority to teach men to see the common humanity which shows through the accidental and finite differences in men, to come to a practical recognition of human equality, and to learn to have a common concern and regard for all mankind.[1]

Anthropology and religion are, therefore, one in believing in the fundamental unity of mankind. It is now the task of religion to see to it that the implications of that belief are put into practice.

Mankind has been painfully groping its way toward the understanding of the truth that all men are brothers, that there is but one world, and that all men must live together in that world in peace and harmony—that man needs fraternity as he needs his daily bread. The consciousness of a common purpose in mankind receives the greatest reinforcement from the recognition of the fact of the common unity of man; the recognition of the truth proclaimed nineteen centuries ago by Paul on Mars Hill in Athens that "God hath made of one blood all nations of men for to dwell on all the face of the earth" (Acts 17:26).

But the common purpose of man goes beyond the "one blood" of all nations, the physical unity of mankind, to the spiritual, the social unity of mankind; in short, to the brotherhood of man and all that that implies to the federation of the

[1] See Lord Lindsay. *The Good and the Clever.* New York: Macmillan, 1945 (p. 18).

world—with national sovereignty a form of social neurosis for scholars to write about but not under which human beings should live. This does not imply a leveling of all cultures to a state of more or less uniformity. On the other hand, it implies the right, without fear or threat, to be different as well as free. It implies respect for beliefs which we may not share and the mutual enrichment and strengthening of us all which the spirit of understanding and co-operation brings.

The scientific validation of the principle of co-operation is an achievement of our own day. It provides the complete answer to the social Darwinists of the "Nature red in tooth and claw" school. The doctrines of "The Survival of the Fittest," "The Struggle for Existence," and "Natural Selection" were fervently embraced by an age which saw the rise of nationalism and imperialism and the waging of aggressive wars against "weaker" peoples who were alleged to be unfit to govern themselves or incapable of exploiting their own lands. In the United States they gave much-needed support to the social philosophy of rugged American individualism and its active state of ruthless competition.

To remain on the biological level for a moment, there is this to say: modern biological investigations reveal that the picture of "Nature red in tooth and claw" has been grossly overpainted. As pointed out in an earlier chapter, we find that, while aggressive drives exist in nature there are also healthy, nonruthless, benign competition, and markedly strong basic drives toward social and co-operative behavior. These forces do not operate independently but together, as a whole, and the evidence strongly indicates that of all these drives those which are directed toward co-operation are dominant and biologically the most important. No group of animals could survive very long were this not the case. It is today perfectly clear to biologists that there exists a "great drive towards natural altruism that extends throughout the whole animal kingdom." [2] It is probable that man owes more to the

[2] Allee, W. C. "Where Angels Fear to Tread; A Contribution from General Sociology to Human Ethics." *Science*, 97, 1943 (pp. 518-525); and "Biology and International Relations." *The New Republic*, 112, 1945 (pp. 816-817).

social elaboration of this natural drive than to any other in his biological and social evolution. His future quite clearly lies with its further development, not with its abrogation.

In 1939 a group of leading scientists formulated the principle naturally operative in governing human conduct as follows: "The probability of survival of a relationship between individual humans or groups of humans increases with the extent to which that relationship is mutually satisfying." This principle is but a special case of the more general one that "the probability of survival of individual or groups of living things increases with the degree with which they harmoniously adjust themselves to each other and their environment." [3]

These formulations express the essence of the principle of co-operation, of mutual aid, the conscious recognition of which has been the cornerstone of most religious and ethical systems. The biological and social corroboration of the soundness of that ethical principle must be counted one of the great contributions of our time. An inspiring discussion of that principle from the standpoint of the biologist is to be found in the final chapter of Sir Charles Sherrington's superb book, *Man on His Nature*. Man, says Sherrington, is "slowly drawing from life the inference that altruism, charity, is a duty incumbent on thinking life. That an aim of conscious conduct must be the unselfish life. . . . Of all his new-found values perhaps altruism will be the most hard to grow. The 'self' has been so long devoted to self as end. A good man's egotism, it is said, is altruism. Perhaps that indicates a stepping-stone on the way."

On the social human level it must never be forgotten that even natural selection tends to be more and more replaced by social selection, and that by socially selecting, by behaving wisely, there is scarcely any limit to what we can do toward securing the greatest happiness of mankind.

Man learns to be co-operative, as he learns to become a social being, by being loved. As a puling infant his greatest

[3] Leake, Chauncey. "Ethicogenesis." In Montagu, Ashley, editor, *Essays and Studies in the History of Science and Learning offered in Homage to George Sarton*. New York: Henry Schuman, 1947 (pp. 261-275).

need is to have his basic urges satisfied—hunger, thirst, air, sleep, being held, caressed, and so on. The satisfaction of his basic needs, of his feelings of dependency, is, for him, love; and it is by being loved that he learns to love and thus to take the first step toward becoming a human being, a social human being. What the human being most needs is security, and security is for him the equivalent of love. Without love he has no security, and without love he suffers in a state of constant anxiety. In such a case he exhibits, as an adult, all the marks of early privation.

Love is an active state which is learned by the infant, and it is a state which is developed in dependency. That is the pattern of love which man seeks to maintain throughout his life. We love only those things upon which we are dependent. Those which are associated with frustration we tend to hate, but those which are associated with pleasure, either present, recollected, or anticipated, we tend to love.

Those who love their fellow men are secure. Without love there is no security; there is only anxiety, fear, and distrust.

Science gives the fullest validation to the commandment to love thy neighbor as thyself. It does more. It demonstrates that man is naturally inclined to love his neighbor, and all that an intelligent society is required to do is to see to it that his natural urges are given an opportunity to develop. Such a society should see to it that he is provided with the conditions for development which will not transform him into the unloving, vicious, frustrated creature he so often becomes.

It is often said that man is born neither good nor evil. My own studies lead me to believe that this is untrue. I think it can be shown that man is born good; good in the sense that were the infant's basic needs adequately satisfied in human society he would develop as a good human being in the ethical or Christian meaning of that term. His drives are toward goodness, and he needs goodness as he needs air. Otherwise he becomes a psychological cripple, unloving and unloved.

It is in the love of the mother that the infant usually finds his satisfaction, the stimulus to develop and grow in goodness. It is from these satisfied urges that the spiritual urges spring;

the strong desires and emotions that are directed toward the attainment of some ideal object over and above all selfish objects of desire: love of truth, love of country, love of others beyond oneself. The biologically founded altruism of the mother is the original stimulus which sets off the development of the altruistic potentialities of man. Altruism is the maternal passion. By seeing to it that the child is enabled to grow and develop to adulthood under conditions which do not deprive him of love, which give him security and the opportunity to observe and to participate in goodness in action, we can be certain that he will rarely develop the perversion of social self-interest. With the proper encouragement altruism and co-operation can become the passion of all men.

In *Science* for November 15, 1946 (p. 469), America's distinguished neurologist, Professor C. Judson Herrick, drew attention to the iniquity of selfish concern for personal, group, and national advantage into which we seem to have fallen. "This," he says, "can be changed if enough of us want to and are willing to pay the price. It is fortunate that under the surface of our present disorder there is, as there always has been, a strong human craving for decency, justice, and social stability based on individual responsibility for the welfare of the group, and the group has now been enlarged to include the whole world. This key to social progress has not been lost, and it is up to all of us to recognize it and use it."

The craving for decency, justice, and social stability cannot be achieved without love. We know that now. Christianity has always known it, and science has at last demonstrated it. More than anything else man not only wants love but he wants to embrace the whole world within his interest and to extend to everything in it his love and his understanding. Heartened by the support for this knowledge which has come from the wholly unexpected quarter of science the Church must go forward in the renewed faith of its principles.

Devotion to human ideals, love, sympathy, understanding, justice, peace, and the embodiment of these values in human relations is the true religion of man. Failure to practice this faith is the only real atheism.

Today, and hereafter, the Church, in leading mankind toward the practice of this faith, will have the support of many loyal allies: the social scientists and particularly the anthropologists. Let us, then, join head, heart, and hands and go forward together.

11

Race and Caste

SOME TIME AGO Dr. Norman D. Humphrey suggested that what in the social context of America is usually referred to as a race, or racial group, in reality constitutes a caste.[1] For example, Negroes, Jews, Japanese, and Indians are, in actual practice, treated by dominant white groups as if they were members of specific castes functioning within a definite caste system. Dr. Humphrey offered a definition of caste based upon those of Warner and of Dollard.[2] Caste is defined as "an endogamous status grouping, which places culturally defined limits upon the individual member in terms of mobility and kinds of interaction, and [upon] his nature as a person."

While such a definition of caste is perfectly acceptable to me, I propose to offer my own definition of caste, not because it is any better than the given one, but merely because it is more meaningful to me. I define caste as the rank assigned by a predominatingly powerful group to practically all persons within a society to specific culturally limited status groups.

From *Psychiatry*, vol. 4, 1941, 337-338.
[1] Humphrey, Norman D. "American Race and Caste." *Psychiatry*, 4, 1941.
[2] Warner, Lloyd. "American Caste and Class." *American Journal of Sociology*, 42, 1936; and Dollard, John. *Caste and Class in a Southern Town*. New Haven: Yale University Press, 1937.

The limiting factors of caste are, in effect, primarily to create barriers against sexual relations between the members of the hegemonic caste and those of the "lower castes," and secondarily, to regulate the social status, privileges, and social mobility of the members of the "lower castes."

When, as students of society and interpersonal relations, we speak of the "race problem" in America, what we really mean is the caste system and the problems which that caste system creates in America. To recognize this fact is, I fully agree with Dr. Humphrey, to effect a clarification and a change in conceptual approach to a problem upon which, perhaps more than any other in our time, clear thinking and accurate concepts are a dire necessity.

When Dr. Humphrey concludes that "the term 'race' should be discarded entirely in the cultural reference, and the more appropriate term 'caste' employed in its stead," I am in complete agreement. But when he goes on to add that "the term 'race' should be retained in its biologic context as a taxonomic category for the delineation of types of mankind" we part company, for Dr. Humphrey here falls into the error of all who commonly assume that because a word or a concept exists there must necessarily be a reality to which that word or concept corresponds. For he obviously considers that while the term "race" has no validity as a sociological concept it does possess some validity as a biological concept with reference to human species.

Hogben,[3] Haddon and Huxley,[4] Huxley,[5] Morant,[6] and myself entertain no doubts as to the meaninglessness, not alone of the popular conception, but also of the anthropological conception of "race." We do not consider that any of the existing conceptions of race correspond to any reality whatsoever; but we do consider that the persistence of the term and of the

[3] Hogben, Lancelot. *Genetic Principles in Medicine and Social Science.* New York: Knopf, 1932 (pp. 230 and 122-144).
[4] Haddon, Alfred Cort, and Huxley, Julian S. *We Europeans; a Survey of "Racial" Problems.* New York: Harper, 1936.
[5] Huxley, Julian S. *Man Stands Alone.* New York: Harper, 1941 (pp. 106-126).
[6] Morant, Geoffrey M. "Racial Theories and International Relations." *Journal of the Royal Anthropological Institute,* 69, 1939 (pp. 151-162).

concept has been responsible for much confused thinking and, what is worse, has rendered possible much confused and confusing action resulting in the most tragic consequences for large numbers of mankind. It is for these reasons that several of us, as biologists, have urged that the term "race" be altogether dropped from the vocabulary, at least, of the anthropologist. If we do no more than resign this term to the oblivion to which it properly belongs, this would in itself constitute a contribution toward clear thinking, for what is implied in the anthropological conception of "race" represents an egregious congerie of errors.

Huxley has suggested that "It would be highly desirable if we could banish the question-begging term 'race' from all discussions of human affairs and substitute the noncommittal phrase 'ethnic group.' That would be a first step towards rational consideration of the problem at issue." [7]

Since Huxley does not venture a definition of an "ethnic group," I do so here. An ethnic group is one of a number of populations, which populations together comprise the species *Homo sapiens,* and which individually maintain their genotypical and phenotypical differences by means of isolating mechanisms such as geographic and social barriers. These differences will vary as the power of the geographic and social—the ecologic—barriers vary. Where these barriers are of low power, neighboring ethnic groups will intergrade, or hybridize, with one another. Where these barriers are of high power, such ethnic groups will tend to remain distinct from each other, or replace each other geographically or ecologically.

From this definition, or description, of an ethnic group, it will be seen that the problem of ethnic variation is really an ecological problem and may ultimately be reduced to the problem of the physical mobility of populations and the consequences resulting therefrom. This is a point which has been emphasized by R. A. Fisher, who writes, "While genetic knowledge is essential for the clarity it introduces into the subject, the causes of the evolutionary changes in progress can only be resolved by an appeal to sociological, and even

[7] *Man Stands Alone* (p. 126).

historical, facts. These should at least be sufficiently available to reveal the more powerful agencies at work in the modification of mankind." [8] Thus, the problem of ethnic variation falls very definitely into the purview of the biosociologist.

If, then, we replace the outmoded concept of "race" by the concept of "ethnic group," we shall have obtained a real clarification and change in the conceptual approach to a problem whose importance requires no emphasis here. The sociologist will then be able to proceed with the study of the problem of caste, intra- and inter-socially, with the clear consciousness of the fact that, as far as he is concerned, the problem is "entirely a social problem" and that, to him at any rate, it is of no biological relevance whatever. Insofar as it is necessary for him to take cognizance of the biological evidence, the old concept of "race" has no more scientific justification in the field of human biology than it has in the field of human sociology.

In summary, the term "race" should be discarded entirely in the cultural reference and the more appropriate term "caste" employed in its stead, while the term "race" should be replaced in the biologic or ecologic context by the term "ethnic group" and should not be used in any human context whatsoever.

[8] Fisher, R. A. *The Genetical Theory of Natural Selection.* Oxford: Clarendon Press, 1930 (p. 174).

12

Antifeminism and Race Prejudice

IN CONNECTION WITH THE MODERN FORM of race prejudice it is of interest to recall that almost every one of the arguments used by the racists to "prove" the inferiority of this or that "race" was not so long ago used by the antifeminists to "prove" the inferiority of the female as compared with the male. In the case of these sexual prejudices one generation has been sufficient in which to discover how completely spurious and erroneous virtually every one of these arguments and assertions were.

In the nineteenth century it was fairly generally believed that women were inferior creatures. Was it not a fact that women had smaller brains than men? Was it not apparent to everyone that their intelligence was lower, that they were essentially creatures of emotion rather than of reason—volatile swooning natures whose powers of concentration were severely limited and whose creative abilities were restricted almost entirely to knitting and childbirth? For hundreds of years women had played musical instruments and painted, but to how many great female musicians and painters could

From *Psychiatry*, vol. 9, 1945, 69-71.

one point? Where were the great women poets and novelists? Women had practically no executive ability, were quite unable to manage the domestic finances, and, as for competing with men in the business or professional world, such an idea was utterly preposterous, for women were held to possess neither the necessary intelligence nor the equally unattainable stamina. Man's place was out in the world earning a living; woman's place was definitely in the home.

The second decade of the twentieth century, substantially assisted by World War I, saw the beginning of the dissolution of most of these prejudices, following the assumption by large numbers of women of occupations formerly considered exclusively masculine. Women, it had reluctantly to be admitted, did at least as good a job in most of these occupations as men and, it was even whispered by some, there were many things which they did a great deal better. Woman's invasion of industry and her entrance into business has on all fronts proceeded apace. Social and political inequalities have been to a large extent eliminated, and women are everywhere in the Western world increasingly being accorded equal rights with men. A certain amount of prejudice still remains and probably always will, but it is nothing compared to what it was fifty years ago.

In the eighteenth century men claimed that no woman had produced anything worth while in literature, with the possible exception of Sappho. Since they had failed to do so up to that time, it was a fair assumption that they would never do so. But within the first half of the nineteenth century feminine writers of genius commenced the assault upon the literary world and took it by storm: Jane Austen, Mrs. Elizabeth Gaskell, Charlotte Brontë (Currer Bell), George Eliot, George Sand,[1] and Elizabeth Barrett Browning. In more recent times have appeared such distinguished writers as Emily Dickinson, Mary Webb, Virginia Wolfe, Edith Wharton, Willa Cather, Edna St. Vincent Millay, Sigrid Undset, Selma Lagerlöf, and Pearl Buck. Nobody any longer doubts that women can write and that what they have to say is worth listening to.

[1] Let it not pass unnoticed that these three writers deliberately assumed masculine names in order to avoid the prejudiced judgments which a knowledge of their sex would have elicited.

But arguments are still heard to the effect that relatively few women have achieved greatness in most of the fields in which men have excelled.

There has been only one great woman scientist, it is said —Mme. Curie. But how many women, it may be asked, have enjoyed the same opportunities as men to become great scientists? What chance does a woman stand to obtain even an instructorship in any of the departments of science in our colleges? I believe that it does not exceed the chance of 1 in 100. The pattern of the antifeminist argument is identical with that of the racist argument. Deny a particular group equality of opportunity and then assert that because that group has not achieved as much as the groups enjoying complete freedom of opportunity it is obviously inferior and can never do as well.

It is a thought worth pondering whether there may not be some relation between the slackening of prejudices against women and the increase in the intensity of prejudices against ethnic and minority groups; that is, whether a certain amount of displaced aggression is not involved here. Man, it would seem, must have a scapegoat, and for his purposes any distinguishable group will do against which the exhibition of aggression or prejudice is socially sanctioned. It is a likely hypothesis that much of the deep-seated aggression which was at one time canalized in an antifeminist direction today serves to swell the tide of that which expresses itself in race prejudice.

However this may be, the parallel between antifeminism and race prejudice is striking. The same underlying motives appear to be at work, namely, fear, jealousy, feelings of insecurity, fear of economic competition, guilt feelings, and the like. Many of the leaders of the feminist movement in the nineteenth-century United States clearly understood the similarity of the motives at work in antifeminism and race discrimination and associated themselves with the antislavery movement.[2] Very similar devices have been utilized in order to keep women, on the one hand, and "races," on the other,

[2] See, for example, Harper, Ida Husted. *The Life and Works of Susan B. Anthony.* Indianapolis: 1898-1908.

in subjection. In each case barriers were created. For centuries it was socially quite impossible for women to enter into activities which were regarded as exclusively the prerogative of the male. It was taken for granted that women could never succeed in such occupations. Women have now broken down many of those barriers and shown that they can do at least as well as men in most occupations previously regarded as "masculine."

Modern race prejudice has erected barriers against almost all ethnic groups other than the group of which one is oneself a member. These barriers are calculated to limit and restrict the social participation of such groups and to prevent their ascent in the social scale. By means of these barriers they are set off from the dominant group as members of an inferior caste. But such barriers are removable. As the late Sidney Olivier wrote in 1923: [3]

> The colored races all over the world are now thinking and aiming exactly as our women have done. The presumption that they are incapable of succeeding is no stronger than the presumption against women was confidently asserted to be two generations ago. Their intellectual leaders are no more convinced than were the women's leaders of the impossibility of their aims. They are trying, they are going to go on trying, to undeceive us.

We know that to gain even so much as a hearing women had to fight every inch of the way. Ridiculed, maligned, opposed at almost every turn, and even imprisoned, the leaders of the women's movement realized that they would actually be forced to fight—and fight they did. More than any other group it was the militant suffragettes who forced the issue of women's rights and brought that issue to a vote. They pitched no battles, although there were a few clashes with the police, but they insisted on making themselves heard—until they succeeded.

The leaders of groups upon whom the egregious epithet "minority" has come to be visited would do well to take a leaf out of the suffragettes' notebook.

[3] Olivier, Sidney. "Colour Prejudice." *Contemporary Review*, 121, 1923 (p. 457).

13

The Myth of "Blood"

WORDS RULE the lives of men, a fact which should be readily understandable since the meaning of most, if not of all words, is to some extent emotionally determined, and man is, to a large extent, a creature of emotion. It is Freud who said, in his *Introductory Lectures on Psycho-Analysis*, that "Words and magic were in the beginning one and the same thing, and even today words retain much of their magical power. By words one of us can give to another the greatest happiness or bring about utter despair; by words the teacher imparts his knowledge to the student; by words the orator sweeps his audience with him and determines its judgments and decisions. Words call forth emotions and are universally the means by which we influence our fellow creatures." And as Henry James remarked, "All life comes back to the question of our speech—the medium through which we communicate."

There are many words in the vocabulary of Western man which are characterized by an exaggerated emotional content; that is to say, such words are distinguished by a high emotional and a low rational, or reasonable, quality. "Race" is such a word; "blood" is another. "Race" is a word which has assumed a high emotional content in relatively recent

From *Psychiatry*, vol. 6, 1943, 15-19.

times; "blood," on the other hand, is a word which, from the beginning of recorded history, has always possessed a high emotional content.

That blood is the most immediately important constituent of the human body must have been remarked by men at a very early period in their cultural development. The weakening effect, or actual death, produced by an appreciable loss of blood can hardly have escaped their notice. Hence, the identification of blood as a vital principle of life and its endowment with special strength-giving qualities must have been almost inevitable steps in the process of attributing a meaning to this red fluid. Among all primitive peoples blood is regarded as a most powerful element possessed of the most varied and potent qualities. To enumerate these, and the functions they are believed able to perform, would alone fill a volume.

In the cultural dynamics of Western civilization the concept of blood has played a significant and important role. From the earliest times it has been regarded as that most quintessential element of the body which carries, and through which is transmitted, the hereditary qualities of the stock. Thus, all persons of the same family stock were regarded as of the same blood. In a community which mostly consisted of family lines whose members had, over many generations, intermarried with one another, it is easy to understand how, with such a concept of blood, the community or nation would come to regard itself as of one blood—distinct, *by blood,* from all other communities or nations. This, indeed, is the popular conception of "blood" which prevails at the present day. Thus, for example, if one turns to the *Oxford English Dictionary* and looks under "blood," the following statement is found:

> Blood is popularly treated as the typical part of the body which children inherit from their parents and ancestors; hence that of parents and children, and of the members of a family or race, is spoken of as identical, and as being distinct from that of other families or races.

It is this conception of blood as the carrier of the heritable qualities of the family, race, or nation which has led to its application in such extended meanings as are implied in terms like "blue blood," "blood royal," "pure blood," "full blood," "half blood," "good blood," "blood tie," "blood relationship," and "consanguinity." Putative racial and national differences are, of course, recognized in such terms as "German blood," "English blood," "Jewish blood," and "Negro blood," so that today the words "race" and "blood" have come to be used as synonyms.

When the meaning of these terms is analyzed, the manner in which the general conception of "blood" operates may be more clearly perceived. Thus, the term "blue blood," which refers to a presumed special kind of blood supposed to flow in the veins of ancient and aristocratic families, actually represents a translation from the Spanish *sangre azul*, attributed to some of the oldest and proudest families of Castile, who claimed never to have been contaminated by foreign blood. Many of these families were of fair complexion, hence, in members of these families the veins would, in comparison with those in the members of the predominatingly dark-complexioned population, appear strikingly blue. Thus, the difference between an aristocrat and a commoner could be easily recognized as a difference in "blood"; one was a "blue blood," the other was not.

The expression "blood royal" refers to the generally accepted notion that only such persons as are of royal ancestry have the blood of kings flowing in their veins. No person, however noble his ancestry may be, can be of the "blood royal" unless he has the blood of kingly ancestors in his veins. Thus, kings are held to belong to a special class of mankind principally in virtue of the supposed unique characters of their blood. In order to keep the blood of the royal house pure, marriages are arranged exclusively between those who are of the royal blood. In England, for example, no member of the royal family who stands in direct line of succession to the throne may marry anyone but a member of another royal house. The most recent example of the consequence of disobeying this rule is, of course, the case of the present

Duke of Windsor, who was forced to abdicate his succession to the throne of England because of his declared intention to marry a person who was not of royal blood.

In common parlance, and in the loose usage of many who should know better, terms like "full blood," "pure blood," and "half blood" very clearly illustrate the supposed hereditary character of the blood and the manner in which, by simple arithmetical division, it may be diluted. Thus, "full blood" or "pure blood" are expressions which are alleged to define the supposed fact that a person is of unadulterated blood, that is, he is a person whose particular ancestors have undergone no admixture of blood with members of another race. Within the last century these terms have come to be applied almost exclusively to persons who are not of the "white race," to persons, in short, who are alleged to belong to the supposedly inferior rungs of the racial ladder. It is possible that this restricted usage has been determined by the fact that these expressions have generally done most service in the description of native peoples or of slaves, as in "full-blooded Negro" and "pure-blood Indian," or merely "full blood" and "pure blood." Such an unedifying association would be sufficient to secure the nonapplication of the term to any member of the "superior races."

A "half blood," in contradistinction to a "full blood" or a "pure blood," is a person whose blood is half that of one "race" and half that of another, for example, the offspring of an Indian and a white. What is actually implied is that while a "full blood" or "pure blood" may claim relationship through both parents, a "half blood" may claim relationship through one parent only. For example, a mulatto, that is, the offspring of a white and a Negro, is for all *practical* purposes classed with the group to which the Negro parent belongs, and his white ancestry is, for the same purposes, ignored. In practice it often works out that the "half blood" is not fully accepted by either of the parental stocks because of his adulterated blood, and he becomes in the true sense of the expression "half caste," belonging neither to the one caste nor to the other, for in Western society the so-called different "races" are in reality treated as if they were different castes.

A person is said to be of "good" or "gentle blood" if he is of noble or gentle birth, or of good family. Here the assumed biological determinance of social status by blood is clearly exhibited, that is to say, a person's rank in society is assumed to be determined by his blood when, in fact, it is in reality the other way round, that is to say, "blood" is actually determined by rank. The ancestors of all noblemen were once common people, plebeians. It was not a sudden metamorphosis in the composition of their blood which caused them to become noble; it was rather an elevation in social status which endowed them with supposedly superior qualities. Such supposedly superior qualities are not biological in any sense whatsoever and belong purely to the ascriptive variety of things. They have no real but a purely imagined existence.

The statement that a person is of "bad blood," in the sense that he is of common or inferior character or status, is rarely encountered for the reason, presumably, that those who use such terms have not considered the blood of such people worth mentioning at all. Thus, for example, while there is an entry in the *Oxford English Dictionary* for "blood worth mention," there is none for blood *not* worth mention. In the sense in which "blood" is considered as the seat of emotion, "bad blood" is taken to be the physiological equivalent of ill feeling. In this sense, of course, "bad blood" may be created between persons of "good blood."

The term "blood relationship," and its anglicized Latin equivalent "consanguinity," meaning the condition of being of the same blood, or relationship by descent from a common ancestor, enshrines the belief that all biological relationships are reflected in and are to a large extent determined by the character of the blood. This venerable error, along with others, requires correction.

This brief analysis of the variety of ways in which "blood" is used and understood in the English language, and in Western civilization in general, renders it sufficiently clear that most people believe that "blood" is equivalent to heredity, and that blood, therefore, is that part of the organism which determines the quality of the person. By extension it is further generally believed that the social as well as the biological status of the person is determined by the kind of blood he has inherited. These beliefs concerning blood are probably among the oldest of those surviving from the earliest days of mankind. Certainly they are found to be almost universally distributed among the peoples of the earth in very much the same forms, and their antiquity is sufficiently attested to by the fact that in the graves of prehistoric men red pigments are frequently found in association with the remains. These pigments were, most probably, used to represent the blood as the symbol of life and humanity, a belief enshrined in the expression "he is flesh and blood," to signify humanity as opposed to deity or disembodied spirit. There in the grave was the flesh, and the pigment was introduced to represent the blood.

As an example of a myth grown hoary with the ages, and for which there is not the slightest justification in scientific fact, the popular conception of "blood" is outstanding. Were it not for the fact that it is a bad myth, harmful in its effects and dangerous in its possible consequences, it might well be allowed to persist; but since great harm has already been done, and will increasingly continue to be done unless this myth is exposed for what it is—one of the most grievous errors of thought ever perpetrated by mankind—it is today more than ever necessary to set out the facts about blood as science knows them.

In the first place, let it be stated at once that blood is in no way connected with the transmission of hereditary characters. The transmitters of hereditary characters are the genes, which lie in the chromosomes of the germ cells represented by the spermatozoa of the father and the ova of the mother, *and nothing else.* These genes, carried in the chromosomes of a single spermatazoon and a single ovum, are the *only* parts of the organism which transmit and determine the hereditary characters. Blood has nothing whatever to do with heredity, either biologically, socially, or in any other manner whatsoever.

The belief that the blood of the mother is transmitted to the child, and hence becomes a part of the child, is an ancient but completely erroneous one. Scientific knowledge of the processes of pregnancy long ago made it perfectly clear that there is no actual passage of blood from mother to child. The developing child manufactures its own blood, and the character of its various blood cells is demonstrably different from that of either of its parents. The mother does not contribute blood to the fetus. This fact should forever dispose of the ancient notion, so characteristically found among primitive peoples, that the blood of the mother is continuous with that of the child. The same belief is to be found in the works of Aristotle on generation.[1] Aristotle held that the monthly periods, which do not appear during pregnancy, contribute to the formation of the child's body. Modern scientific knowledge shows that this notion is quite false and thus completely disposes of the idea of a blood tie between any two persons whether they be mother or child, or even identical twins. Hence, any claims to kinship based on the tie of blood can have no scientific foundation whatever. Nor can claims of group consciousness based on blood be anything but fictitious since the character of the blood of all human beings is determined not by their membership in any group or nation but by the fact that they are human beings.

The blood of all human beings is in every respect the same. To this the only exception is in the agglutinating properties of certain blood factors, but most of these factors are present in all varieties of men and in different groups differ only in their statistical distribution. This distribution is not a matter of quality but of quantity. There are no demonstrable or known differences but statistical ones in the character of the blood of different peoples. In that sense the biblical obiter dictum that the Lord "hath made of one blood all nations of men to dwell on the face of the earth" is literally true.

Scientists have for many years attempted to discover whether or not any differences exist in the blood of different peoples, but the results of such investigations have always been the same—*no fundamental differences are to be discovered*. In short, it cannot be too emphatically or too often repeated that fundamentally the blood of all human beings

[1] *De Generatione Animalium.*

is similar, no matter what class, group, nation, or "race" they belong to.

Obviously then, since all people are of one blood, such differences as may exist between them can have absolutely no connection with blood. Such facts, however, do not in the least deter propagandists from continuing to use the "blood" myth to set people against one another. The official Nazi view of the matter was presented to the congress of the party at Nuremberg, exactly six years before the invasion of Poland, by the official Nazi distorter of the truth, Arthur Rosenberg.

> A nation [he said] is constituted by the predominance of a definite character formed by its blood, also by language, geographical environment, and the sense of a united political destiny. These last constituents are not, however, definitive; the decisive element in a nation is its blood. In the first awakening of a people, great poets and heroes disclose themselves to us as the incorporation of the eternal values of a particular blood soul. I believe that this recognition of the profound significance of blood is now mysteriously encircling our planet, irresistibly gripping one nation after another.[2]

The extravagant and utterly preposterous claims which the Nazis were able to make on the basis of the "blood" myth were equaled only by the superstitions which prevailed among others in the same connection. During World War II these were given much publicity when the Red Cross segregated the blood of Negroes for purposes of transfusion. In other words, the myth of "blood" seemed almost as strongly entrenched in the United States as it was in Germany. It will be generally admitted that this was and continues to be an undesirable and dangerous situation. The sooner the facts about blood are made known the better.

The astonishing thing about the objection to Negro blood is not so much that it is based upon a misconception but that the same person who refuses to accept Negro blood may at the same time be perfectly willing to have his children suckled by a Negro wet nurse! The same person will be ready to submit to an injection of serum derived from a

[2] *Vossische Zeitung,* September 3, 1933.

horse or cow or some other animal. Yet while he himself may have been suckled by a Negro wet nurse, and even entertain the greatest affection for Negroes, he will violently object to any "pollution" of his "blood" by the injection of Negro blood into his own.

Quite clearly this is a false belief, a superstition for which there is no ground in fact but much in traditional belief. In actual fact the blood of the Negro is identical with that of all other human beings, so that for the purposes of transfusion or for any other purposes it is as good as any other blood.[3]

The objection to Negro blood is, of course, based upon the antique misconception that the blood is the carrier of hereditary characters. Since the Negro is regarded as possessing racially inferior characters it is feared that these may be transmitted to the recipient of the transfusion. Both prejudices are groundless.

What modern science has revealed about blood, then, renders all such terms as "blood royal," "half blood," "full blood," "blood relationship," and the others to which reference has been made utterly meaningless in point of fact and dangerously meaningful in the superstitious social sense.

Is it too much to expect that this false belief, the myth of "blood," will soon make way for the scientifically established universal truth that all human beings, no matter of what creed or complexion, are of one and the same blood?

[3] For an excellent analysis and discussion of the character of the blood in the varieties of mankind see Mourant, A. E. *The Distribution of the Human Blood Groups.* Springfield, Ill.: Thomas, 1954.

14

Theognis, Darwin, and Social Selection

A s illustrative of the practice of eugenic selection among the ancient Greeks, Darwin quotes a poem by Theognis.[1] This poem, because it has so often been quoted in a similar context, is perhaps the best known of all the works of the Greek poet.[2] Darwin writes:

> The Grecian poet, Theognis, who lived 550 b.c., clearly saw how important selection, if carefully applied, would be for the improvement of mankind. He saw, likewise, that wealth often checks the proper action of sexual selection. He thus writes:
>
>> With kine and horses, Kurnus! we proceed
>> By reasonable rules, and choose a breed
>> For profit and increase, at any price;
>> Of a sound stock, without defect or vice.

From *Isis*, vol. 37, nos. 107-108, 1947.

[1] Darwin, Charles. *The Descent of Man*, 2nd ed. London: 1874.
[2] Another writer to refer to the poem (Gittler, Joseph. *Social Thoughts Among the Early Greeks*. Athens, Ga.: The University of Georgia Press, 1941.) interprets Theognis as applying "the idea of eugenics to the perfection of the human race. The author begins with the question of breeding, believing that nothing can be good of its kind, whether man or animal, unless its progenitors are good. He would treat man like any other species of animals; viz., compulsorily breed the good with the good."

But, in the daily matches that we make,
The price is everything: for money's sake,
Men marry: women are in marriage given
The churl or ruffian, that in wealth has thriven,
May match his offspring with the proudest race:
Thus everything is mix'd, noble and base!
If then in outward manner, form, and mind,
You find us degraded, motley, kind,
Wonder no more, my friend! the cause is plain,
And to lament the consequence is vain.[3]

Darwin clearly understood Theognis to be speaking in a biological sense and this is the sense in which all readers have taken the poem. This is readily understandable in view of the fact that the opening lines refer to biological phenomena, and to a modern reader the remainder of the poem reads as if it continues this biological theme. There is, however, good reason to believe that such a reading is a misinterpretation of the poet's meaning. Interestingly enough this very question of the true meaning of Theognis' poem had already presented itself to one writer, Xenophon, in antiquity. Xenophon writes:

> This poet's theme is simply the virtues and vices of mankind, and the poem is a work on man just like the treatise on horsemanship which might be written by a horseman. The beginning of it therefore seems to me to be quite as it should

---

[3] Frere, W. E., editor. *The Works of the Right Honorable John Hookham Frere* (Edited by Basil Montagu), London: Pickering, 1872 (vol. 2, p. 334). The Loeb Library translation is more literal than Frere's and more accurate. It follows: "In rams and asses and horses, Cyrnus, we seek the thoroughbred, and a man is concerned therein to get him offspring of good stock; yet in marriage a good man thinketh not twice of wedding the bad daughter of a bad sire if the father give him many possessions, nor doth the wife of a bad man disdain the bed of a wealthy, but is fain rather to be rich than to be good. [A more accurate reading of this last sentence suggested by Professor Aubrey Diller, is: "nor doth a woman disdain the bed of a bad man if he is wealthy, but wanteth a rich husband instead of a good one."] For 'tis possessions they prize, and a good man weddeth of bad stock and a bad man of good; race is confounded of riches. In like manner, son of Polypaüs, marvel thou not that the race of thy townsmen is made obscure; 'tis because bad things are mingled with good." Edmonds, J. M. *Elegy and Iambus.* Loeb Classical Library. Cambridge: Harvard University Press, 1931 (vol. 1, pp. 250-251).

be: the author begins with the question of breeding or good birth, believing, no doubt, that nothing can be good of its kind, whether man or any other creature, unless its progenitors are good. And that is why he chose to do with men as he would with other animals, which we do not keep without consideration, but give each kind the particular skilled attention which will produce the finest strain. . . . The meaning of these verses is that men do not know how to produce their kind properly, and the result is that the human race is not so good as it might be because the good is always mingled with the bad. But the generality of men take these lines as proving that the poet accuses his fellow-men of busying themselves in vain matters, and of knowing how to make money compensate for low-birth and viciousness. My own view is that the poet is accusing them of ignorance of the nature of their own lives." [4]

Xenophon apparently understood the poem as a commentary on the bad eugenic practice of Theognis' fellow aristocrats, "but," he says, "the generality of men take these lines as proving that the poet accuses his fellow-men of busying themselves in vain matters, and of knowing how to make money compensate for low-birth and viciousness." In short, the poem was commonly understood in the social sense. The evidence, I believe, indicates that this is the sense in which the poet intended his poem to be understood.

Theognis' poem must be studied in its context. Theognis, a native of Nisaean Megara, lived and wrote during the great democratic revolution of the sixth century B.C. Indeed, Theognis—who at one time appears to have held a position of authority—was one of the first members of the aristocratic party to foresee the coming revolution. As an aristocrat he deplored the rising power of the lower classes and feared the contamination and displacement of the qualities and culture of his own class by those of the inferior classes. A great part of his poetry represents an expression of that

---

[4] Stobaeus, Joannes. *Anthologium.* IV, 29, 53, from Xenophon's treatise *On Theognis.* Edmonds, J. M. *op. cit.* (pp. 220–223). There has been some question as to the correctness of the ascription of this passage to Xenophon but the consensus of opinion is that it is correct. See Edmonds, *ibid.* (p. 220) and Harrison, E. *Studies in Theognis.* Cambridge: University Press, 1902 (pp. 73-87).

fear. It is with political, social, and cultural problems that Theognis is concerned, not with their biological bases.

The conception of caste and class throughout the history of Greek culture was based on purely social considerations into which no clearly conceived element of a biological nature entered. There were differences between classes and there were differences between castes; there were slaves and there were barbarians. These were not, however, held to be so upon biological grounds but because, in the scheme of social or cultural life, slaves and barbarians, noblemen and workers were judged by the standard of social status as determined by birth, γένος.[5] Slaves for example, belonged to the lowest class within Greek society, whereas barbarians didn't belong within Greek society at all. The repugnance which the Greeks felt for barbarians was purely national, the outcome principally of the Persian Wars, and was not in the least based on so-called biological grounds.

As Professor Aubrey Diller has said, "On the whole, the biological conceptions of the Greek thinkers were not very clear or vivid, especially in respect to mankind. They tended to regard them as intellectual curiosities rather than as the immutable facts of existence."[6] The Greeks as a whole, with the exception of a few isolated thinkers, seem never to have entertained the notion that biological factors as such could possibly determine either class, caste, cultural, social, or national differences. This is essentially an idea which was developed for the first time during the nineteenth century of our present era.

Read in the light of the above remarks it will be seen that Theognis' poem is open to an interpretation quite different from that which is usually given it. What Theognis laments in this poem is the intermarriage of members of the superior classes with those of the inferior classes, the "good" with the

[5] Aristotle was exceptional in that he believed in the existence of biological differences between the classes. He held, for example, that the slave was so by nature. *Politics*, I, 5. See also Plato. *The Republic*, V, VIII.
[6] Diller, Aubrey. "Race Mixture Among the Greeks Before Alexander." *Illinois Studies in Language and Literature* (University of Illinois at Urbana), 20, 1937.

"bad," ϰαϰοί. The meaning of "bad" here is distinctly not "bad heredity" but "low class." Referring to Greek writers and orators of this period, and to another poem by Theognis in particular, Ure has pointed out that "bad" is the regular term in aristocratic writers for their political opponents.[7] It should be remembered that in writing of the ϰαϰοί Theognis was referring to those whom he regarded as his political enemies. He laments the fact that a man in virtue of the possession of a large amount of money may become a member of the upper classes. Such a person, however, cannot become a member of a superior caste unless he was born into it.

Hence, for an aristocrat to marry for money or possessions into a base family, that is to say a family of low social status, is to degrade the social purity of his stock and of himself. We are much more careful in the selection of our domestic animals, says Theognis, than we are in the selection of our own mates. With animals we proceed by reasonable rules, but in our daily matches wealth, not social status or "breeding," is the main consideration. By this means any churl can put his children into society on a par with the best stock. Theognis uses the term εὐγενέας, "stock," here in the sense of "the best people" or aristocrats and not in any restricted biological sense such as would be suggested by the mistranslation of the word as "race."

To conclude: in the poem cited by Darwin, Theognis is, it is here suggested, bemoaning the mixture of good and bad social stocks. He is not thinking of the biology of the stocks for the reason that the Greeks simply did not think in such terms. Hence, it is unlikely that he could have had any ideas of a eugenic kind in mind. What he wished to see preserved was the social integrity of his class and its caste status. The threat to the preservation of that integrity by the rich parvenus of lower-class origin is the theme of his poem. It is not a eugenic Jeremiad.

[7] Ure, P. N. *The Origin of Tyranny.* Cambridge: University Press, 1922 (p. 8).

15

Behavior From Two Points of View

BEHAVIOR AS VIEWED by students of the behavioral sciences is not quite the same thing as behavior viewed by American educators. The disparity is of the kind that often exists between theory and practice, the pure and the applied, science and art, the technical and the technological. There is at present a considerable lag between the verified and verifiable findings of the behavioral sciences and their practical application in education. This is interesting because there appears to be no really significant lag between publication of the relevant findings of the behavioral sciences and their incorporation in the educational literature.

Under the prevailing circumstances a certain time lag is both necessary and desirable, for it renders possible the leisurely evaluation of the findings of the scientists. Time is needed for the proper weighing of the findings provided by the behavioral scientists. Since we are in the midst of such a ruminating period, it may be useful to take stock of some of the principal findings of the behavioral sciences in

From *Teachers College Record,* 1959, 440-448.

recent years with a view to estimating their value for American education.

According to the late Walter Pitkin, life begins at forty. This is perhaps a more accurate statement than employability ceases at forty or life begins at birth.

We are all aware of the existence of critical developmental periods during the early years of postnatal life, but very few of us are aware of the fact that there exist vastly more important critical developmental periods during the prenatal life of the individual and that what happens during prenatal life far outweighs in significance anything that could possibly happen to the individual during postnatal development. With that prescient illumination which so often characterizes poets, Samuel Taylor Coleridge more than one hundred and fifty years ago wrote, "Yes, the history of man for the nine months preceding his birth would, probably, be far more interesting, and contain events of greater moment, than all the threescore and ten years that follow it." Facts accumulated in this connection in recent years abundantly serve to confirm the truth of Coleridge's speculation. Those facts are of considerable significance for the fuller understanding of human postnatal behavior. Together they constitute a subject far beyond the limits of this discussion.

The older view that the developing prenatal organism is virtually completely insulated from the assults and insults of both the uterine and the external environment is still widely prevalent. Since, it was argued, both the mother's nervous system and her circulating blood are in no way connected with the same systems in the uterine organism, there was no possible means by which changes in the mother's nervous system or anything carried in her blood could get through to the developing organism. The oxygen carried on the surface of the red blood corpuscles could pass through the placenta as a detached gas, whereas the blood corpuscles could not. Some forty years ago that was what was taught and it is still widely believed. But the facts as we have come to know them lead us to very different conclusions.

The structure and functions of the nervous system were, in

the past, too narrowly conceived. Today we understand that the nervous system is properly to be regarded as the neuro-humoral system, that is, the process and effects of interaction of the conventional nervous system with the endocrine system of glands through the fluid medium of the blood and its gaseous content. The manner in which the neurohumoral system functions makes it possible for us to understand how it can be that, although the nervous systems of mother and child are quite separate, changes in the mother's emotional state—to mention but one complex variable—can immediately affect the physical and behavioral development of the uterine organism.

On the subject of emotional influences upon the developing organism we have, at present, a small number of experimental studies on lower animals and a few on man. All these studies agree that more or less prolonged emotional disturbance experienced by the pregnant woman, or relatively short emotional crises, may seriously affect the developing uterine organism. The degree of damage done physically will depend upon the developmental age of the organism and will follow the general embryological law: the earlier the developmental age of insult, the greater the damage done. The same law probably applies to development of the substrates of mind in the prenatal period, but very little critical evidence can be offered.

Both for experimental animals and for human beings we now have evidence which indicates that emotional disturbances in the maternal organism during the period, for example, when the palate is being formed (in man, between the seventh and tenth weeks) are capable of producing cleft palate.

This is an impressive finding. What can be the mechanism involved? Complex as it is, that mechanism is not difficult to understand. Any description of it must be something of an oversimplification. Bearing that in mind we may proceed. An individual who is severely emotionally disturbed is initially disturbed in the gray matter of the brain. From the gray matter, impulses pass down to the midbrain and hypothalamus and out into the stalk at the end of which the pituitary gland is situated. Here the anterior portion of the gland is activated to secrete unusually large amounts of ACTH (adrenocortico-trophic hormone) into the blood stream, with a resulting hypersecretion of the cortex of the adrenal gland, cortisone. In the case of a pregnant woman, the molecules of ACTH and cortisone are small enough to pass through the placenta into the circulation of the uterine organism, and if this occurs at the critical developmental period, when the maxilla and premaxilla are in process of developing, cleft palate is likely to result—presumably because of the interference of these chemical substances with the normal processes of development.

To check this, experiments have been performed in which pregnant mice were severely emotionally disturbed during the critical developmental period of formation of the upper jaw. In such experiments it was observed that 80 per cent of the offspring were born with cleft palates.[1] In a second group of experiments, ACTH was injected into undisturbed pregnant mice during the same critical developmental period, and it was found that very nearly 100 per cent of their offspring were born with cleft palates.[2] In a third series of experiments, in which cortisone rather than ACTH was injected, similar results were obtained.[3]

It is reasonable to suppose that a similar series of events is involved in human beings where emotional disturbances in the pregnant woman produce changes in the uterine organism which result in observable behavioral disturbances in the postnatal organism. Such behavioral disturbances have

[1] Strean, L. P., and Peer, L. A. "Stress as an Etiologic Factor in the Development of Cleft Palate." *Plastic and Reconstructive Surgery*, 18, 1956 (pp. 1-8).

[2] Fraser, F. C., Kalter, H., Walker, B. E., and Fainstat, T. D. "Experimental Production of Cleft Palate with Cortisone and Other Hormones." *Journal of Cellular and Comparative Physiology*, 43 (supp. 1), 1954 (pp. 237-259).

[3] Ingalls, T. H., and Curley, F. J. "The Relation of Hydrocortisone Injections to Cleft Palate in Mice." *New England Journal of Medicine*, 256, 1957 (pp. 1035-1039).

been described by several workers,[4] but a vast amount of work needs yet to be done in this area in which scarcely a beginning has been made. Fuller exploration of the area will teach us much about the nature of human nature and may put at our disposal the means of assisting that nature to realize itself to the optimum degree.

It is but a short time since the evidence became available that the fetus is capable of learning *in utero*. In a classical series of experiments reported in 1948 by Spelt, it was shown that it was possible to condition a human fetus at the seventh month of prenatal age to respond to an original stimulus, in this case the vibration of a doorbell buzzer from which the buzzer-head had been removed.[5]

We have evidence, then, that learning is capable of occurring before birth. How much is the fetus capable of learning? We don't know. Does a fetus normally learn anything *in utero*? At present the answer to this question must be largely speculative. If the fetus does learn *in utero*, how does that prenatal learning affect its postnatal behavior? Again we don't know but it is important for us to find out. We are at the frontier of a new and important realm of knowledge. We know that after the fifth month of prenatal age, at least, the human fetus can discriminate between certain tastes, for example, between sweet and nonsweet. It can hear and respond to pitch, vibration, and tone, and it is capable of being influenced by a wide range of chemical and physiological stimuli.

Work emanating from Teachers College, Columbia, indicates that, on the whole, pregnant women fed on an adequate diet have children who subsequently make higher scores on intelligence tests than do those whose mothers' diets were

[4] Sontag, L. W. "The Significance of Fetal Environmental Differences." *American Journal of Obstetrics and Gynecology*, 42, 1941 (pp. 996-1003); and "War and Fetal Maternal Relationship." *Marriage and Family Living*, 6, 1944 (pp. 1-5); Halliday, J. L. *Psychosocial Medicine*. New York: Norton, 1948; Montagu, Ashley. *The Direction of Human Development.* New York: Harper, 1955.
[5] Spelt, D. K. "The Conditioning of the Human Fetus *in utero*." *Journal of Experimental Psychology*, 38, 1948 (pp. 338-346).

not adequate during pregnancy.[6] There is a good deal of confirmatory evidence from other sources on the relation between prenatal nutrition and behavioral development.[7]

The period of birth has in the past tended to be dismissed as simply a transitional phase in the passage from prenatal to postnatal life, but we now know it to be much more than that. Among other things, there is now strong suggestive evidence that the experience of the birth process constitutes a very real complex of factors influencing subsequent behavior; that the conception of the trauma of birth is, in many cases at least, a very real thing; and that in the cultures of the Western world we serve to render the process of birth more difficult for the fetus.

Adjustment of the organism from the prenatal to the post-natal environment is extremely complicated and precarious. Birth is the process by means of which the fetus is prepared, not for the assumption of the demands and responsibilities of postnatal existence, but merely for initiation into them. As I have already said, there has been a tendency to regard the period of birth as a mere incident in the passage of the fetus from the microcosmic womb into the macrocosmic world. The knowledge we have acquired in recent years concerning the physiology of birth and something of the effects of the different kinds of experiences undergone by the fetus during this critical period of its development has rendered the older view obsolete.

Thus far it has been possible to establish associations between only the grosser kinds of insults to the fetus during the birth period and subsequent development. Of the artificially produced insults, high forceps delivery resulting in

[6] Harrell, R. F., Woodyard, E., and Gates, A. I. *The Effect of Mothers' Diets on the Intelligence of Offspring.* New York: Bureau of Publications, Teachers College, Columbia University, 1955.
[7] Tisdal, F. F. "The Role of Nutrition in Preventive Medicine." *The Milbank Memorial Fund Quarterly,* 23, 1945 (pp. 1-15); Sontag, L. W., and Wines, J. "Relation of Mothers' Diets to Status of Their Infants at Birth and in Infancy." *American Journal of Obstetrics and Gynecology,* 54, 1947 (pp. 994-1003); Rogers, M. E., Lilienfeld, A. M., and Pasamanick, B. *Prenatal and Paranatal Factors in the Development of Childhood Behavior Disorders.* Baltimore: The Johns Hopkins University, School of Hygiene and Public Health, 1957.

damage to the brain is known, in many cases, to be the direct cause of cerebral palsy and is highly suspect in quite a number of other disturbances of behavior.[8] Heavy sedation, by robbing the fetus of its already reduced supply of oxygen, has undoubtedly been responsible for the death of many fetuses at birth, and among the survivors the foundations have thus been laid for behavioral disturbances ranging all the way from amentia to the very slightest degrees of mental retardation. The anoxia that is produced as the result of various possible kinds of failure in the functions of the placenta, such as placenta previa or premature cessation of placental progesterone, may produce similar effects. The few studies that have been made on the relation between exogenous factors at birth and later behavior problems, such as those of Wile and Davis, and others,[9] indicate that quite marked behavioral disturbances may be associated with the birth experience.

Important as is the understanding of these endogenously and exogenously originating pathologies—and the more we can learn about them the better able we shall be to avoid their often tragic consequences—it is to the variables involved in the normal process of birth and their relation to behavior that we need to pay most attention, for these are the variables which are most frequently operative and about which we need to know so much more than we do at present. But such knowledge as we do have indicates that variations in the normal experience of birth are differentially capable of affecting the later behavior of the person. Phyllis Greenacre,

[8] Pasamanick, B., Rogers, M. E., and Lilienthal, A. M. "Pregnancy Experience and the Development of Behavior Disorder in Children." *American Journal of Psychiatry*, 112, 1956 (pp. 613-618); Ernhart, C. B., Graham, F. K., and Thurstion, D. L. "The Relationship of Perinatal Anoxia to Intelligence and to Neurological Deviations in the Preschool Child." Presented to the American Psychological Association, August 28, 1958.

[9] Wile, I. S., and Davis, R. "The Relation of Birth to Behavior." *American Journal of Orthopsychiatry*, 11, 1941 (pp. 320-324); Greenacre, P. *Trauma, Growth, and Personality*. New York: Norton, 1952; Schroeder, P. L. "Behavior Difficulties in Children Associated with the Results of Birth Trauma." *Journal of the American Medical Association*, 92, 1929 (pp. 100-104); Boland, J. L. "Type of Birth as Related to Stuttering." *Journal of Speech and Behavior Disorders*, 16, 1951 (pp. 40-43).

for example, has pointed out that in the economy of birth there is an enormous and sudden increase in sensory stimuli,[10] and there must be very considerable differences in the varieties and amplitude of such stimuli as experienced by the newborn. It is reasonable to suppose that such differences in birth experience are reflected in the subsequent behavioral development of the organism. That this is so is borne out by the fact that prematurely born children tend to exhibit somewhat different behavioral responses to the same stimuli from those displayed by normally born children.[11] For Caesarean-delivered children we have virtually no data whatever. Here is another interesting piece of research that cries out to be done.

From what has thus far been said it should be clear that a wholly new and complex dimension has been opened up for investigation—that of prenatal life—and that the findings of this field must hereafter be taken into consideration when evaluating the behavior of the person.

The intrabirth process brings us to the immediate postnatal period. It is here that the work of the modern students of animal behavior—the ethologists, chiefly associated with the names of Lorenz and Tinbergen—fits in most naturally. These men and their co-workers have shown that fish, birds, and the several mammals thus far investigated are born equipped with releaser mechanisms which cause the organism to respond to certain sign stimuli in a particular manner. Seemingly complex social behavior in these animals is constituted by a relatively few such releaser mechanisms. These mechanisms do not determine what particular stimuli shall release the response any more than genes determine the characters or traits with which they are connected, but a particular releaser mechanism will be activated in a particular manner by a particular class of stimuli. Any object or stimulus within such a class to which the organism is exposed during the appropriate critical developmental period will

[10] Greenacre, op. cit.

[11] Shirley, M. "A Behavior Syndrome Characterizing Prematurely-born Children." Child Development, 10, 1939 (pp. 115-128); Howard, P. J., and Worrell, C. H. "Premature Infants in Later Life." Pediatrics, 9, 1952.

usually become fixed as the particular stimulus—and no other—which will elicit the particular releaser mechanism. This phenomenon is known as "imprinting." Lorenz has shown that graylag goslings, for example, accept as their mother the first living creature to which they are exposed and thereafter refuse to accept any other as such. Freshly hatched mallards will not respond to the visual stimulus but will respond to the call note and will accept as mother the first creature whose call note they hear.[12]

The question is, do releaser mechanisms exist in man? The parental response to the baby has been cited as one such example. It is, however, at the very least questionable whether upon careful analysis the response would not turn out to be dominantly learned.

Is there anything akin to imprinting in man? The Freudian concept of fixation is certainly a close ally. Fixation, in Freud's own words, refers to "a conjunction of impulses with impressions and with the objects connected with those impressions. This conjunction has to be effected very early, is very hard to resolve, and has the effect of bringing the development of the instincts concerned to a standstill." [13] The difference, however, between imprinting in animals and fixation in man is that in the former the process is permanent while in man the process of fixation need not be so.

Tinbergen, and to a lesser degree Lorenz, in the light of the criticism their views have received, have modified their conception of the innateness of the releaser mechanism and are willing to grant that in the ontogeny of all behavior processes something akin to learning may occur.[14] However, no matter what the component of learning may be, there can be no doubt that certain complex patterns of behavior in lower animals are largely, if not entirely, innate; that is, they are present at birth. But every animal has a prenatal experience and, in light of our earlier discussion, it should be clear that we cannot be quite certain that all the elements that have entered into the

[12] Lorenz, K. Z. *King Solomon's Ring*. New York: Crowell, 1952.
[13] Healy, W., Bronner, A. F., and Bowers, A. M. *The Structure and Meaning of Psychoanalysis*. New York: Knopf, 1930 (p. 117).
[14] Lorenz, K. Z., and Tinbergen, N., in *Group Processes*. New York: Josiah Macy, Jr. Foundation, 1955 (pp. 75-218).

conditioning of the behavior observed at birth were entirely unlearned.

To overcome this difficulty and at the same time help us to discover what is going on, Ewer has suggested that the innate behavior we observe at birth be regarded as self-differentiating, as coming into being as part of the normal development of every individual. On the basis of its innate behavioral responses the animal can learn to the limit of its capacity, "but unless there is self-differentiation of the basis on which to learn, the animal will die, or remain in permanent infantile dependency." [15]

In the human species, in which the dependency period is so prolonged, parental care becomes an indispensable stimulus to the self-differentiating process, and the behavioral equipment for beginning life in the outside world is limited to the automatic functioning of needs which must be satisfied mostly by the behavior of others. The human infant must be fed, kept clean, allowed to sleep and to rest, caused to be active, kept out of harm's way, and protected from noxious stimuli.

This is the situational context in which the member of the species *Homo sapiens* learns to become human, in the functional sense of that term. This is the socialization period which, while it differs in its details in every culture and in every family, has precisely the same over-all function in every culture, namely, to enable the individual to become a person who has learned what his relationships are to others and what their relationships are to him—in short, what he owes to or should do for others and what he may expect from them.

Cross-cultural studies in personality development are too familiar to need discussion here, but one should at least pause to underscore the fact that the findings of all the relevant sciences point to the important conclusion that no matter what the genetic limitations of individuals may be, within the range of normal variation what the average individual in any one ethnic group can do can be done by the average individual in any other ethnic group, provided his group is af-

[15] Ewer, R. F. "Ethological Concepts." *Science*, 126, 1958 (pp. 599-603).

forded adequate opportunities; and also that by far the most important complex of variables in the making of a human being is the cultural environment in which he is nourished and caused to grow. Allowing for all genetic differences between individuals—and those differences can be very considerable—the culturalization process, the social differentiation, that the individual is made to undergo exceeds all else in importance.

It is here that the analysis of the concept of basic needs has received some attention. The basic needs are those drives of the organism that must be adequately satisfied if the organism is to survive. They are the need for oxygen, food, liquid, rest, sleep, activity, bowel and bladder elimination, protection from danger, and the avoidance of pain.

Observe that sex has been omitted from the list of basic needs. Obviously the organism can survive without satisfaction of its sex drive, but the species cannot; hence the enormous active specific energy which is attached to this nonvital basic need. Under conditions of stress, such as emotional disturbance, physical starvation, or illness, the energy of the sex drive is the first to decline.

The most important of all the basic needs is the need for love. Love is a somewhat curious entity for a behavioral scientist to be considering, and that, indeed, is why it has been considered by so few behavioral scientists. I am not speaking for behavioral scientists in general. I am speaking for only a handful of scientists, such as Spitz, Bowlby, Maslow, Foote, and a few others.[16]

Love is still a four-letter word to most scientists, not excluding most behavioral scientists, who haven't yet experienced the shock of recognition and are therefore likely to raise their eyebrows at any scientist who has, and to regard

[16] Spitz, R. "Hospitalism" in *The Psychoanalytic Study of the Child*, vol. 1. International Universities Press, 1945; Bowlby, J. *Maternal Care and Mental Health*. New York: World Health Organization, UNESCO Publications, 1951; Maslow, A. *Motivation and Personality*. New York: Harper, 1954; Foote, N. N. "Love." *Psychiatry*, 16, 1953 (pp. 245-251); Prescott, D. A. "Role of Love in Human Development." *Journal of Home Economics*, 44, 1952 (pp. 173-176); and Suttie, I. D. *The Origins of Love and Hate*. New York: Julian Press, 1953.

him as a sort of Elvis Presley who is causing his cerebral hemispheres to comport themselves in a somewhat dubious manner. This is all the more surprising because it is what Freud was talking about during the greater part of his life, and Freud's influence on the behavioral sciences has been not inconsiderable. The very important work on this subject by Adler and Ferenczi,[17] not to mention others, seems to be almost forgotten. Whatever the reasons for this may be, there is now sufficient evidence available from a variety of sources to prove beyond any question that love stands at the very center of the system of basic needs and that its satisfaction is fundamental if the organism is to develop in health. Love stands like the central sun of our solar system, holding all the basic needs in their courses as they revolve about it. The Elizabethan dramatist George Chapman put it very well:

> I tell thee Love is Nature's second sun,
> Causing a spring of virtues where he shines.

It would seem that the most remarkable truths concerning human behavior can be arrived at by methods unlike those of the behavioral scientist. But, then, poets belong to a special class of visionary humanity. Behavioral scientists must plod behind them by scores of years, even centuries.

It has been found that unless children are adequately loved during their first six years all sorts of harm may be done to their development as psychophysical organisms—and that much of this damage is irreversible. The principal disorders produced assume a very recognizable form, consisting chiefly in the inability of the individual to love or to relate himself adequately to others. Such individuals have been called "the institution child," "the affectionless character," or simply "the cold fish." The Western world, unhappily, is populated by far too many persons of this kind, and I put in the judgment implied in the world "unhappily" because I feel strongly that among the principal tasks of the educator must be the prevention of such disasters being visited upon the individual

[17] Adler, A. *Social Interest: a Challenge to Mankind.* New York: Putnam, 1938; and Ferenczi, S., see deForest, I. *The Leaven of Love.* New York: Harper, 1954.

by means of proper teaching not only inside the classroom but long before the child arrives at school age. I should consider a discussion such as this entirely valueless unless it contributed to this end, for the meaning of a word lies not in the sound it makes but in the reverberations in the form of the action it produces.

Whereas the lack of love has been found to produce all sorts of disordered conditions—diminution in capacity for abstract reasoning, narrowness of attention span, inability to relate, and the like—the provision of adequate love has been shown to be the best of all the stimuli to healthy development.

It is no longer a theory but a matter of established fact that most functional behavioral disorders are caused principally by the absence of love suffered during the person's first six years. By the time the educator formally comes upon the scene most of the damage has been done. But this is so only because we have consistently failed to recognize the role of the educator in the making of human beings, indeed, because we have regularly failed to appreciate the nature and meaning of education itself. We need to rethink and revalue our conventional conception of education and our explicit function as educators.

What is the function of education? To help create healthy human beings. By "healthy" I mean the ability to love and the ability to work. Training in the three "R's" is to be regarded simply as instruction in the techniques subserving the functions of the healthy human being. Our principal troubles at present result from the fact that we confuse instruction with education. Instruction is not education. Today more than ever we in America need to be quite clear upon the nature of the difference, for in the hysterical attempt to outdo our bogeymen in the design and manufacture of rockets there is danger that the distinction may be altogether submerged by the concentration on technology. To be human ought to mean to be humane first, and to be instructed should always be secondary to that. It is vastly more important to be civilized than to be clever, meaning by "civilized" urbane in a humane and refined manner. A humane man is unlikely to misuse his knowledge; a merely instructed man is very likely to do so. But this is only one reason for insisting upon recognition of the distinction between instruction and education. There are others, all of which can be subsumed in the statement that it is only through a soundly based system of education that human beings can be enabled to realize their best potentialities for being human.

By "a soundly based system of education" I mean one that is based on the findings of the anthropological and behavioral sciences concerning the nature of human nature, and the functioning of that human nature in the context of human society.

Summarized very briefly, the findings are that man evolved in a manner such that a high premium was placed upon cooperative behavior on the part of the individual. As greater demands were made upon intelligence those individuals who relied less on instinct and more on intelligence were favored in the struggle for survival, so that eventually man became a virtually instinctless creature who must learn most of what he does in relation to his environment. To negotiate that environment, cultural as well as physical, he requires an extended learning period. For the first half-dozen or more years of this learning period he is wholly dependent upon other human beings, and it is what those human beings do to him during his formative years that largely determines the personality of the individual.

Analysis of the nature of human nature tells us that the human organism possesses a built-in value system in the form of the basic needs. These represent the inner necessities, the inner requirements, of the organism which must be satisfied if the organism is to develop in health. The operational form which these basic needs take is not consciously so much the need to survive as the need to relate—to relate to others and to be related to, which, in somewhat deceptively plain English, means the need to love and to be loved. To love means to behave in a manner calculated to confer survival benefits upon others in a creatively enlarging manner.

I read all the relevant evidence as indicating that the satisfaction of the organism's need to love and to be loved is the key which opens all the doors to its healthy development, and that insofar as this satisfaction is inadequately achieved the behavioral development of the organism is disturbed. To come to the point at once, we conclude that the function of education should be principally to help the individual realize his potentialities for being a healthy human being, that is to say, one who is able to relate himself in a harmonious and creative manner to others; to enable him, in short, to function as a warm, loving human being. This should be the whole meaning and purpose of education—anything that is not this is not education. We have then, in light of the facts, to ask ourselves as educators whether we are going to remain part of the problem or to make ourselves part of the solution.

16

Is Sexual Behavior Culturally or Biologically Determined?

IN THIS CHAPTER I propose to discuss how physical and mental sexual status has developed in human societies.

The status occupied by the individual in any human society is determined by purely cultural factors. Whether it be inherited, acquired, or assigned—and whatever its nature may be, based or not on some natural characteristic—it is the sanction of a *social group* which gives it being. Social status is not something which is innate or organically determined. It is true that organic differences between individuals in any given society may be socially evaluated in such a way as to serve in certain respects to influence the subsequent status of such individuals. In these cases it is always the cultural sanction which is the determining factor; it is not the organic character as such. There have been frequent claims that the so-called "superorganic achievement of man"—namely, his culture—is the one great accomplishment which serves to separate him from the rest of the animal kingdom. But this anthropocentric claim is, upon examination, found to mean no more than that man is an animal characterized by behavior

From *University Review*, vol. 7, 1940, 313-317.

(whether in the form of institutions or conduct) which is apparently more elaborate and complex than that of which other animals are presumed to be capable. The difference is, in reality, one of degree rather than of kind.

Social studies on animal groups other than man have for the most part been limited to the subhuman primates—the chimpanzee, the baboon of South Africa, and the rhesus monkey of India having served as the chief subjects for study.[1] The few studies on the social life of these creatures are extremely illuminating, for they prove that no matter under what artificial conditions such groups are studied the mere "accident" of the association of a number of individuals inevitably leads to the development of a series of social situations which may be more or less knit into something of a formal, though rudimentary, organization in which it becomes obligatory that each individual conduct himself in definite ways. Zuckerman, who has written a valuable account of the social life of the baboon in *The Social Life of Monkeys and Apes,* would probably not agree with this statement, but his own observations, it seems to me, provide abundant confirmatory evidence in support of its essential truth. The clear-cut and determinate social relations which Zuckerman has shown to exist, not only between the individuals of the same family but also between the individuals of different families among his baboons, indicate the existence of a pattern of behavior which can in no way be differentiated from human behavior. Zuckerman has clearly shown that the family basis of baboon society rests on the dominance of an overlord who gathers a harem of females about him and keeps all others at a distance —with the exception of an occasional bachelor who is admitted into his family upon certain clearly understood terms.

Such conditions are alone sufficient to produce a fairly complex social situation, and they do. The strongest males in baboon society determine the status of all other individuals in it by the use of force and fear. The relations between the strong

[1] For example, Yerkes, R. M. "Social Dominance and Sexual Status in the Chimpanzee." *Quarterly Review of Biology,* 14, 1939 (p. 115); Zuckerman, S. *The Social Life of Monkeys and Apes.* New York: Harcourt, 1932; and Marais, E. N. *My Friends, the Baboons.* London, 1939.

188 MAN IN PROCESS

and the weak, the aggressive and the timorous animals, are
of a very definite order, as their behavior very strikingly demonstrates. This behavior is social behavior in precisely the
same way as our own behavior is social behavior, and it is
socially determined by sanctions which are made and maintained by the strong and applied to the weak. When human
behavior regresses to this elementary level we call it not
baboon behavior but "fascism," [2] another form of social behavior based on force seized and held in the hands of a few
above the heads of the many. But even in monkey societies,
as Dr. Abraham Maslow has shown in "The Rôle of Dominance in Social and Sexual Behavior," [3] the proletarians sometimes rebel. This investigator reveals the fact that among
rhesus monkeys a tyrannous overlord who maintains his superior status by force of strength may be overthrown and put
in his proper place by the simple expedient of the "ganging
up" of the weaker animals on the tyrant, who will generally
be so severely chastised that he will thereafter keep a respect-
ful distance from each individual member of that gang. When
the workers of the monkey world unite they have nothing to
lose but their pains!

The behavior of these social groups of monkeys proves
that such status as each individual may enjoy is actually produced and maintained by factors of a social nature akin to
those which are operative in human societies. Living, as they
do, at a far more elementary level than man has lived for, let
us say, these last ten thousand generations, and being perfectly
adapted to a natural environment which for them has scarcely
changed, monkeys have little need of complex social or cultural relationships. It is not, however, that they are incapable
of developing them. But such relations as they have developed fully prove—and this is for us the important point—that

[2] Compare Mussolini's conception of the state with the baboon overlord's
conception of baboon society: "The foundation of fascism is the conception of the state, its character, its duty, and its aim. Fascism
conceives of the state as an absolute, in comparison with which all individuals or groups are relative, only to be conceived of in their relation
to the state." Mussolini, B. *The Political and Social Doctrine of Fascism.*
London, 1933.
[3] *Journal of Genetic Psychology,* 1936 (p. 261).

status among the subhuman primates, even though it is more often than not based on organic characters, physical strength, or dominance, is able to function only if it is socially allowed or, as it were, sanctioned. The parallel between human and monkey society is a close one, for in both cases the social sanctions in the ultimate analysis rely upon force for their maintenance, and in both societies they may by the same means be modified or canceled. The difference, then, between human and monkey society would for the most part appear to lie in the degree to which force has been converted into a power for the development and maintenance of social relationships. Monkey overlords use their power to gratify their immediate desires, human overlords to fulfill both their immediate desires and their remote wants. It is a difference of degree and not of kind.

As in monkey society, so in human society the social status of the sexes is greatly influenced by the physical differences existing between them. The most important of these differences is physical strength, for it is in virtue of this one factor alone that men are able to enforce their will upon a group of individuals who are principally distinguished from themselves by the possession of peculiar primary and secondary sexual characters subserving functions peculiar to one sex alone. The superior physical strength with which the male is naturally endowed is the one factor which has weighted the balance of power in his favor in human as in monkey society. Indeed, in every living society the correlation is so complete that one may lay it down as a general law that, wherever one sex is larger or stronger than the other, the larger or stronger sex will occupy a position of dominance with respect to the smaller or weaker sex. Thus, in those animal groups in which the females are larger than the males, as among certain fishes and insects, the subservience of the timorous male to the dominant female is complete. This elementary fact—the relationship between strength and sexual dominance in human societies—is often neglected or overlooked by those who are inclined to attribute the differences in sexual status to exclusively cultural factors. In human societies the stronger male is able to establish a physical and social supremacy over the female, which is the starting point of that social supremacy of the male that we find in practically all human societies. From such an initial gross mammalian advantage arise the variegated ways in which the social status of the sexes is expressed.

In the past too much importance has been placed upon the role played by physiological differences related to reproduction in determining the status of the sexes or, rather, the universal supremacy of the male. This view was based on the idea that the processes of pregnancy, parturition, and lactation put the female at a disadvantage in comparison to the male. The facts, however, are that in the vast majority of human primitive societies women are not very greatly incommoded *physically* by these processes. It is only when cultural prohibitions exist in relation to them that any disadvantage becomes apparent. Even among the women of our own social group the physical correlates associated with reproduction are in themselves or their effects hardly a handicap in their rivalry with men. In food-gathering cultures, such as those of the Australians or the Bushmen of Africa, the fact that a woman is pregnant or that half an hour ago she may have given birth to a child is generally responsible for no deviation whatever—except the additive one of nursing—from her customary manner of living. It often happens that on the march she falls out, gives birth to her child, catches up with her companions, and carries on as if nothing had happened. If another child happens to be born to her a little too soon after the last one, it is killed, for now it constitutes a real disability, since under the conditions of a food-gathering existence it is difficult to take care of more than one infant at a time. There must be adequate spacing between children, not alone for this reason but also because the business of raising a child is considered to be a serious matter.

It would be wrong to underestimate altogether such disadvantages as may exist in the case of the female in relation to childbearing as compared to the male, but it is important that, if the female of the species were the more powerful animal, it is almost certain that childbearing would, in all societies, be esteemed yet another of the physical advantages of the dominant female as compared to the submissive male. In this sense it should be clear that the processes associated with reproduction are irrelevant, whereas physical strength is primary in the actual determination of sexual dominance or subservience. Reproduction does not organically constitute a disability; it is only rendered so *culturally*. As Linton has put it:

> All societies prescribe different attitudes and activities to men and women. Most of them try to rationalize these prescriptions in terms of the physiological differences between the sexes or their different rôles in reproduction. However, a comparative study of the statuses ascribed to women and men in different cultures seems to show that while such factors may have served as a starting point for the development of a division the actual ascriptions are almost entirely determined by culture.[4]

If the point be grasped clearly that the "starting point" for the original division of the sexes into the dominant male and the subservient female was and continues to be the greater muscular power of the male, it then becomes possible to understand that the original basis of male dominance everywhere is determined by the same single organic factor—an organic factor upon which man proceeds to erect a great cultural superstructure of differences which, universally, he then claims to represent the expression of biological factors. It is this ascription to biological factors of the determinants of the differences between the sexes that we must now examine. If we have not arrived at this point earlier it has been due to the fact that it was felt necessary to make clear what has generally been neglected in the discussion of these matters, namely, that sexual dominance rests upon an organic basis which gives one sex a certain amount of power over another, whether this power be expressed in physical force or in the creation of laws or customs to the advantage of the male and the disadvantage of the female. Perhaps it may be suggested here that the measure of a people's progress in this connec-

[4] Linton, Ralph. *The Study of Man.* New York: Appleton-Century, 1936 (p. 116).

tion is the extent to which the male has relinquished some of his muscular power over the female.

If, then, sexual dominance may be taken to have its origins in an organic difference between the sexes, it may well be asked whether it is not possible that all or most of the behavioral differences observable between the sexes are not similarly determined by organic factors. Even though our knowledge of all the factors involved is still far from complete, it is none the less possible to return an answer to this question in terms of a very high degree of probability.

Let us first briefly inquire into the nature of the physical differences which exist between the sexes. From the anatomical standpoint the sexes are distinguished by one marked characteristic, the essential genital system, and by nothing else—at least, at birth. Subsequently developed physical differences are limited to the primary functions of ovigenesis in the female and spermatogenesis in the male, the secondary differences being represented simply by changes in form or in such characters as the distribution of the subcutaneous fat and of the hair. The differences in the genital systems of the sexes, it is obvious, have their being in the furtherance and realization of the function of reproduction, and it is to be noted that all the functions of this system of organs in the sexes operate in the service of this end—that is, in a purely physiological sense. In the female, for example, the pelvic girdle is a very important part of this system of organs. Since it plays a considerable role in supporting the gravid uterus and in giving passage to the child at birth, the female pelvic girdle differs to the extent necessitated by the actual or potential existence of these conditions from the same organ in the male, which, as far as we know, has never yet been called upon to serve in a similar capacity. Structure in each of the sexes is intimately correlated with function. Even so, the differences between the male and the female pelvis are so slight that the expert will be wrong in his sexing of skeletal pelves almost as often as he will be right. The male is structurally organized to produce fertilization, the female to act as host to the developing organism and as its nutritive agent postnatally.

From the standpoint of the zoologist, mankind, regarded as a noncultural animal, is classified into two sexes in virtue of these functions rather than upon the basis of physical characters which normally serve merely as indices of these functions. Apart from the primary sexual characters, such differences as exist between the sexes are, from the standpoint of the zoologist, purely quantitative, being characterized, for instance, by the *intensity* of local hair growth, distribution of subcutaneous fat, deposition of bony material, and the important characters of body weight and body size. These are examples of secondary sexual characters. The primary sexual characters are immediately recognizable in any human group, in children as in adults; the secondary sexual characters become apparent only with the development of adolescence. From the zoological or morphological standpoint these are the only demonstrable differences which exist between the sexes.

It is evident that the primary sexual characters are fundamentally associated with the different roles played by the sexes in reproduction and that the secondary sexual characters are by-products, as it were, of the systems subserving these different roles; the regulators of bone or hair growth, for example, functioning in a different manner in each sex in consequence of the different hormones poured into the blood stream by the glands associated with each of these systems. Apart from these basic differences for which, incidentally, there is some evidence—at least in respect to the development of several of them—that cultural or sexually selective factors have played a part, it is impossible to say whether there exist any other significant differences between the sexes, physical or otherwise, which are in their immediate origins of a "biological" nature. Are there, for instance, any mental differences between the sexes which can be attributed to a fundamental biological or structural difference?

If there exist such biological or physical bases for the mental differences which we may observe as existing between men and women in practically all societies, then they have defied demonstration. All that has been written upon this subject, no matter how impressively supported by statements and the citation of figures to the effect that man has a greater brain weight than woman, is purely speculative—or, as in the case of the brain weight arguments, simply without any foundation whatsoever. That great psychical differences may be recognized to exist between the sexes in almost any human society is a fact which requires no demonstration, but it is quite another thing to assume that such mental differences represent the effects of physical, organic, biological, or structural differences between the sexes. For such an assumption there is not a particle of evidence which will withstand critical examination. The important fact is that no correlation of any significance has ever been established between normal physical differences in the structure of the body and mental functions, not even in relation to the reproductive functions. It is probable that in a general way certain physical factors are operative in each sex which may exert some influence upon the physical functions, but, whatever the nature of these factors may be, they most certainly cannot be allowed to play any significant part in determining the expression of those functions; for these are fundamentally and almost continuously determined by cultural factors, and, as far as the evidence permits us to judge, by cultural factors alone. It is not what man's internal or external environment does to him that matters so much as what man does to his environment.

Such mental differences between the sexes as have customarily been attributed to the operation of biological or innate factors can be shown to be completely determined by cultural factors, and by cultural factors alone. If biological factors are arbitrarily and customarily taken as the pegs upon which to hang the socially determined mental differences, that, too, must be esteemed no less a cultural device than the mental differences themselves. *Mind, it must always be remembered, is a social product; without society there is no mind.* Of a physical, a biological, or nonsocial mind, we know nothing. But before proceeding further let us return to the physical characters. In what follows an attempt will be made to show that there is reason to believe that some, at least, of these physical characters have, in the case of the female, in large part been brought about by the operation of cultural factors. If we examine, for example, the nature of a character such as the human female breast, we find that in the order of mammals to which man belongs—the Primates—it is really a unique character. Among man's closest relatives in the animal kingdom, the African anthropoids—the gorilla and chimpanzee—even during pregnancy and lactation the breast is comparatively flat and not much more developed than it is in the male of the species. The conclusion would appear to be obvious: If man originated from some apelike stock, then the characteristic form of the human female breast must have developed during some period after the separation of the human stock from the ancestral Primate group. What brought the peculiar human female breast into being we cannot with certainty tell, but it does seem highly probable that a combination of factors was responsible, of which sexual selection was only one.

In the same manner was probably produced steatopygy (the excessive deposit of subcutaneous fat in the buttocks), favored by so many widely separated peoples of the Paleolithic and the Neolithic, and which today is still to be found among a very high proportion of the Bushman women of South Africa. Fat as an object of food is highly prized among all primitive peoples, and as a mark of beauty in women is greatly esteemed. Even in our own society flat-chested, boyish-breasted women are in the esteem of most men to some extent at a disadvantage as compared to the woman showing something of a bosom. In connection with steatopygy it is of interest to recall that in the rococo period, and again in the early 1880's, the bustle found favor with the fashionable world, chiefly, so it is said, because the poet Jean Paul, like Albrecht von Haller before him, had maintained that it gave an appearance different from the apes. It has even been suggested that the bustle became popular in Europe because it gave an actual appearance of steatopygy. This may or may not have been the case.

Whatever other factors may have played a role, the possibility remains that the female breast, as well as steatopygy, developed as a result of conscious, arbitrarily determined, socially selective processes favoring the women possessing such appendages. It would hardly seem possible to explain these characters upon any other hypothesis. This being so, we have here positive evidence of the effects of the operation of a cultural preference upon the actual physical form of the female, determining not alone the distribution of the subcutaneous fat but also its local intensity or density, as well as the form of the breasts. This is an important point, for if the frequency with which certain forms of the body can be determined by the long continued operation of cultural factors, it will readily be understood how preferred types of beauty would come to be established by sexual selection over the course of time, according to a definite cultural pattern.

Differences such as the angulation of the upper and lower arms to one another in the sexes are immediately traceable to purely mechanical factors which result from the sexual differences in the form of the pelvis; they need therefore not detain us here. Differences such as have been said to exist in the weight of the brain between the sexes need keep us here for no more time than it takes to state that the functions of the mind are not dependent upon the size or weight of the brain, but are dependent rather upon its cultural organization. Concerning its structural organization and the relation of that organization to function we know absolutely nothing. Furthermore, the weight of the brain in relation to total body weight is greater in the female than in the male.

What, however, are we to say of the differences which exist between the sexes in such oft-cited fundamental characters as the blood? Here surely is something which is independent of the cultural factor? As one writer upon this subject has put the matter:

> A very remarkable sex difference, and one which in its fundamental importance is not generally assessed at full value, is in the blood. Our blood, as we all know, consists, for the greater part, of the blood fluid "plasma," and the corpuscles (red and white) which float in the fluid, or to put it more correctly are "suspended" in the plasma. The blood has the very important function, on the one hand, of carrying to all parts of our system the material necessary for the life processes, and, on the other hand, of eliminating and passing out

waste matter useless to the organs, the products of metabolism. The red corpuscles have also the particular function of adjusting the gas exchange, that is of extracting the oxygen from the air drawn into the lungs, and delivering it to the various organs, a task which they are enabled to perform by reason of their haemoglobin content. The blood of the adult woman by comparison is richer in plasma and in water-content (80:75 per cent) and produces far less red corpuscles (in one cubic millimetre of blood, 4.8:5.3 million), and thereby the haemoglobin content is less (13:14 per cent). It seems that this sex difference becomes especially marked at puberty. This gulf between the sexes cannot be bridged and no further evidence is required to show how extraordinarily important the blood is in the whole life-process.[5]

Strangely enough this unbridgeable gulf turns out, as has many an unbridgeable gulf before it, to be merely another *pons asinorum* to cross, a privilege which is apparently granted only to those who are able. Hemoglobin is a measure of the functional power of the blood, and stands in a very definite relation to the size of the body and the work that that body is called upon to perform. And while these elementary physiological facts have been known and understood for a considerable period of time, no one, it seems, has ever thought of putting them together and examining them closely for whatever light they might be able to shed upon the causes of man's alleged superior amount of red corpuscles and hemoglobin. Yet the evidence has always been available which should have led to the correct explanation. But when anyone is bent on finding differences in support of a theory, he is content to rest upon the discovery and statement of them— the meaning of the differences found being generally predetermined to fit the theory.

Woman is smaller than man and the amount of work done by her body is physiologically absolutely less than that of man. Her lungs are smaller, hence her oxygen-combining capacity is less than that of man, all this in the absolute sense. In relation to her size, however, it is doubtful whether there can be said to exist any significant difference in the relative

[5] Heilborn, A. *The Opposite Sexes*. London, 1923 (p. 38).

amount of the hemoglobin in the two sexes. If there does exist a difference in favor of the male beyond the *relative* amount of hemoglobin for body size (and we would expect to find such a difference in our own social group at least), then this difference is most probably to be attributed to factors which are largely social in origin, for we now have very definite evidence that economic and occupational factors have a very significant influence upon such an "unbridgeable" fundamental character as the hemoglobin content of the blood. It has also long been well known that the oxygen-combining capacity of the lungs is greater in athletes than in normal untrained individuals, and that it is also less in sedentary men as compared to active men.[6] Many years ago an English investigator, Lloyd Jones, and, following him, Havelock Ellis, showed "that good physique is associated with high specific gravity of the blood, and poor physique with a low specific gravity; the blood of Cambridge undergraduates [being] of very high specific gravity." "This difference," wrote Ellis, "in the quality of the blood of men and women is fundamental, and its importance cannot be exaggerated; although," he added as an afterthought, "it is possible that its significance may be to some extent neutralized by other factors."[7]

What these other factors may have been was never suggested, but the direction has already been indicated here in which they might be sought—and found. To put the matter briefly, the differences in the hemoglobin content of the blood of the sexes is, when the relative somatic differences have been considered, probably determined by the differences in occupational status or, more definitely, by the economic activities of the sexes in our society. To the same extent, other things being equal, the pulse, respiration, and metabolism are determined by similarly operative cultural factors.

We may now turn to a brief examination of the nature of the mental differences which exist between the sexes. These differences, it is still generally believed, are due to the innate differences in the neural structure of the sexes plus, it is now

[6] Dill, David Bruce. *Life, Heat, and Altitude.* Cambridge: Harvard University Press, 1938.
[7] *Man and Woman.* London, 1926 (p. 271).

fashionable to add, the differential operation of the glandular system. For this belief the evidence is none too good. In the present state of our knowledge this belief would appear to represent a rationalization devised to account for differences not clearly understood; at the very best it represents an extrapolation from the evidence. In the first place it requires to be stated that though many have tried no one has yet succeeded in demonstrating a difference in the structure of the nervous system of the sexes; nor has anyone yet been able to demonstrate a difference in the functioning in the glandular system, with the exception, of course, of those glands which are directly associated with the reproductive functions, both primary and secondary. That the glands have *normally* anything to do with giving the mind its peculiar cast of masculinity or femininity is a superstition for which there is at present no real foundation whatever. The corrective to a notorious book entitled *The Glands Regulating Personality*, which sought to show how dependent the functions of the mind were upon the glandular system, would be another entitled *The Personality Regulating the Glands*, showing how much the glandular system is regulatively dependent upon the mind. Pathological disorders of the endocrine glandular system do not constitute a satisfactory basis upon which to erect a normal physiology of behavior.

With respect to the innate mental inheritance of male and female there is no reason to believe that this is in any way unequal at birth. At any rate, there is good reason to believe that such mental differences and inequalities as exist in various societies between the sexes are produced through the force of custom and education. The truth would appear to be that an individual's mental endowment or inheritance at birth consists of no more than certain broad psycho-physical dispositions which are common to all mankind without distinction of race or sex, and secondarily, perhaps, of certain tendencies or patterns which are inherited from one's forebears and which may possibly determine to some extent the so-called individual color or quality of behavior. The manner in which these dispositions and tendencies will subsequently come to function is determined entirely by the particular cultural experience undergone. We do not inherit primary or tertiary sexual characters of the mind. The mind at birth is sexually undifferentiated, but in every known society the process of differentiation is at that time initiated and thereafter consistently maintained throughout the lifetime of the individual. From the appearance of the body the cultural status of the infant is at once determined. By their external genitalia ye shall know them. In our own society, when a child is born bearing the external genitalia of a female it is at once declared to be a *girl*, or if it bears the genitalia of a male then it is declared to be a *boy*. These are formulas which by traditional heredity have assumed the power to bring about the development of individuals according to the terms in which they are strictly and differentially understood by each culture.

Everyone is familiar with the details of the education of boys and girls in our society; how, from the earliest days, the mind and even the body of each sex is formed upon distinctively disparate lines. As a consequence of such conditioning, of cultural differentiation, it is surely not surprising that such marked differences—differences which it has been actively sought to produce—should exist between male and female. It is well known that the boy who has been brought up exclusively in the society of women tends to be very much more feminine than the boy who has been brought up by a father and a mother, while a girl brought up by males tends to be very much more masculine in her ways than a normally brought up girl.

In recent years the case for the cultural determinance of sexual role behavior has been clinched by the findings of the endocrinologists. In all, at the time of writing (1960), about one hundred cases have been reported of the masculinization of the external genitalia in female infants born of mothers who had been given certain synthetic progestins (hormones) in early pregnancy. In such cases the fusion of the labioscrotal folds in these infants may be so complete and the enlargement of the phallus so great that the infant is usually identified as a male and raised as such. The result of being reared as a male is to produce an individual who is psychologically, in attitudes and in gender role, in every way a male. Yet such individuals are physically, except for the slight alteration in the appearance of the external genitalia, in every way perfectly normal females. As Drs. Money and Hampson write, "It is indeed startling to see, for example, two children with female hyperadrenocorticism in the company of one another in a hospital playroom, one of them entirely feminine in behavior and conduct, the other entirely masculine, each according to upbringing. As a social observer, one gets no suspicion that the two children are chromosomally and gonadally female, for psychologically they are entirely different." [8]

There are now a good many cases on record of such psychologically masculinized females who have married normal females, adopted children, and lived perfectly normal lives as the husband and adoptive father of the children in the family.[9] And, as Money and Hampson have shown, gender role and orientation unequivocally correspond not with biological sex but with the sex of assignment and rearing.[10] There can no longer be any doubt of the dominant role played by cultural conditioning in determining masculinity and femininity.

Margaret Mead in her excellent book *Sex and Temperament* [11] has provided at once the best and the most important illustrations, based on the study of three primitive societies, of the manner in which different cultures group their social attitudes toward temperament or personality. The Arapesh, the Mundugumor, and the Tchambuli of New Guinea each have constructed their own peculiar and, as between themselves, contrasting types of personality for the sexes, illustrating in a most striking fashion how the psyche

[8] Money, John, and Hampson, Joan G. and John L. "Imprinting and the Establishment of Gender Role." *A.M.A. Archives of Neurology and Psychiatry,* 77, 1957 (pp. 333-336).
[9] Money, John, and Hampson, Joan G. and John L. "An Examination of Some Basic Sexual Concepts: the Evidence of Human Hermaphroditism." *Bulletin of the Johns Hopkins Hospital,* 97, 1955.
[10] Money, John, and Hampson, Joan G. and John L. "Sexual Incongruities and Psychopathology: the Evidence of Human Hermaphroditism." *Bulletin of the Johns Hopkins Hospital,* 98, 1956; and "Hermaphroditism: Recommendations Concerning Assignment of Sex, Change of Sex, and Psychologic Management." *Bulletin of the Johns Hopkins Hospital,* 97, 1955.
[11] New York: Morrow, 1935.

is irrelevant to and independent of the biological facts of sex gender. Among the Arapesh, Mead found both the men and the women displaying a personality that we from our own cultural standpoint would call maternal in its parental aspects and feminine in its sexual aspects. Among the Arapesh the sexes were trained to be co-operative, unaggressive, and responsive to the needs of others. The idea that sex is a powerful driving force was altogether unknown to this people. Among the Mundugumor, in strong contrast to these attitudes, men and women developed equally as ruthless, aggressive, positively sexed individuals, with the maternal cherishing aspects of personality at a minimum. Both men and women approximated to a personality type that in our culture would only be found in an undisciplined and very violent male.

> Neither the Arapesh nor the Mundugumor profit by a contrast between the sexes; the Arapesh ideal is the mild, responsive man married to the mild, responsive woman; the Mundugumor ideal is the violent aggressive man married to the violent aggressive woman.[12]

In the third tribe, the Tchambuli, a striking reversal of the sex attitudes of our own culture was discovered to be the rule; here the woman was the dominant, impersonal, managing partner, the man the less responsible and the emotionally dependent person. From these three situations Mead concludes:

> If these temperamental attitudes which we have traditionally regarded as feminine—such as passivity, responsiveness, and a willingness to cherish children—can so easily be set up as the masculine pattern in one tribe, and in another be outlawed for the majority of women as well as for the majority of men, we no longer have any basis for regarding such aspects of behavior as sex-linked. And this conclusion becomes even stronger when we consider the actual reversal in the Tchambuli of the position of dominance of the two sexes, in spite of the existence of formal patrilineal institutions.

[12] *Ibid.*

From observations such as these it should be quite clear that, as Mead remarks, "the personality traits which we have called masculine or feminine are as lightly linked to sex as are the clothing, the manners, and the form of the head-dress that a society at a given period assigns to either sex." Masculinity is not a function determined by a particular set of organs but by a particular cultural emphasis or *habitus*. Hence, strictly speaking, there is no equivalence between such concepts as "male" and "man" or "female" and "woman," for with a reversal of dominance a male may take on the mental characters which in other societies are the prerogatives of the woman and the female the mental characters which in other societies are the privilege of the man.

In the light of such evidence it becomes apparent that with respect to the mental differences between the sexes in any given society we are dealing not with the effects of biological factors, but rather with *cultural determinants*—cultural determinants which derive their force from a social heredity which we conventionally accept as if it were equivalent to what we understand by our organic or physical heredity. Traditional thinking here serves to preserve the practices and beliefs, the errors, the prejudices, and the injustices of primordial ages, and by its authority makes certain that whatever changes must take place in our thinking concerning the status of the sexes shall take place slowly. Whatever the origin of these beliefs it is clear that they have too long outlived the conditions which created them.

17

Beds, Babies, and Familial Bonds

T HE FAMILY constitutes the basic interpersonal unit. The
character of family cohesion depends upon a very large
number of different factors; a good many of these have
been analyzed and discussed by numerous writers. There are,
however, two factors or groups of factors which, as far as I
am aware, have never been so much as mentioned in scientific
discussions of the family. The first group of factors relates to
the sleeping arrangements of husband and wife, and the second group relates to the handling of the immediate post-
parturitive situation.

In Western society the sleeping habits of husband and
wife vary a great deal. In by far the larger number of instances husbands and wives sleep together in the same bed;
a large proportion occupy separate beds in the same room;
and a smaller proportion occupy separate beds in separate
rooms.

It would seem highly probable that a husband and wife
occupying the same bed are, on the whole, likely to be in
every way closer to each other than a husband and wife who
occupy separate beds or separate bedrooms. The fact alone
that husband and wife share the same bed is in itself a symbol of unity to them and to their children. Where separate
beds are occupied there develops a peculiar sense of separate-

From *Psychiatry*, vol. 7, 1944, 349-352.

ness which imperceptibly has significant effects upon both parents and children. The worst form of this separation is, of course, the occupation of separate bedrooms by the parents.[1]

Another phase of this problem, but one not immediately relevant to the discussion at the moment, is that presented by the sleeping arrangements to which the children themselves are exposed. It surely makes some difference to the developing personality of the child whether he is or is not permitted to sleep in the same room with one or more of his siblings and to enjoy all those experiences which result from such an arrangement. The period of development at which such arrangements are terminated and the sex of one's siblings should also play something of a part in the development of personality and in subsequent interpersonal relations.

It is my impression that throughout the Western world the greatest proportion of cases where husband and wife occupy the same bed is to be found among the lower classes. One explanation of this would be first, the economic factor: it is cheaper to have one bed than two, it occupies less space, makes less work, less laundry, while in winter one keeps warmer with two in the bed than one. Then there is the influence of custom, the feeling of husband and wife toward each other, and I dare say several other factors.

[1] There is a reference to this subject in Lillian Smith's novel, *Strange Fruit* (New York: Reynal, 1944, p. 74), when the author has Alma, the wife of Dr. Tracy, or "Tut," reflect in the following terms: "Sometimes all she could remember of her's and Tut's nights together was the lifting of his leg off her body. There was something almost *dissipated* about the way Tut slept, letting himself go, so, so uncontrolled, you might say. Alma had thought of twin beds but had never done anything about it, for she doubted in her heart that husbands and wives should sleep separately. It was all a little vague to her, but sleeping together, cold weather or hot, seemed a necessary thread in the fabric of marriage, which, once broken, might cause the whole thing to unravel.

"Just how she was not certain. She was convinced, however, that her own mother's custom of sleeping in a room separate from father's had caused their family life to be not as successful as it should have been. 'I can endure your sermons on Sunday,' Mother used to say, throwing back her head and laughing gaily as she said it, 'but to listen to you talk in your sleep is beyond my strength.'"

The occupation by husband and wife of separate beds in the same bedroom is, I should imagine, most frequently found among the middle classes. It is possible that some of the reasons for this are the development of prudery, a desire to ape the upper classes, and an expectation of comfort.

Among the upper classes the occupation of separate bedrooms by husband and wife has long been the general rule. Here some of the operative reasons are probably to be found among the following: first, the possession of a large income makes possible the employment of a personal maid who could certainly not function very well in a bedroom also occupied by her lady's husband; second, it is vastly more comfortable and convenient for persons whose lives are spent in "society" to occupy different suites of rooms; third, marriages of convenience occur most frequently in the upper classes and there is frequently no great desire to see more of one's wife or husband than is necessary; and, fourth, it is generally considered quite "barbaric," in "bad taste," to do anything other than occupy separate rooms or suites, so that anyone deviating from this rule would tend to lose caste.

It seems highly probable that the affection, the degree of interaction and of unity which exists within the family is greatest among the lowest classes, somewhat less so in the middle classes, and least of all in the upper classes. This, at least, is what my own observations lead me to conclude. I do not for a moment suggest that such cohesiveness is wholly due to the sleeping arrangements of the parents; such a suggestion would unjustifiably neglect a host of other important factors. But I do suggest that those sleeping arrangements constitute an important contributory factor not only to the degree and quality of the cohesion of the family but also to the personal development of each member of it.

It seems to me that the experience of sharing the same bed being one of the most intimate and prolonged forms of behavior which two persons can enjoy together, as between husband and wife, will inevitably tend to produce an identification of one with the other, a feeling of "togetherness," amounting as near to identity as it is possible to achieve.[2] Taken together with all the other experiences which husband and wife share in common, this constitutes one of the strongest means of cementing the marriage tie conceivable. How long can ill feeling or misunderstanding endure between persons who share the same bed? Certainly nowhere nearly as long as between persons occupying separate beds or bedrooms. One might even suggest that were the double bed for husband and wife the rule in this country the divorce rate would probably be appreciably lower than it is. It may or may not be of some significance but it is a fact that the divorce rate in the various social classes is highest in the separate-bedroom class and lowest in the double-bed class.

I have here dealt with these matters so far as they relate to conditions encountered in Western society, but these are factors which, in varying ways, are to be found in all societies. In studying any culture it is highly desirable that this group of factors shall be carefully recorded and analyzed, and integrated into the final account of the culture with which one is presented.

The second group of factors of which I spoke relates to the custom of dealing with mother and infant immediately following childbirth and the effect which this may have upon the whole family.

In former years it was the custom for a woman to give birth to her own children in her own bed in her own home. The infant was kept either in the same bed with the mother or in a crib nearby where the mother could see and hear it at will. The infant was put to the breast shortly after birth, at least as soon after as was possible, and was often fed whenever it cried as well as at other intervals. Today things are becoming increasingly very different. A day or so before

[2] It may be suspected that the opposite of this is produced in those many instances, among the lower classes, where children have been forced to occupy the same bed with lodgers taken in by the mother to help keep the household going. The resentment of children to such forced arrangements and the effort to avoid any physical contact with strangers may play a significant role in the development of the personality. Hostility toward others or mankind in general, the avoidance of any contact with strangers, and many other forms of rejection and withdrawal may have their roots in such experiences.

the onset of labor is expected the mother goes to a hospital where, at the appropriate time, under a condition of "twilight sleep" during which she is blissfully unaware of anything, the baby is delivered. During the first day or two after delivery the mother may see her baby once or she may not see it at all. Following the traumatic experience of birth the baby is isolated from its mother and put in a crib in the nursery where it is indifferently handled by "baby-hardened" nurses and left absolutely alone except for the crying of other babies in the same condition. What a change from that wonderful environment within the mother's womb to this bleak, cold, indifferent world!

When the baby is at last brought to nurse at its mother's breast he is "a little stranger." What should be for both mother and infant a warm and happy experience is rendered a rather cold and flat mechanical affair at which time the mother is often heard to exclaim "Oh, I'd forgotten all about the baby" or "Are you sure it's mine? Sure you've taken it out of the right crib?" It might be anybody's baby for all the mother knows. In every well-conducted maternity division the wrong baby is occasionally given to nurse to the wrong mother. I have been informed by several intelligent women with whom I have discussed this matter that they had very little interest in the infant during the first few nursings, that had the child never been brought to them they would not have missed it, and that interest in and love for it began to manifest itself only toward the end of the first or the beginning of the second week. Attitudes of this kind on the part of the mother are probably due to the dissociation of the child from her. It is an attitude which is good neither for the mother nor the child. I suspect that among the poorer classes, where the infant remains with the mother throughout the confinement and later, that the mother takes almost immediately to the infant and the infant to her with benefit to both.

It might be a good plan not to separate mother and child. If the confinement must take place in a hospital or nursing home, it might be better for mother and infant to occupy the same room. The hazard of visitors could be overcome by forbidding all but the husband and grandparents. Visitors are, in general, not good for the nursing mother or child, as obstetricians and pediatricians are aware and systematic observation has demonstrated.[3]

It seems likely to be more true than otherwise that the relations between mother and infant during the first few days are of the utmost importance for each of them, that the newborn needs the presence of a loving, solicitous voice, the warmth and softness of its mother's body, the caressing atmosphere of the home, rather than the cold comfort of a dissociated crib and the indifferent detached care of a nurse.

If birth is a traumatic experience, then surely what the newborn requires after suffering that birth is something a little more calculated to inspire a feeling of being wanted than what it at present receives. In short, everything should be done to reassure it that it is among friends and that, although the journey has been a rough one, there is a haven right here and now which gives promise of even better things to come. This sort of consciousness is certainly not achieved in the rather semidetached universe of the hospital, and this failure very likely has serious effects upon the newborn infant. The sense of separateness should never be allowed to develop in mother and child; they should from the first be closely identified. By bringing them closely together from the onset, I suspect that a significant contribution toward the production of better human beings would thus be made.

Another difficulty about confinement in a hospital is that when there are other children in the family a situation may arise which may do permanent injury to the development of good interpersonal relations within and without the family. Unless the situation is well handled the children may feel that the new baby is the cause of depriving them of their mother and hence they will resent it; this may be the begin-

[3] A recent investigation has shown that infants delivered of one hundred mothers who were not disturbed by visitors at initiation of breast feeding more frequently regained their birth weight by the time they were discharged from hospital and suffered a smaller initial loss than did one hundred infants of mothers who had visitors. Undisturbed mothers had a more abundant supply of breast milk. Darner, C. B., and Hunter, G. Wilson. "The Importance of Rest in the Initiation of Breast Feeding." *American Journal of Obstetrics and Gynecology*, 45, 1943 (pp. 117-120).

ning of difficulties of various sorts for each and every member of the family.

In conclusion, it may be said that while the difficulties of confinement at home are great and the physical disadvantages considerable these are, I believe, worth suffering for a brief while in view of the probability that the newborn child is likely to enjoy a happier arrival and sojourn in this world than would have been the case had he been born in a hospital under the conditions described. Furthermore, each member of the family is likely to have a happier time, as is the family as a whole. In other words, the hospital is no substitute for the home.

18

Why Man Weeps

"TEARS, IDLE TEARS, I know not what they mean, . . ." When Tennyson wrote his famous line he was stating neither more nor less than the fact. Tears appeared to be idle in the sense that no one quite understood the function of emotional weeping; and as for its meaning, in the sense of its functional origins, *that* remained a profound mystery defying all attempts at analysis.

Today, the function and origin of weeping are no longer problems as obscure as they once were. Research during the last generation in many seemingly unrelated fields of knowledge has cast a shaft of illumination upon matters which today enable us to see more clearly what the function of weeping really is and how it may have become established within the human species as pervasively as it has.

The theory of the function, origin, and evolution of weeping which will be offered here has the advantage of being internally consistent and externally in complete harmony with evolutionary theory and the contemporarily verifiable facts.

In spite of references to "crocodile tears," and stories about weeping dogs and horses that shed tears, man is, in fact, the only animal that weeps. Indeed, with respect to the alleged tears of crocodiles one researcher attempted to induce the

From *Think,* IBM, vol. 26, 1960, 7-9.

212 MAN IN PROCESS

crocodiles of several different species to shed tears by squeezing onion juice into their eyes. The crocodiles most obstinately declined to lacrimate, and the conclusion was drawn that crocodiles no more shed tears than other nonhuman animals do. Of course, an occasional droplet of lacrimal fluid will fall from an animal's eye and this may, upon occasion, even have something to do with its emotional state, but the copious flow of tears which is characteristic of emotional weeping appears to be exclusively limited to human beings.

Darwin devoted considerable attention to the subject of weeping in his *Expression of the Emotions in Man and Animals* (1877), but, though his investigations were admirably carried out, it was simply impossible for him to solve the problem since the necessary information which would have enabled him to do so was not available in his day. He did, however, make some brilliant suggestions. He pointed out that when the infant cries the blood vessels of the eye become engorged and the muscles around the eyes contract in order to protect the eyes. "At the same time," wrote Darwin, "the spasmodic pressure on the surface of the eye, and the distension of the vessels within the eye, without necessarily entailing any conscious sensation, will have affected, through reflex action, the lacrimal glands. Finally . . . it has come to pass that suffering readily causes the secretion of tears, without being necessarily accompanied by any other action."

This is perfectly sound, as far as it goes, but it is only a very small part of the story, and even though Darwin does develop it somewhat, he nowhere indicates how it has come about that man is the only creature that weeps. The conditions to which Darwin attributes the cause of weeping might have occurred in any number of other animal species possessing the necessary lacrimal glands and muscles around the eyes.

How then, it may well be asked, does it happen that man is the only animal that weeps? Are there any adaptively valuable functions that weeping may have in addition to protecting the engorged eye?

Babies do not usually cry with tears until they are about six weeks old. This late development of weeping in the human being suggests that it was a late acquisition in the human species as a whole. If, as seems probable, weeping was a trait acquired not *with*, but some time *after*, the assumption of human status, we have to ask ourselves what factor or combination of factors it was in the development of early man that may have been responsible for the appearance of weeping.

The length of the infant's dependency period immediately suggests itself. During the first year or more of his life the human infant is without speech or the ability to help himself. His principal means of drawing the attention of others to his own needs is by crying. It is now known that even a fairly short session of tearless crying in a small infant produces a drying effect upon the mucous membranes of its nose and throat. Excessive intake and expulsion of air even in adults will quickly dry mucous membranes, and it is this intake and expulsion of air in the tearless crying infant that may be closely associated with the origin and development of weeping. Equally important is the fact that tears normally flow down the nasolacrimal duct from the eye to the nose and reach the mucous membrane of the nose. It is this mucous membrane that constitutes the most immediate contact of the respiratory system with the external world. No living cells are so directly exposed to the insults and assaults of the environment. The nasal mucous membrane must withstand the impact of respired air laden with bacteria, dust, particles, and gases. Discharges from the eye entering by the nasolacrimal duct leading from the eye into the nose trickle down over it. The air may be dry or moist, at subzero temperature or very hot, and changes in the temperature of the respired air may vary rapidly from hot to cold. The mucous membrane is adapted to meet all these contingencies.

The bacteriocidal and bacteriostatic efficiency of the mucous membrane is quite remarkable, for 90 to 95 per cent of bacteria when placed on its surface are inactivated within five to ten minutes. Viruses also suffer a similar fate. The bacteriolytic action of the nasal secretions is principally due to the enzyme lysozyme, discovered by Sir Alexander Fleming, who also discovered penicillin (in 1922).

By drying it with a jet of air, one can easily demonstrate that the mucous membrane becomes inactivated within a few minutes, and death of the ciliated cells follows very quickly. When, for any reason, drying is produced in the mucous membrane, the hairlike cells that keep mucus moving tend to lose their function and soon die. This is followed by a piling up and drying of mucus, and permeability of mucous membrane. In that state the gelatinous mass of mucus constitutes a most hospitable culture medium for bacteria, which may then in large numbers easily pass through the permeable nasal mucosa. The consequences of this are not infrequently lethal. In passing, it may be noted that the chronic drying of mucous membranes as a result of winter overheating in American homes and offices has probably resulted in more damage to the health of Americans than any other single condition.

The theory of the origin of weeping proposed here is that, in man, weeping established itself as an adaptive trait of considerable value because it served to counteract the drying effects, indeed to prevent the drying effects, of more or less prolonged tearless crying upon the nasal mucosa of the infant. Infants who cried for prolonged periods of time during the early years of their lives without benefit of tears would stand less chance of surviving than those who cried with tears. Dry crying is dangerous because it renders the organism vulnerable to the invasions of harmful bacteria and viruses through a dried-out mucous membrane, the autosterilizing functions of which have been substantially reduced. Crying with tears, on the other hand, serves to keep the mucous membrane wet—via the nasolacrimal duct—and to assist in the task of maintaining as well as reinforcing its functions.

Sir Alexander Fleming showed that tears contain, among other things, an enzyme elaborated by the lacrimal glands in high concentration, namely, lysozyme, which, as we have already mentioned, is also secreted by the mucous glands of the nasal mucosa. Lysozyme is highly bacteriocidal, that is, it is lethally damaging to bacteria, and it has also been demonstrated to be a powerful killer of various viruses. The action of lysozyme indicates that one of the functions of weeping, especially in the infant and child, is to act principally as a physiologically protective device against the depredations of potentially noxious organisms. In addition, it should be mentioned that tears contain sugar and protein which are nutritious both to the eye and the mucous membranes of the nose and its associated parts. Weeping, furthermore, activates the mucosa, increasing the blood supply and thereby causing the mucosal glands to secrete additional lysozyme.

The theory is, then, that weeping originated as an adaptively valuable trait in a species in which the crying of the young is extended over a much longer period of time than in any other species, as a protective adjustment against damage to the nasal mucous membrane of the young, and the consequent reduction in fitness. Early in the development of man those individuals were naturally selected in the struggle for existence who were able to produce an abundant flow of tears as they cried, as a preventive of mucosal dehydration. Those who were not able to do so would be likely to succumb more frequently at all ages and to leave the perpetuation of the species increasingly to those who could weep.

Having now proposed a theory of the origin and physiological functions of weeping, we may now proceed to ask a further question: what are the consequences, if any, of the establishment of weeping through natural selection upon man as a human being? What we have done thus far is to discuss the physical origins and functions of weeping. This is the first and fundamental part of the story, but there is a second and perhaps not less equally important part which we have now to consider. It is no less than the influential role played by weeping in the social evolution of man.

It is reasonably evident that weeping, in addition to serving the physical functions it does, is also a highly significant means of communication. Between the tears of sorrow and those of profound joy there lies a whole spectrum of conditions under which human beings weep. In almost every instance, whatever special state each may represent or communicate, the effect produced upon the beholder is almost invariably one of sympathy. A bond and an involvement are immediately established in a manner as instantaneous and profound as occurs in no other form of human behavior. Weeping is a powerful means of expressing distress and constitutes an equally powerful means of eliciting sympathy and help from others.

It is suggested here that the sympathy evoked by weeping originated in the recognition by early man of the meaning of weeping in the infant, and the identification of weeping as a signal of distress and an appeal for sympathy and help; that, as man evolved, the weeping and the responses made to it, which he increasingly observed, increasingly sensitized him to the emotional behavior of his fellow men, the members of his community. Like the infant's cry, weeping at later ages is a signal for fellow sympathy, for help. It is, therefore, for the most part something that is not, as a function, limited to the individual, but is a matter of the group, of the community, a form of behavior that is eminently evocative of response from others.

The emotional distress of which weeping is the external manifestation demands a delicacy of response of a peculiarly humane kind. It is suggested here that weeping, therefore, has exercised a humanizing effect upon man as a person and upon the human group as a community; in short, that in the manner described, weeping, the show of tears, has been a powerful factor in the evolution of man as a compassionate creature. Or to resume it all in the words of a great poet of nature, William Wordsworth, man

> More skilful in self-knowledge, even more pure,
> As tempted more; more able to endure,
> As more exposed to suffering and distress;
> Thence also, more alive to tenderness.

Where words may fail, tears may often succeed. Even the most uncomprehending male, or the most resistant to the appeal of words, will not fail to understand or be moved by a woman's tears—or, for that matter, the tears of anyone else. The profound social significance of weeping is thus once more underscored. Weeping will often move men to action when every other form of behavior has failed.

In those highly sophisticated cultures which have placed a

negative sanction on any display of emotion, children and sometimes women may be permitted to weep, and there may be occasions when men may be permitted to weep, as at a wake or a funeral. In such societies, weeping as a socially cohesive force is a form of behavior that has been lost. In those societies in which weeping is permitted as a normal, healthy expression of human beings, as among Latins, there seems to be a great deal more human warmth, reflecting a deeper involvement in humanity generally.

Thus, the freedom to weep contributes to the more complete development of the personality of the individual and at the same time tends to deepen his involvement in the welfare of his fellows.

19

Why Man Laughs

MAN IS THE ONLY ANIMAL that laughs. Why? And
what is the function of that "happy convulsion," as
someone has called it?

We are not short of theories to explain the mystery.
Thomas Hobbes, in the seventeenth century, said that the
"passion of laughter" arises from a "sudden conception of
some eminency in ourselves" which accrues to us "by comparison with the infirmities of others." Later, in the early
twentieth century, Bergson theorized that the function of
laughter was intimidation by humiliation. Nietzsche had taken
the opposite view, suggesting that we laugh in order that
we should not cry. British psychologist William McDougall
held that "laughter is primarily and fundamentally the anti-
dote of sympathetic pain," and its biological function is
"defence of the organism against the many minor pains to
which man is exposed. . . ." Psychologist J. C. Gregory finds
the function to be "enlightenment," that is to say, "relief."
Max Eastman makes out as good a case as any for the notion
that laughter may be a response to any pleasant stimulus,
and to any unpleasant one that can be taken playfully.

Almost every theory has been concerned either with the
structure or the function of laughter, while relatively few

From *Think*, IBM, vol. 26, 30-32.

have been devoted to the question of its origin. In this chapter I propose to offer a theory which, so far as I am aware, has not previously been proposed. If, in addition to novelty, the theory has any merit, that merit lies perhaps in fitting both the requirements of evolutionary theory and the findings of contemporary psychosomatic medicine.

Laughter is defined as an emotional response, expressive normally of joy, involving characteristic sounds of the voice and movements of the features and the body. The joy may take the form of mirth, amusement, ridicule, and so on.

Those of us who have observed chimpanzees under various favorable conditions feel quite confident that the chimpanzee exhibits behavior which looks very much like a primitive precursor of human laughter. Under certain conditions of obvious elation, or when tickled, the juvenile chimpanzee certainly looks as if he is engaging in something resembling soundless laughter. But this is behavior elicited in a human context. It is not known, and it is greatly to be doubted, whether chimpanzees under natural conditions indulge in such behavior. But whether they do or not, the fact that under any conditions an ape is capable of behavior which is even a primitive precursor of laughter is of more than passing interest, for it indicates that early man probably did not have to start, as it were, from scratch.

The suggestion I am going to make here is that those animals alone are capable of laughter who are alone capable of speech. Man, being the only animal that speaks, is therefore the only animal that laughs. What is the association of laughter with speech? The suggestion is that laughter originated along with, more or less, the origin and evolution of speech as a kind of quasi-verbalized social expression of pleasure. As a result of the development of speech, that is, the verbal expression of symbols and symbol relations, the occasions producing the sudden experiences of pleasure, of "sudden glory," would greatly multiply. The breaking of the sound barrier, as it were, would enable early man to express in full voice what the anthropoid could not express in the same way, firstly because of the infrequency of situations producing similar pleasurable states to those occurring in man, and secondly because of the anthropoid's lack of speech.

In 1947, in an article in *Science*, Professor Theodosius Dobzhansky and I proposed the theory that in the evolution of man the trait that was from the very beginning, and throughout the greater part of human history, at the highest premium was the ability to get along with one's fellows—the trait of plasticity, flexibility, malleability, or educability. This hypothesis was proposed on the basis of what is known to transpire in virtually every society, in order to explain how it has come about that the average mental capacities of the so-called "races" of mankind are so very much alike. Having considered this question we concluded that there had been no significant differentiation of mental abilities in the different ethnic groups or "races" because special abilities were not given any special preference over the long period of man's evolution.

The evidence, on the other hand, seemed unequivocally to indicate that the one ability that was continuously valued, whatever form the preferred behavior might temporarily assume, was the ability to get along with others. This hypothesis has been favorably received by most scientists, and reference is being made to it here in order not merely to suggest that the "good mixer" has a long and honorable history but that the individual who was able to communicate his "sudden glories" in an expressive manner would certainly enjoy social advantages over those individuals who were less able or inclined to feel or to express their feelings that way. Even today, the "coefficient of risibility," as it might be called, varies considerably from individual to individual. Those who possessed the ability to express their pleasurable states in what we may now call laughter would tend to be socially preferred over those who were not so capable. In other words, those who tended to laugh would be socially selected and would thus enjoy advantages over those who were not as able to do so.

Social selection would in itself be sufficient to establish laughter as a capacity among all or nearly all human beings.

Those, in short, who spoke their laughter were socially selected in preference to those who did not.

Everyone likes a good laugher. He brings good cheer
with him wherever he goes; the very thought of him makes
life more bearable. It is not for nothing that even today our
highest paid entertainers should be not tragedians but come-
dians. Laughter is infectious, and most of us go out of our
way to acquire the infection. We cannot think that it was
otherwise in the earlier days of man's evolution, and if that
was indeed so, then it would follow that the capacity to laugh
would tend to become increasingly distributed as a trait
common to all men—one, moreover, that exercised an increasingly humanizing effect upon man.

Laughter is essentially an interactive, a social, phenomenon,
in which interacting persons reciprocally engage. Whatever
contributes to such social reciprocity tends to exercise a
humanizing effect, especially when there is an increasing
humanization of the occasions upon which one laughs. It
is, for example, no longer permissible, as it was in Hobbes'
day, to laugh at the infirmities of others. The risible and the
ridiculous change with the times. What we laugh at is to
a large extent culturally determined. It is not the custom
of the Western world to respond to the reprimand of a
superior with a smile, but it is in Japan. Movie stars should
smile or laugh in their photographs, but professors should
look serious. Again, the social function of laughter is underscored.

Let us now proceed to the second stage of our hypothesis:
consider the manner in which natural selection would operate to favor those able to express their pleasurable states in
laughter as compared with those not so able. It is well known
that laughter has a tonic effect. It is good for the health. It
suffuses the organism with a feeling of well-being which
virtually nothing else is comparably able to do. It refreshes
and enlivens. It relieves and enlightens. It renders all burdens
bearable and brightens every prospect. It is like the sun, a
"sudden glory," casting light and warmth all about it.

Physiologically, this "happy convulsion" involves the whole
body, since the action of the diaphragm and trunk muscles

produces a bellowslike action of the lungs resulting in an accelerated intake and output of air. The effect of this is a greater oxygenation of the blood, more efficient circulation, and the experiencing of a freshening effect. Involuntarily, laughter has the effect of good voluntary exercise since virtually every part of the body is involved.

The psychophysiological effects of laughter would quite obviously confer survival benefits upon laughers and negatively select the nonlaughers for survival. In this manner, in the course of time, laughter would become established throughout the human species as a function of biological value, as one with considerable psychological and social value.

Just as the development of speech has been an indispensable factor in the development of man's capacity to think and to establish a mastery of his environment, so speech has been, it is here suggested, the basic condition in the development of man's capacity to laugh.

Finally, how shall we account for the convulsive nature of hearty laughter? Here, perhaps, we need appeal to no more than the fact that the kind of nervous excitation experienced during laughter is likely to overflow into many segments of the body, resulting in reflex muscular, glandular, and other changes, among them tearing from the eye and nose-blowing—all of which have very definite physiological functions, namely, to assist the more rapid respiration and to prevent the mucous membranes of nose and throat from becoming dehydrated as a result of the rapid respiration.

Why the loud noises so characteristic of much hearty laughter? Possibly because early man was fairly uninhibited about expressing his pleasurable states, so that this lack of inhibition was also at a highly selective advantage and thus became an indissoluble and characteristic part of the function of laughter.

And now, to wind all this up, there remains but one matter with which we must deal. It is the relation of the smile to laughter, insofar as it bears upon our theory of the origin of laughter. Infants begin to laugh at about twelve weeks; they will sometimes smile as early as six days. The smile is

obviously the precursor of the laugh. A twelve-week-old infant will laugh because he is a comparatively sophisticated
creature compared to the neonate (first two weeks of postnatal life). This suggests that the older infant laughs not
because he is physiologically better able to do so than the
neonate but because he is psychologically rather better
equipped to do so. The older infant laughs because he understands; the neonate does not laugh because he is not yet
capable of understanding. The smile is to the laugh as the
dawn is to the noon's glorious sun. Even though he is himself
unable to speak, it is with the infant's beginning understanding of the general meaning of some uttered human sounds that
he begins to laugh. Hence, the connection of the origin of
laughter with the origins of speech would appear to be indicated by the gradual development of these two capacities
in the human infant.

Whatever the future fate of the hypothesis proposed in
this chapter, it may perhaps be appropriately concluded with
the enjoining words of John Masefield:

> Laugh, for the time is brief, a thread
>   the length of a span.
> Laugh and be proud to belong to the
>   old proud pageant of man.

20

On the Physiology and
Psychology of Swearing

THERE IS GOOD REASON to believe that swearing is a form of behavior coeval with the origin of man and the birth of language. There is also good reason to believe that swearing, in one form or another, occurs among every group of human beings of whom there is knowledge. It is, therefore, likely that swearing constitutes a basic response to some fundamental urge deeply woven into the fabric of man's being. This likelihood seems to have been recognized by almost everyone who has ever devoted any thought to the matter, and with ready insight most people have unambiguously understood the function of swearing to be a sort of safety device for letting off excess steam. It is interesting to note what some of the authorities, among them some of the most original and valiant swearers, have had to say upon this matter.

François Rabelais (1494-1553), the greatest, most proficient, and most imaginative swearer the world has yet known, causes Panurge to cry out against the swearing of that accomplished cusser, Friar John, and in so doing gives the first account of the *easement* function of swearing:

From *Psychiatry*, vol. 5, 1942, 189-201.

> Oh, said Panurge, you sin Friar John . . . . it goes against my heart to tell it to you: for I believe this swearing doth your spleen a great deal of good; as it is a great ease to a wood-cleaver to cry hem at every blow; and as one who plays at nine-pins is wonderfully helped if, when he hath not thrown his bowl right, and is like to make a bad caste, some ingenious standerby leans and screws his body halfway about, on that side which the bowl should have took to hit the pin.[1]

Earlier in the same work, in that exquisite chapter in which Panurge consults the ephectic and pyrrhonian philosopher Trouillogan on the question whether he shall marry or not, being much exasperated by the philosopher's evasive replies, Panurge exclaims. "By the death of a hog, and mother of a toad, O Lord, if I durst hazard upon a little fling at the swearing game, though privily and under the thumb, it would lighten the burden of my heart and ease my lights and reins exceedingly. A little patience, nevertheless, is requisite." Panurge's patience is sorely tried by the slipperiness of Trouillogan; none the less, he finds he must stay in hopes of getting something out of the philosopher and so he calls upon a page to swear by deputy for him: "Page, my little pretty darling, take here my cap,—I give it to thee. Have a care you do not break the spectacles that are in it. Go down to the lower court. Swear there half an hour for me, and I shall in compensation of that favour swear hereafter for thee as much as thou wilt."

Good Doctor Rabelais has here stated the law of easements as well as it could be, and no book has given that law a greater amount of exemplification than his.

Laurence Sterne in *Tristram Shandy* provides the following illuminating discussion:

> "Small curses, Dr. Slop, upon great occasions," quoth my father, "are but so much waste of our strength and soul's health to no manner of purpose."
> "I own it," replied Dr. Slop.
> "They are like sparrow-shot," quoth my Uncle Toby (suspending his whistling), "fired against a bastion."

[1] Rabelais, François. *Pantagruel.* London and New York: Bodley Head, 1927.

"They serve," continued my father, "to stir the humours, but carry off none of their acrimony; for my own part, I seldom swear or curse at all—I hold it bad, but if I fall into it by surprise I generally retain so much presence of mind ("Right," quoth my Uncle Toby) as to make it answer my purpose, that is, I swear on till I find myself easy. A wise and just man, however, would always endeavour to proportion the vent given to these humours, not only to the degree of them stirring within himself, but to the size and ill-intent of the offense upon which they are to fall."

"Injuries come only from the heart," quoth my Uncle Toby.[2]

Coleridge considered the swearers' oaths as serving the function of "escape-valves to carry off the excess of their passions, as so much superfluous steam that would endanger the vessel if it were retained." [3]

To Julian Sharman the fact that the mildest of men are prone to swear under certain conditions

. . . would seem to suggest some remarkable underlying motive as accounting for the wonderful omnipotence of swearing. It is possible that an occult virus congenial to its development is so insinuated into the composition of the human mind as to defy the power of ethics wholly to eradicate it. Can it be that the habit owes its existence and source of delight to some soothing and pleasureful qualities which like the solace of the tobaccoleaf or balm of the night shade, the world will not willingly forego?

We are disposed to think that the instinct of swearing is very deeply rooted in the mental constitution.[4]

Mr. Robert Graves, in his little volume on swearing, writes:

There is no doubt that swearing has a definite physiological function; for after childhood relief in tears and wailing is rightly discouraged, and groans are also considered a signal of extreme weakness. Silence under suffering is usually impossible. The nervous system demands some expression that

[2] Sterne, Laurence. *The Life and Opinions of Tristram Shandy, Gentleman.* London: Dent, 1935.
[3] Coleridge, Samuel Taylor. "Fire, Famine, and Slaughter."
[4] Sharman, Julian. *A Cursory History of Swearing.* London: J. C. Nimmo and Bain, 1884 (p. 39).

does not affect towards cowardice and feebleness and, as a nervous stimulant in a crisis, swearing is unequalled.[5]

Mr. Graves considers the function of swearing to act as a nervous stimulant. This may well be but it is soon discovered that its principal function is to produce a sedative rather than a stimulant effect.

In *The Journal of a Disappointed Man*, W. N. P. Barbellion reports the following conversation setting out his views on the function of swearing:

> "Don't you ever swear?" I asked. "It's a good thing, you know, swearing is like pimples, better to come out, cleanses the moral system. The person who controls himself must have lots of terrible oaths circulating in his blood."
>
> "Swearing is not the only remedy."
>
> "I suppose you prefer the gilded pill of a curate's sermon; I prefer pimples to pills." [6]

In *Love's Labour Lost* Shakespeare puts this view into three words when he makes Biron say ". . . abstinence engenders maladies."

The view of the function of swearing expressed by the authorities previously quoted—and it is one which has been put forward by more serious thinkers—may be said to assign to it the function of acting as a relief mechanism whereby excess energy is allowed to escape without doing anyone serious injury, while doing the swearer some good. Those who have concluded that this was the function of swearing, even when they have thoroughly disapproved of swearing, have recognized its deep-seated nature and have wisely allowed that some forms of strong expression must be permitted in any properly organized society. This view may be illustrated from an article published in the *Biblical World*. The writer, Mr. Henry Woodward Hulbert, says:

> One of the notable theories of the origin of human speech, and a very plausible one, is that man began his invention of

[5] Graves, Robert. *Lars Porsena; or the Future of Swearing and Improper Language.* London: Kegan Paul, 1927 (p. 32).
[6] Barbellion, W. N. P. (Bruce Frederick Cummings). *The Journal of a Disappointed Man.* London: Chatto, 1919 (entry for November 14, 1914).

language by the use of interjections, cries of fear or pain or joy. At any rate the demand for expression along those lines may be accounted primitive and universal in man and not to be eradicated. We may be sure it will never cease to be a constituent part of the race. Utterance must be had for every phase of human life. Vigor of body, mind and heart will always call for definite, strong, emotional expression. No study of our theme can stop with the negative side of it. It is imperative that, however imperfect human speech must always remain, it shall yet furnish man with words fitted to ease the mind under conditions of deep emotion and to convey one's feelings with force and effectiveness to others.

Music is a parallel instrument, rousing the soul of the performer to high states of feeling and conveying the same to others in a marked degree.[7]

The reference here to music is a happy one and calls to mind the story told of Mark Twain, a noble swearer, whose swearing upon one occasion so much tried and exasperated his wife that she, in order to prove to him what he sounded like to others, treated him to a somewhat unusual performance of really eloquent swearing. Mark listened for a while and then drily remarked, "The words are there, my dear, but the music is wanting."

The fact is that swearing is an instrument, which like all others, can be effectively played only when there is a sufficient amount of devotion to it.

Mr. Hulbert's recognition of the "ineradicable nature of the tendency to strong utterances," and his acknowledgment of the desirability of furnishing "man with words fitted to ease the mind under conditions of deep emotion and to convey one's feelings with force and effectiveness to others," is really an event worthy of jubilant celebration, for it represents the first statement of its kind ever to have been published in a respected organ of the Christian Church. In the year 1920 the sun was not observed to dance, the stars in their courses pursued the usual tenor of their way, the skies were not unduly lighted up, and no swearer, as far as I am aware, stopped in his tracks to cry out the news. Yet

[7] Hulbert, Henry Woodward. "Profanity." *Biblical World*, 54, 1920 (pp. 69-75).

when it is considered to what extremes the misunderstanding of the swearer's nature has been carried by the Church, all these things should have occurred, if only for a moment, to mark the glory of the sudden illumination which had descended upon one of its ministers. For this represents the first instance of such an act of understanding which has been granted to a representative of the Church from its foundation to this very day. Mr. Hulbert's is, however, a lone voice within the Church, and it is doubtful whether he, or anyone else within it, has uttered another word upon the subject. Yet had the Church shown such understanding of the nature of swearing as Mr. Hulbert has done, it is certain that the whole course and history of swearing would have been altered, and the Church would by such means have achieved all that it has by every means—but those based on the understanding of the facts—failed to achieve. It is one thing to know the facts, it is another to understand them.

The deep-seated nature and ineradicability of the tendency to strong expressions under the influence of certain conditions have been noted by many writers upon the subject, and have been referred to by some already quoted. As one writer on swearing has put it, "Swearing is in the nature of things. Somewhere, deep down in the 'onta,' the noumenon, the 'thing in itself,' the immanent, the Seyen, in 'Das Ich,' or 'Das Nicht-Ich,' in substance, swearing must be. Now and then, in the collision and impact of matter, it emerges into phenomena, and emitting a spark or two, dives under again, into the rock-bottom of noumena." [8]

It is good to have so many different writers agree that swearing is a fundamental form of human behavior, and that its function is relief-producing. But actually very little is thus far known about swearing. What is the character of the stimuli which induce swearing, and what are the physiological and psychological mechanisms through which it operates? These are the most really essential questions which one can ask about swearing, and their answer constitutes the principal purpose of the present discussion.

Is there any general law or principle which could be ap-

[8] Steinhoff, B. G. "Of Swearing." *East and West*, 12, 1913 (pp. 992-998).

plied to the conditions which induce swearing? I think that there is. I will begin with the behavior of children, first with the infant. An infant begins to weep at about six weeks; it begins to speak at about fourteen months; and it begins to walk alone, on the average, at about fifteen months. The human infant will exhibit signs of anger at an early age; these signs are usually observed in connection with some deprivation which it has just suffered: the withdrawal of the nipple, the forcing of a rattle or some other object out of its hand. Under such conditions all that the defenseless, speechless infant can do is to express his rage by the only means available to him, by howling at the top of his voice—a performance which is usually brought to an end either by the return of the object, the loss of which caused the outburst, or from sheer exhaustion. This represents the elementary form of the human swearing situation. With the acquisition of speech and experience the child learns to weep less and less, and to express himself in ways which are more effective and "naughtier." When he grows to adolescence, weeping and childish naughtiness are left behind for more manly forms of conduct; where one formerly wept one now swears.

When a three-year-old accidentally knocks his head against the edge of the table he either cries or runs complainingly away, and is on bad terms for a long time afterward with the table; or else he gives it a thorough spanking until, by either the first or the last means, he has relieved his feelings and has re-established normal relations between himself and the table. The second mode of response, that of a whining retreat, offers no relief, no means of "letting off steam," and thus serves to preserve the feeling of anger toward the table. With age the child learns that a table is not an animate being, so that when he again knocks his head against the table it is highly significant that he now responds by *swearing* at it, however mild his oaths may be—"Oh, shucks!" "Oh, damn that table!" As a "grown" person, as a man, he knows that even though the pain be sufficient and the occasion great enough to cause him to weep, he cannot do so because he has learned to consider such conduct unmanly. Relief by this means is closed to him, more especially in the presence of others. To belabor the table physically, as with a kick or with a blow of the fist, is never entirely satisfactory. Even when in the privacy of his own chamber there is no one to laugh at his childish lack of restraint, and he is free to behave so, there is no satisfactory relief in such conduct, and so he swears at, he curses the table. In this way everyone tends to behave, not because of a private belief in the animate nature of the table, but because something in the nature of personality motivates behavior, as if the cause and object of angry feelings were something animate. Swearing may be used as an alternative method for belaboring things which cannot, for some reason, be directly chastised.

Such, in brief, is the ontogenetic development of swearing in the person. But the principal point which requires emphasis here is that the predisposition to swearing is already present in the newborn infant, as is proven by its responses to all forms of deprivation and frustration. Its only means of reacting to such deprivations and frustrations is by crying; it uses the only instrument available to it. Later, when the child acquires the instrument of speech, he reacts verbally to such situations and with the appropriate intensity. This is to recognize that swearing is a form of human conduct which not only has its basis in the constitution of man, but that in its earliest form it is exhibited by the infant in the crying or howling of frustration. If swearing is merely the speech-invested form of infantile crying in the developed person, this then is the answer to the question: What is the cause of swearing? The cause of swearing is to be discovered, it would seem, in those conditions which arouse angry feelings of an aggressive quality which for one reason or another cannot be expressed in any other way. The function of swearing would appear to be an effective substitute for the means which might be desired, but which would be impracticable to apply, in order to "belabor" the object or to secure a certain end, and thus to serve as a means of relief to the overwrought person by giving an adequate release to his aggressively angry feelings until a normal state of equilibrium is reestablished. The infant's crying of frustration, and the adult's swearing, are due to the same kinds of causes and are calculated to produce the same effects upon both the subject and the object.

The tentative theory, then, which may be proposed here is that swearing is always a reaction to frustration of some kind, and its function is to provide an outlet for the aggressive feelings thus induced and so to restore the normal psychophysical equilibrium.

Consider now in the light of this theory of the origin and nature of swearing the various situations which are customarily productive of swearing.

What are the conditions of everyday life that evoke swearing? On the basis of broad personal experience one may say that thwarting or frustrative conditions generally evoke swearing; that sudden shocks, surprises, disappointments, mortifications, and many similar conditions which produce angry feelings of great or little intensity are often relieved by, or are provocative of, swearing.

Frustration may be defined as the consciousness of the thwarting—or the deprivation—of an expected satisfaction. The response to frustration is always a feeling of aggressiveness. But not all aggressive responses to frustration take the form of swearing, although they are generally marked by hostile behavior of some sort. The relation of frustration to aggressiveness has recently been illuminatingly worked out by Dr. John Dollard and his colleagues at Yale University,[9] but these thinkers have failed to note the significance of this relationship for the phenomenon of swearing. The present writer first proposed this theory in connection with swearing in 1928, and in 1940 applied it to the analysis of the problem of race prejudice.[10] But this frustration-aggression explanation of swearing was actually first put forward by Professor G. W. T. Patrick of the University of Iowa in 1901, in an article on "The Psychology of Profanity." In that article Professor Patrick wrote:

[9] Dollard, John, and others. *Frustrations and Aggressions.* New Haven: Yale University Press, 1939.
[10] "Problems and Methods Relating to the Study of Race." *Psychiatry,* 3, 1940 (pp. 493-506); and *Man's Most Dangerous Myth: the Fallacy of Race.* 3rd ed. New York: Harper, 1952.

Profanity is a primitive and instinctive form of reaction to a situation which threatens in some way the well-being of the individual, standing next to that of actual combat. Like all instinctive reactions, it does not generate emotion but allays it. The emotion arises when the reaction is delayed or inhibited. We are thus able to account for the "katharsis" phenomenon of profanity. It seems to serve as a vent for emotion and to relieve it. It really acts as a vent only in this sense that it brings to an end the intolerable period of inner conflict, of attempted inhibition, of repression and readjustment, and allows the habitual attitude to assert itself. The relief is only that of any completed activity.[11]

Without commenting in detail here upon Professor Patrick's remarks, it should be evident that he has not only stated the function of swearing correctly but that he has fully recognized the frustration-aggression relationship of swearing.

At this point the conditions which have been named as normally leading to swearing may be examined in an endeavor to ascertain whether frustration and angry aggressive feelings are the indispensable elements involved in the state of mind which gives rise to swearing. Among everyday experiences which provoke swearing are sudden physical shocks, such as hitting one's knee or elbow, or running into the edge of an open door. Mr. Eric Linklater, like the uncompromising artist that he is, has chronicled for all time the violence of the aggressive reaction which is likely to occur on such an occasion. In his novel, *Magnus Merriman*, the following incident is recorded:

> He got up to look for a drink. The syphon was empty and he went to the pantry for another. The passage was dark and the door stood ajar. He hit his forehead hard against the edge of it, and flew into a rage.
>
> "Good God damn and blast the bloody fool who made that door to everlasting hell, the lousy bastard!" he shouted, and kicked the dumb wood with all his strength.[12]

This example illustrates, as it were in high relief, every element and aspect of the present theory of swearing. Here

[11] Patrick, G. W. T. "The Psychology of Profanity." *Psychological Review*, 8, 1901 (pp. 113-127).
[12] New York: Farrar and Rinehart, 1934 (pp. 295-296).

is a person who wants a drink. He fully expects to have it without any thought of hindrance. He rises and walks toward the pantry with every assurance that the anticipated drink will soon be bringing solace to his palate—when, crash! he comes into violent and painful collision with the edge of an open door. His feeling of well-being, of anticipated satisfaction, is suddenly and rudely thwarted by this altogether unexpected and painful interposition of the door between himself and his objective. And here the sudden frustration results in a verbal assault upon the maker of the door and a physical assault upon the innocent door itself, as if both by their stupidity and malevolence had planned this piece of frustration from the beginning. The absent offender is cursed; the present offender is physically assaulted.

Here is another example of a common experience. You are walking contentedly along the street when suddenly you stub your toe against the curb, and for a moment almost stumble. As likely as not you will give utterance to some expletive, like "Oh damn!" Here the anticipated placid state of walking is suddenly frustrated, an aggressive feeling immediately takes possession, and vent is given it in an expletive.

If you are expecting to hit the nail which you are attempting to drive into the wall on the head, but instead hit your thumb, you may respond with an "Ouch!" but the probability is that you will say something more appropriate to the occasion, or at least feel like saying it. Here, too, the anticipated process is rudely frustrated by the deviation of the hammer from the nail to what it was not intended for, the thumb, and a feeling of aggression at once takes hold and results in an expletive, or a series of them.

The classic case of the invariably hurried gentleman attempting to coax his collar stud into place and being continually frustrated in his purpose can be put into language which, translated in another medium, would be enough to dye his white shirt all the colors of the rainbow. Frustration, aggression, and the outlet of the feeling of aggressiveness in swearing is here obvious.

Mental shocks, surprises, or disappointments involving frustration all obviously contain the fundamental elements which make for swearing. The desire that something which *is* should continue or not continue to be, or that something hoped for or anticipated should come about, results in a feeling of aggressiveness when that desire is frustrated, the aggressiveness arising out of the strong desire, although it may not consciously be perceived as such, to remove or punish the frustrating agent.

It will have been noted that whether the cause was an animate or an inanimate object it seems almost always to be treated as if it were a conscious being capable of receiving to the full the charge of shotted words. The door, the curb, the nail, and the stud are belabored as if they were capable of being affected by verbal blasts, and, surely enough, when sufficiently enraged one is capable of kicking them, stamping upon them, and attempting to knock them out of shape. Interestingly enough, to provide for such a method of working off one's accumulated frustrations, there was put on the market, in the year of grace 1940, an assortment of pottery articles the sole function of which was to break into smithereens when propelled by those who felt impelled to let off excess steam in some active way.

The relation of swearing to the process of chastising a living person has been referred to in the quotation from Patrick, in which he refers to it as "standing next to actual combat," and it is one which has been recognized in popular speech in the phrase "What a *tongue lashing* he (or she) gave him!" Shakespeare puts this view when he makes Philip the Bastard exclaim, in *King John:*

> He speaks plain cannon fire, and smoke and bounce,
> He gives the bastinado with his tongue:
> Our ears are cudgell'd, not a word of his
> But buffets better than a fist of France.
> Zounds! I was never so bethumped with words
> Since I first call'd my brother's father dad.

I recall seeing a young man in Union Square who pretended to receive every oath that an outraged Irishman hurled at him as if it were a physical blow. The verbal assault of swearing would appear to be a substitute form of physical assault.

By knocking the enemy about, so to speak, in scurrilous language, by applying all the degrading epithets of which one can think, he is brought down, in imagination at least, to that condition in which, in reality, one would like to see him. Surely there is something of a family resemblance between such a form of behavior and that of the aboriginal who maltreats the image of his enemy?

To a greater or lesser extent this element of "physical assault" is present in practically every form of swearing. Even the curse, with its delayed action, was "laid upon" the victim like the physical assault of the plague. Is it perhaps possible that swearing is a natural form of behavior whose function has been replaced, among uncontrolled men, by physical violence? If physical combat between persons and between nations could be replaced by the more natural arrangement of a swearing contest, how much more would it profit their souls, and what a happier world this would be to live in!

The most cultivated form of swearing is invective. The shafts aimed in this form of verbal assault are often, as we shall later see, of the highest artistic merit. Persons and groups at whom they have been aimed have not only been none the worse for being exposed to them but have, on the whole, been greatly benefited. The social function of ridicule, persiflage, and invective has not gone altogether unrecognized, and in the education of the child and adolescent these play a considerable role. So too, have nations a great deal to learn —and precisely at those times when they are preening themselves on their great qualities—from the criticism and the ridicule of those who see them as they do not see themselves.

Some day, when man has risen from the status of "Homo sap" to that of *Homo sapiens,* it will be thus that personal conflicts and wars between nations will be fought—not with the destructive powder of cannon but with the constructive power of words. To a certain extent this has already long been recognized by many societies. Insults are no longer considered to be properly dealt with by a duel—dueling has been outlawed by all civilized societies—but society approves that man most who takes action, not in a court of law, but in such manner as to turn the tables upon his adversary by the art and virtuosity of his own words.

Physical combat is brutal and horrible in any shape or form. There can be neither biological nor social justification for it. It is at the very best an undesirable form of behavior which any society that would lay claim to being "civilized" and reasonably intelligent would relegate to the limbo of the remote past and forever banish from the present.

Despite the widespread belief to the contrary, animals do not fight with anything like the frequency that the so-called civilized peoples do. Man's collateral relatives, the gorilla and chimpanzee, although they are possessed of enormous strength, do not fight except on the rarest occasions and are, on the whole, very peaceable animals. "Primitive" peoples are very little given to fighting, and their personal and group combats are very mild affairs indeed. As a rule, as soon as first blood is drawn the fight is at an end. Man therefore cannot use his ancestral past as a scapegoat and speak of the survival of brutish or savage instincts in him which cause him to fight. There is no such thing as an instinct or urge to fight or to warfare. Men who are given to physical violence, however so rarely, are either crude personally unorganized and uncontrolled persons or else they are of the cool calculating variety. Soldiers will shoot to kill and maim others because they understand it is their "duty" to do so. In none of these cases is any question of instinct involved. In the first type of case one is usually dealing with an uncultivated person who has never really been under his own control and who therefore gives himself up freely to the play of his emotions, and for their expression makes use of his fists whenever possible because, in his class, that is the usual custom. The cool calculators make use of physical violence for every reason but an instinctive one. Strike breakers will attack workers because they are paid to do so. Newspapers and others will engineer wars and beat up the battle cry against the enemy because there is profit in it. And men will fight as soldiers to "defend their country" because they have been made to feel that their lives and the lives of their families are at stake. But in all this there is nothing that is instinctive.

It is not instinctive for men to fight. There is no general urge in man to combat or physical violence. The instinct theory of man's innate tendency to violence and warfare is a complete myth, as I have earlier in this book endeavored to show.

It would seem that man has been sufficiently provided with a means of restoring himself to his usual state of equilibrium without having to resort to any other means to do so. This means is the urge which takes the overt form of swearing. Physical violence is man's own invention.

Whether there is any form of behavior among the lower animals which may in any way be regarded as akin to the swearing of man is uncertain. The snarling of the dog and other animals looks suspiciously like a form of behavior analogous to swearing. There can be no mistaking the fact that the snarl of the dog is a sign of anger; but the function seems rather to be to serve as a warning, a caution to others, that it is dangerous to proceed further rather than as a frustration-aggression relief mechanism. The bark is certainly not of this nature, for it is clearly a direct expression of developed anger, and certain forms of barking may well represent the equivalent of human swearing. This is a matter which deserves further inquiry.

Among the Order of Mammals to which man belongs, the Primates, behavior akin to the swearing of man has been frequently observed in monkeys and among the anthropoid apes. This takes the form of violent shaking, repeated baring of the teeth, crashing and kicking with the feet, but with rarely any kind of vocal display at all.[13] Man's swearing is, I believe, merely the vocalized form of such behavior.

It is seen, then, that there is good reason to believe that swearing is not only one of the oldest forms of human behavior, but that it is also among the most fundamental of these forms.

Having set out to find the conditions which were invariably sufficient to form the cause of swearing, I think they have been found in the frustration-aggression equation. The Law of Swearing may thus be formulated. Swearing is the verbal

[13] Yerkes, Robert M. and Ada W. *The Great Apes.* New Haven: Yale University Press, 1929.

expression, or venting, of the aggressiveness which follows upon frustration. Hence, the desire to swear will always be experienced under conditions which give rise to the frustration-aggression syndrome.

Although the function of swearing has not yet been fully considered, the subject has been sufficiently dealt with in the first part of this chapter to indicate something of the nature of that function. From examination of the character of the causes of swearing and from what has thus far been learned of its function, it seems probable that swearing is a form of behavior which is not only so deep-seated in the constitution of man as to be ineradicable but also serves a function of the very first importance. In grief, it would appear to be physiologically and psychologically as deeply grounded in the constitution of man as weeping and laughing.

Swearing, laughter, and weeping have in common the function of acting as relief valves for sudden surges of energy which require the appropriate form of expression, the ultimate function of these separate activities being the re-establishment of a state of psychophysical equilibrium in the person.

The most simple incongruity between events of any kind will produce laughter. The same events invested with a meaning of another kind will produce tears and, under still other circumstances, swearing. Let us take an example in illustration of this. When, just before the game is about to open, the star pitcher sends a message to the effect that owing to the development of hemorrhoids he will be unable to play, the announcement will be greeted by the crowd in different ways. Supporters of the opposing team will laugh with joy, with the pleasurable unexpectedness of this advantage to their side, and the incongruity between the cause and the effect will stimulate them to further laughter. To the fiancée of the player the announcement will come as a painful disappointment or shock, and she will weep with chagrin. To the supporters of the star pitcher, upon whom most of them had placed their hopes for the game, the announcement will be a great blow, a tremendous frustration of their expectations, and they will swear in order to relieve their feelings.

This example serves to illustrate the obvious fact that whether one will laugh or weep or swear depends mainly upon the attitude of mind which the person bears toward the things which elicit his response. One's attitude toward certain groups of conditions may, at various times, undergo a series of changes, so that where one once laughed and then wept, one now swears or else is quite indifferent. Furthermore, upon occasion a person may laugh when he might more adequately, or more naturally, have wept, and vice versa; or he may swear when he might more appropriately have laughed or wept; or he may altogether inhibit his desire to laugh or weep or swear. It is even possible to telescope any two of these activities and give expression to them at one and the same time, as in hysterical weeping and laughing, or swearing and weeping, or swearing and laughter—although in the latter case the swearing will generally be of the jocular kind.

Now, while laughter and weeping may be regarded as innate urges to react to specific stimuli in a specific manner, can the same be said of swearing? Infants, for example, are able to laugh and cry, but no case of an infant who could swear has ever been reported. Nor has any case ever been reported of an infant being capable of sexual intercourse, yet no one would be so bold as to deny that the sexual urge is an innate disposition in the infant which can function only when he is physiologically mature. To swear, one must have speech. The nearest thing to speech in the infant is crying, and so he lets off the aggressiveness of his frustrations in howling. This is the form which his aggressiveness takes. When later he acquires speech he will have this as an additional instrument for the purposes of venting his aggressiveness. At first the child will use all the instruments available to it, physical assault, weeping, and name calling, such as "you naughty girl," "you bad boy!"—"naughty" and "bad" being the emotionally most heavily weighted words with which it is acquainted. On the other hand, some children having from birth been exposed to the most horrendous swearing will, like Tom Sawyer and Huckleberry Finn, not be at a loss for the proper words. The actual swearing vocabulary is, of course, purely a matter of experience, and in many instances—particularly among youths who have been privately educated and shielded from all "doubtful" contacts—a minimal swearing vocabulary is not acquired until relatively late, at college or in the world at large. But no person can be so shielded that he does not overhear some expletives, however mild, and these, one may be sure, he will adopt for his own use together with those which he may have invented. Patrick quotes a very amusing example of the way in which "properly" brought-up children feel. The six-year-old son of a clergyman, a sturdy and combative child but of good habits and careful training, having suffered some serious childish trouble with his playmates, came home and said, "Mama, I feel just like saying 'God damn'; I would like to say 'Jesus Christ,' but I think that would be wrong." [14]

The fact is that no person has ever failed to experience the desire to swear, and it is improbable that there has ever been one who has never done so. Even the greatly respected Quaker who abjures all swearing has probably been guilty of the sin as a child. That the Quaker is able to refrain from swearing as an adult is simply an illustration of the fact that it is possible to control the expression of most innate urges, just as it is possible for some men to inhibit the desire to weep and for others to inhibit the desire to laugh. The urges to weeping, laughter, and swearing may not, in the inhibiting person, have ever been given overt expression, but the continued existence of these urges in the constitution of the person cannot be questioned.

The fact that the phenomena of weeping and laughter appear, as it were, full-fledged in the human infant, while verbal swearing does not, merely means that the frustration-aggression urge must wait upon the development of speech just as the sexual urge must wait upon the physiological development of the reproductive organs before it can function properly. In short, it would appear that swearing is based upon a fundamental urge in the constitution of man which does not attain its normal expression until speech is more or less completely developed. This is indubitable, but the ques-

[14] Patrick, *op. cit.*

tion which has to be settled is whether there exists an urge to swearing or whether swearing merely represents an arbitrarily selected form out of a large number of possible forms of response to a fundamental urge to anger or aggressiveness. I believe that the evidence so far considered strongly suggests that swearing is not merely a possible and arbitrarily selected form of response to a fundamental urge, but rather that it is the only and specific form of response associated with the particular urge which gives rise to it. Anger is a fundamental urge which will give rise to some hostile response—it may be an oath, it may be a lampoon, it may be a laugh, or a hundred and one other things—but in the case of swearing it is a peculiar kind of anger which calls it forth. Although this kind of anger has gone unrecognized and unnamed, it exists and must be distinguished from the general blanket concept of anger which is generally recognized. All that can be said about it here is that it is a quick anger, an anger which rises suddenly as the result of a sudden stimulus, a stimulus of a frustrating kind, and is unlike the anger which has been slow in its inception and is calculated in its expression. Whatever the truth may be, it is clear that different conditions call for different forms of anger, and that with one of these forms of anger the desire to swear is invariably associated. At this point, therefore, I shall leave the question of swearing as a fundamental urge open until further evidence has been considered, and particularly that for the striking kinship of swearing to laughter and weeping.

Swearing, weeping, and laughter are all characterized by the presence of certain very definite physical accompaniments and physiological changes. Thus, laughter is characterized by definite muscular contractions of the diaphragm, of the vocal chords, and of the face, by an accelerated flow of the blood, by changes in respiration and so on—the whole resulting in a general heightening of the psychophysical tone of the body. Weeping is also characterized by muscular contractions of the diaphragm, of the vocal chords, and of the face, but instead of an acceleration it is characterized by a deceleration in the flow of the blood and in the rate of respiration, while there is an hypersecretion of tears from the lacrimal gland—the whole resulting in a general lowering of the psychophysical tone of the body. In swearing, there is no specific contraction of the diaphragm, but there is a general increase in neuromuscular tension, an increase in blood pressure and an acceleration of its flow, and a rise in the amount of sugar in the blood; respiration is accelerated and there is a general feeling of tension which is gradually reduced as the swearing proceeds, and a state of relief ensues.

Thus, it has been observed that, from the standpoint of psychophysiology, swearing, weeping, and laughter appear to be closely related and to have in common the function of serving to restore or preserve the normal psychophysical equilibrium of the person. Thus, whatever the causes which evoke laughter may be,[15] its function seems to be to produce a temporary heightening of vital energy throughout the body of such an intensity that the possibility of any noxious stimuli taking possession of the mind is completely precluded; the feeling of relief which ensues signifies that whatever tension there may have been is broken, and proclaims the return to a state of equilibrium.

Weeping, by lowering the general feeling tone of the body, breaks or reduces the shock of the stimulus and keeps the subject less intensely aware of it, meanwhile exerting a distinctively soothing effect upon the mind until, by allowing the painfully induced and temporarily dominant energy of the shock to be worked off gradually, a return is made to the state of normal feeling tone. In the adult as well as in the child this not infrequently declares itself in a distinct sigh of relief.

In swearing, potentially noxious energy is converted into a form which renders it comparatively innocuous. By affording the means of working off the surplus energy of the emotion induced by frustation, the tension between the emotion and the object of it is decreased, the final dissolution of the tension being expressed in a feeling of relief which in its place is a sign of the return to a state of equilibrium. A "good cry," a "good laugh," and a "good swear" have each in their

[15] Gregory, J. C. *The Nature of Laughter* (New York: Harcourt, 1924), contains a discussion of the theories and nature of laughter.

way long been esteemed as serving the useful function of bringing relief to the harassed soul.

It is clear, then, that in common with weeping and laughter swearing serves a very useful function as a cathartic, that is as an outlet for emotions which results, as it were, in a purifying effect as well as a pacifying one. As Campbell has remarked in connection with swearing, "the shouting and gesticulation which accompany an outburst of passion act physiologically by relieving nerve tension; and, indeed, as Hughlings Jackson has suggested, swearing may not be without its physiological justification. Passionate outbursts are generally succeeded by periods of good behaviour and, it may be, improved health." [16]

This relieving, purifying, pacifying function of swearing has been recognized by many thinkers, some of whose views have already been referred to. Steinhoff has put the matter very succinctly. Swearing, he writes, "is a seton for harmlessly drawing off wrath and peccant humours. As it does not require to be taught, it may be safely inferred that it comes by instinct, or intuition, and thus it may finally be placed among the 'a priori' ideas." [17] More succinct even than this is the remark made by a colleague of mine when discussing the problem of swearing with me. "If we didn't have volcanoes," he said, "we would all blow up." [18]

Shakespeare, who fully understood the significance, and every form and aspect, of the function of swearing, clearly stated the relief function of swearing when in *Coriolanus* he made Volumnia say:

> I would the gods had nothing else to do
> But to confirm my curses! Could I meet 'em
> But once a day, it would unclog my heart
> Of what lies heavy to't.

To unclog the heart of all those dull and noisome vapors which oppress it is the service which swearing performs for

[16] Campbell, Harry. "The Therapeutical Aspects of Talking, Shouting, Singing, Laughing, Crying, Sighing, and Yawning." *The Lancet*, 2, 1897 (pp. 140-142).
[17] Steinhoff, *op. cit.*
[18] Dr. Henry Bull, in conversation, July 6, 1932.

man. What poisons circulate in the system of him who hoards his noxious "humors"! For him the complexion of life becomes the color of bile, a world full of unavenged personal wrongs, and hated creatures for the announcement of whose death he looks hopefully in the obituary columns of his daily paper. His biliousness robs him of laughter and the friendly token of a smile. His digestion becomes disordered, a clogging heaviness descends upon him and invades every part of his body, his thoughts and vital processes become bogged in a mire of thickening bile which is continually being added to by new upsurges of poison. As Mr. John Fothergill, that deipnosophistical innkeeper, has put it, "All the steam, manufactured for use, is pent up, it can't escape through the natural channel but goes into the blood and bones and poisons." [19]

It was to prevent such a sorry state that the Apostle Paul urged though "ye be angry, sin not"; and further, "let not the sun go down upon your wrath." [20] He does not say "Be ye angry," as the King James version mistranslates, but "Ye be angry," that is, "You are angry, don't be violent, don't swear, don't harbor malice but make peace before the day ends." If this is what he meant, as he seems to have, then he just missed doing mankind a great service. How, being in anger, can one best be relieved of it without giving effective expression to one's anger? It is not enough to go out and climb a tree, or to chop one down, or to chop one up that has already been chopped down; at least it is not anywhere nearly as satisfactory as the real thing, that is to say, a good swear. To forgive is admirable, but a good swear is more effective. It is unfortunate that this was not early recognized by the wise men of the East who laid down the canons of moral life for the West, for the Apostle's advice to "let not the sun go down upon your wrath" would have been perfect if he had added "by swearing your fill like the good men that ye are, and bearing no malice."

The ill effects of not swearing are likely to be so great, while the evil effects of swearing are likely to be so much

[19] Fothergill, John. *An Innkeeper's Diary.* London: Chatto, 1932 (p. 125).
[20] Ephesians 4:26.

less than the good effects, that mankind, having everywhere discovered this for itself, continues to swear and blast away despite all the interdictions and prohibitions of the politicians, whether they be secular or ecclesiastical, whose concern is not with truth but with the maintenance of the *status quo,* and particularly their own *quo.*

It has thus been seen that swearing is a psychological means of keeping the organism physiologically clean. It is a way of getting rid of noxious humors. Its function is to provide an outlet for the boiling over of emotions under pressure. Like laughter and weeping it represents a specific response to a specific urge and, while producing a feeling of relief in the organism, is itself perfectly harmless. Upon the psychophysiological turmoil and pressure of anger, swearing produces a tranquilizing, a pacifying effect, a feeling of relief, of emotional satisfaction. Indeed, in a very real sense swearing may be regarded as an emotional orgasm, of greater or less intensity, as the case may be.

Any inhibition of swearing merely serves to pile up an enormous amount of aggressiveness, and unless this aggressiveness can be expressed in some more acceptable manner, as in the business of the "attack" upon social problems of the Quaker or upon the enemy with whom one is at war, it is likely to prove disadvantageous to the general well-being of the person.

Thus, the important conclusion is reached that, as a functional form of human behavior, swearing, biologically—that is to say psychologically and physically—belongs with the group of fundamental urges of which laughter and weeping are the other two. Beyond all else it is observed that the function of swearing is, as it has been so eminently well described by the cockney, "to let off steam."

Now, it may have occurred to the reader that something is still wanting in this explanation of the nature and function of swearing. If swearing is a natural urge, he may well ask, why is there such a difference in the expression of it between men and women? Are they differently endowed in this respect? To this one may profitably reply with another question: Why is it that men do not, as a rule, weep while women do? Are they differently endowed here, too? I think that the probability is high that there is no difference in biological endowment in any of these respects, and that such differences as are observed in the sexual expression of any of these functions is for the most part, if not entirely, determined by cultural factors.

In this society woman is definitely of the "gentler" sex, to whom violent activities and expression of any sort were, until very recently, forbidden. It just wasn't done. Woman was too fragile and sensitive to be exposed to anything but the most refined expressions. She was too tender. As the Queen remarks in *Cymbeline*, when Posthumus swears by Jove and Iachimo swears by Jupiter:

> Beseech your majesty,
> Forbear sharp speeches to her: she's a lady
> So tender of rebukes that words are strokes
> And strokes death to her.

At least that was the Victorian view. And so in the days of Victoria, under conditions in which a male would swear, a female would resort to tears. This is still an outlet for her frustrated angry feelings which is always available to her and to which she may resort without incurring the contempt of her fellows. This accounts for the fact that up until recently women rarely swore, for weeping rendered swearing unnecessary. It is of the most significant interest to note here that prostitutes, who have always been as notorious for their swearing as they have for their easy virtue, rarely weep but unpack their hearts with words "and fall a-cursing." [21] If women wept less they would swear more, a statement which derives some support from the fact that many modern women have grown to be ashamed of tears and quite aggressively proud of swearing.

[21] Note the following passage in *Hamlet:*

> O, Vengeance!
> Why, what an ass am I! This is most brave
> That I, the son of a dear father murder'd,
> Prompted to my revenge by heaven and hell,
> Must, like a whore, unpack my heart with words,
> And fall a-cursing, like a very drab,
> A scullion!

Hence, it may be seen that up until recently swearing in women was replaced by the infantile expression of weeping, and that with the growing emancipation of woman from her former inferior status she has now altogether renounced the privilege of swooning and has reduced the potential oceans of tears to mere rivulets. Today, instead of swooning or breaking into tears, she will swear and then do something useful and helpful. It is in my view a great advance upon the old method.

21

Nature, Nurture, and Nutrition

IT WAS DURING that overdetermined period of materialism at the midpoint of the nineteenth century that Ludwig Feuerbach remarked that "Man is what he eats," a remark which, if not altogether silly, is nearly so—for man is what he is, not because he eats what he eats, but because he is the most educable of all the creatures upon the face of the earth. It is not eating which makes man, but educability.

Those who are concerned with human nutrition must be continuously alive to the fact that it is the human aspect of the equation rather than the nutritional which is the more important. The human aspect of the equation is the more important, not simply because it is the more difficult to understand and to manage, but because it is the most significant factor in determining the nutritional behavior of human beings. As we shall see, the schemes of men go oft agley because of their failure to take the human factor fully into consideration.

In this chapter I propose to discuss some of the cultural-psychological aspects of the problems attaching to food, with a view of bringing into high relief something of the nature of the creature with whom nutritionists have to deal; hence, the title "Nature, Nurture, and Nutrition."

From Proceedings New England Conference on Human Nutrition, Boston, March 22, 1956, 42-51.

By nature man is the most adaptively versatile of all creatures. Insofar as food is concerned, the fact is that anything that is edible has constituted food at more than one period of man's history and in more than one human group. Today this is still true of the nonliterate peoples who live at the subsistence level in many different parts of the world, such, for example, as the Australian aborigines, the Eskimos, the Bushmen of South Africa, the Andaman Islanders, and the tribes of Tierra del Fuego. It is not merely that these peoples eat what they *think* is edible, but that they eat everything that is in fact edible.

By nature, then, there is no food that man cannot eat and, in fact, in certain human societies does not eat. How then does it come about that so universal an eater can become as ornery as he does about the foods he will eat and those he will not? The answer is: nurture, or what the anthropologist calls *culture.*

Even among the nonliterate peoples I have mentioned, ideas relating to the qualities of food and their significance for human welfare are present. Indeed, these ideas are often more complexly developed than their equivalents in more civilized societies. For example, among the Andamanese, foods that are difficult and dangerous to procure, such as dugong, the *komara* fish, some snakes, and the like, are considered dangerous to eat. Other foods, considered less dangerous, are nevertheless assigned a rated danger value on the food scale. Immediately after the consumption of such foods it is the custom to decorate the body with white clay. Failure to do so, it is avowed, would lead to more or less severe illness. Since the procurement of food is the principal social activity of the Andamanese, it is believed that the painting of the body after the consumption of the "dangerous" foods is a ritual solemnizing the recognition, not only of the value of food, but of the social bonds which through food relate one to one's fellows.[1]

This socially binding aspect of food is encountered in all human societies. It persists even in our own atomized societies

[1] Radcliffe-Brown, A. R. *The Andaman Islanders.* New York: Cambridge University Press, 1922 (pp. 267 ff.).

of the Western world, in which the individual and the group tend to become separated from any profound understanding of the meaning of the institutions and customs which characterize the group. We still tend to recognize that a meal is a socially binding occasion, that "to break bread" with the stranger is to transform him from a stranger and possible enemy into a neighbor and friend. We generally like to discuss matters of moment over a meal, for men are persuasively at their best at such times. In order to prepare the members of an audience for the benevolent reception of a speech, we generally provide them with relaxing liquids and quasi-stupefying foods, the one acting as a vasodilator resulting in a warm capillary glow, the other producing a reduction in C.C.C.—the Coefficient of Critical Consciousness.

But that is to put it somewhat crassly. In more human terms we recognize that a good meal is likely to bring the group more closely together and thus more agreeably and securely achieve its purposes. In passing, it may be remarked that the physiological and psychological bases underlying the sociality of the group meal would more than repay investigation—particularly in a society in which the institution of the family meal appears, like so much else, to be breaking down.

In all human societies ideas influence what men do about food. These ideas are usually transmitted to the individual by an already existing tradition. So that what one eats, how one eats, and where and when one eats are largely culturally conditioned. Thus, it is principally the habits in which he has been nurtured that determine how the individual shall behave in relation to the consumption of food—as the advertising confraternity so well understands.

It seems natural to many Americans to begin the day with a cup of coffee and a cigarette. But coffee and cigarettes are obvious examples of habits which have been learned in a particular culture and are quite unknown in other cultures, just as coffee was unknown in Europe till the late seventeenth century, and cigarettes until the late nineteenth century. Though clearly artificial habits, and certainly not natural in any sense of the word, it is very necessary to understand that such artificial habits can become a powerful second nature which is virtually as strong as any of the natural drives. It is the recognition of this fact that is essential if one is to understand the character of the forces with which one is dealing in the field of practical nutrition.

Just as the making of a good human being starts in the home, so does the establishment of good nutritional habits. These are not likely to be achieved in a home in which the mother, puffing on a cigarette between sips of coffee, feeds her baby from a bottle. The only advantage accruing to anyone in such a relationship is that the bottle-fed baby doesn't get as much cigarette ash in his eyes as the breast-fed baby. Indeed, perhaps no more cogent illustration could be found of the profound desensitization to human need into which our society has fallen than our attitudes toward breast-feeding. We have lived to hear so-called experts tell us that no woman who doesn't want to need feed her baby, and that any good doctor can prepare a formula that is as good as mother's milk. I have heard experts say, and the general run of physicians echo their statement, that colostrum is a useless liquid, hence, there is no reason for putting the baby to suck at its mother's breast until the transitional milk begins to come in.

Such statements and the beliefs to which they give rise exhibit not only a shocking ignorance of the clinical comparative biochemistry and immunology of colostrum and mother's milk but, what is equally destructive, they exhibit a failure to recognize the important biosocial and psychobiological factors and relationships which obtain in the undisturbed maternal-infant nutritional situation.

I dwell on our contemporary handling of the maternal-infant situation because it so strikingly demonstrates the nature of our failure—namely, the *understanding of the situation as a whole,* the understanding of the fact that there is no substitute for the "milk of human kindness"; that the best of bottle formulas cannot make up for the substantive psychological and biological losses suffered by both the artificially feeding mother and the artificially fed infant.

It is beyond all other things necessary to realize that the problem of nutrition is fundamentally a cultural problem. By "culture" the anthropologist understands the man-made part of the environment, whatever is invented, transmitted, and perpetuated—in other words, the socially acquired habits of man: man's past working together with the present to mold man's future.

Because the problem of nutrition is largely a cultural one, the approach to its solution must be principally through cultural means. But what is the problem of nutrition which we are concerned to solve? It is, surely, how one can get human beings to eat foods which at every stage of their growth and development are those most likely to contribute to their optimum health. The achievement of this is, surely, the goal to which all the activities of nutritionists are directed. Toward the attainment of this goal I think it would be wise were nutritionists to acquire unto themselves an anthropological dimension. I can best illustrate the necessity for this by citing some actual examples. No matter how complete our knowledge of the biochemistry, the physiology, and the nutritional value of food may be, unless we attend to the sociopsychological or cultural factors first, we are not likely to succeed in our endeavors. This is what the following experiences in the field illustrate.

In the first place I should like to refer to Goldberger's famous discovery of the cause of pellagra. Pellagra is a severe nutritional disorder due to a deficient intake of vitamin P.-P (Nicotinamide) or vitamin B_7, as it is sometimes called. In 1914, when Goldberger was sent South by the U.S. Public Health Service to investigate the disease, there were somewhere in the vicinity of 200,000 persons in the Southern states who were suffering from pellagra. Pellagra was soon shown to be a disease of the three M's—maize meal, molasses, and meat (salt pork)—a diet associated with poverty and an insufficiency of the antipellagra vitamin. In 1955 there were less than 500 cases of pellagra reported for the whole of the United States—most of these cases still being reported from the Southern states.

The important point to note here is that pellagra is a disease of poverty, and that with improvement in standards of living pellagra becomes a vanished disease. Pellagra is not so much a vitamin deficiency disease as it is a socioeconomic

254 MAN IN PROCESS

deficiency disease. The vitamin deficiency follows upon the socioeconomic deficiency rather than the socioeconomic deficiency following upon the pellagra, although that happens as a tertiary result, too. The principal condition is the socioeconomic deficiency—the poverty which leads to an inadequate diet, which leads to the deficiency, which leads to the disease. To make pellagra an unknown disease, all that one has to do is to raise the socioeconomic standard of living in the areas in which it is endemic—nothing more, nothing less.

If we would improve upon the nutrition of the socioeconomically depressed segments of the population, we can best do so by providing them with better opportunities to elevate their socioeconomic status. Pellagra, in the United States, has in part been reduced by this means and also in part by making freely available information and the reason for adhering to a well-balanced diet.

But reason sometimes does not appear to be enough. Upon analysis, however, it is usually found that it was not a case of reason not being enough, but of reason not having been carried far enough—as the following case report may serve to illustrate.

In 1946, after what appeared at the time to have been a thorough survey of the situation, a county extension agent of the United States Department of Agriculture succeeded in interesting the Spanish-American farmers in the Rio Grande valley of New Mexico in substituting hybrid corn for their own poor Indian variety. The native corn was of poor quality and poor yield, while the hybrid corn was of excellent quality and yielded about three times as large a crop as the native variety. Forty of the eighty-four growers in the village planted hybrid corn the first year and doubled the production per acre of the preceding year. The following year sixty growers planted hybrid corn, but in 1948, although the high yield had continued, only thirty farmers planted hybrid corn. The other thirty returned to the traditional variety. In 1949, there were only three farmers planting hybrid corn. All the rest were planting the old variety.

The county agent was on good terms with the farmers, spoke their language, and was interested in their welfare. He had carefully studied their problems, discussed them with the leaders, and then presented his plan at a special meeting. He showed movies and cartoons illustrating the advantages of the hybrid corn. There was a free discussion and everyone agreed upon the advantage of the new corn. A demonstration plot was set up showing the threefold yield of the new corn as compared with the old. The new seed was made available in exchange for the old.

The yield, quality, and appearance of the hybrid corn planted by the farmers fulfilled all the promised expectations. Why then did they cease to plant it? The answer was very simple: Never underestimate the power of a woman. Their wives didn't like it. "My wife doesn't like that hybrid, that's all." That was the answer.

The corn had not been popular from the first harvest. All the wives had complained. Its texture was wrong; it didn't hang well together for tortillas; the tortillas came out the wrong color. Few had cared for the flavor. But though it made abundant food for the animals, and though there was even a hope that one might get used to the taste, the flavor and texture and the revolt of the wives constituted a combination of conditions which could not be resisted—and so the farmers, after having tried their best, returned to the Indian corn. Domestic harmony was restored, tortillas looked and tasted as they should, and once again custom declared itself king.

The story is a common one. But let us examine this particular nutritional tragicomedy and attempt to discover what went wrong and how a happier denouement might have been brought about.

The county agent had made a study of the physical conditions, the economic conditions, the environment, and the farming practices. He had concluded that increased farm production would greatly benefit the community. He had obtained the agreement of the farmers to this conclusion. All seemed to be well.

Now let us see what he failed to do.

He failed to inquire into the food habits of the people.

He failed to inquire into the uses to which the corn was habitually put.

He failed to recognize that there might be a problem of taste.

He failed to recognize that the customary courtesy of the people prevented them from expressing themselves freely in the presence of an expert, and thus failed to learn what some of the problems which could have been forestalled might be.

He failed to reckon with the preparers of food, the women, and thus paid the penalty of those who ignore the fact that women constitute, at the least, one half of the human race.

In the light of this post mortem it has been suggested that a possibly successful procedure would have included the following steps: (1) trial of several varieties of hybrid corn, in full recognition on the part of everyone that this was experimental, in order to discover which corn the people liked best; (2) testing to see how the corn selected really fitted into the culture patterns; (3) continued work with the farmers in order to see that they fully convinced themselves of the advantages of the new corn; (4) continued contact to obviate all difficulties and to make any modifications that might be called for. By such means the taste problem might have been forestalled and met, and the society as a whole benefited.

This case report presents a good illustration of what I mean by the approach to the nutritional situation as a whole, and particularly from the cultural point of view. But what cases such as this should teach us is not that it is difficult to modify food habits, but rather that with the proper approaches it is probably possible to modify any habit, whether of food or otherwise. The whole of human history, and especially recent history, stands as a testament to that fact. Perhaps no better illustration can be given of the modifiability of human food habits than that which is afforded by the history of the potato.

Brought back from Peru by Spanish explorers in the sixteenth century, it was at first rejected by Europeans. The rumor was spread that it poisoned the ground and caused diarrhea. That the potato first took root in Ireland was due entirely to the condition of virtually continuous famine to which the populace had been reduced by the English. Introduced into Ireland by Sir Walter Raleigh, potatoes were being widely cultivated and eaten by the middle of the first half of the seventeenth century. As is well known, the potato became the staple food of the Irish, and it was to the tragic failure of the potato crops in the middle of the nineteenth century that Boston owes so great a part of its population. The Irish undoubtedly took to the potato not because they originally liked it but because they were reduced to it. It took the English another half century before they accepted the humble tuber, and the rest of Europe took even longer before it succumbed. *The History and Social Influence of the Potato* [2] has been ably written by Dr. Redcliffe N. Salaman, the potato's vicissitudes and eventual conquest being fully set out in the book. The ruses by which people were persuaded to overcome their prejudices and eat the potatoes they had cultivated form an entertaining chapter in the history of nutrition.

As late as 1771 the potato was held so much under suspicion that the French government appealed to the Medical Faculty of Paris for its considered judgment. The faculty returned a report to the effect that the potato was a good and healthy food, in no way injurious to health, and of great utility.

In Prussia it was the general belief that the potato gave rise to scrofula, rickets, and consumption, among other evils. It required all the influence that Frederick the Great could bring to overcome this prejudice. When Frederick sent a wagonload of potatoes to Kolberg after the famine in 1774, in the hope that the people would grow potatoes themselves, the answer he received was, "The things have neither smell nor taste, not even the dogs will eat them, so what use are they to us?" The opposition was overcome by sending a uniformed Swabian gendarme, who, by persuasion and example, taught the people how to cultivate and grow the tubers.[3]

Benjamin Thompson, better known as Count Rumford (1753-1814), who as a Royalist had to leave his native Massa-

[2] New York: Cambridge University Press, 1949.
[3] Bruford, W. H. *Germany in the Seventeenth Century.* New York: Cambridge University Press, 1935 (pp. 115-116).

chusetts in 1776, in later years as head of the army and ordinance of the Elector of Bavaria ingeniously introduced the cultivation of the potato into that country by ordering every soldier to plant and cultivate a patch of potatoes, and also to cook and eat them. The length of military service gave the soldier more than enough time for raising tubers and developing a taste for them. When the men returned to their farms and villages potatoes came at last into their own.

The opposition to the potato and to other new kinds of foods raises an interesting question: "What is the mechanism behind such opposition?" In the case of the potato, Salaman suggests that the fear of disease was simply a rationalization of unconscious fears—the fear of breaking with a Bible-permeated common tradition and the fear of eating a new food, which was akin to eating the forbidden fruit of the Garden of Eden, "a sinful act which, even if its effects were physically harmless, was bound to create a feeling of personal guilt, which demanded some kind of expiation lest the individual be smitten with some dreaded disease."

That such unconscious motivations are often involved in the individual's response to certain foods has now a well-authenticated body of case histories and knowledge to support it. Such knowledge has led, for example, to a revolution in the way meat is packaged and displayed in our food markets, owing to our better understanding of the unconscious avoidance reactions of young housewives when meat is dealt with in the old manner.

The resistance to this day in Europe to Indian corn as a food for human beings is based largely on the fact that it is believed to be a food fit only for hogs and cattle to eat. Since I myself believed this for the first twenty-one years of my life and am now a perfervid corn eater, I offer myself as a living example either of a regression to the barnyard or of a progression in the art of eating without a knife and fork.

Man by virtue of his great plasticity, or what I have earlier called educability, is able to learn new habits and unlearn old ones.

It is well known, and has been repeatedly demonstrated by tests, that the unlearning of habits becomes more difficult with age, particularly when the habits are enjoyable ones. Furthermore, we know that it is well nigh impossible to un-learn a habit one enjoys in the absence of a sufficiently com-pelling motivation. For example, the knowledge that they may develop cancer of the lungs does not constitute a sufficiently compelling reason to cause millions of smokers to relinquish the habit. On the other hand, some thousands of smokers have abandoned the habit; but here we cannot be certain that the compelling reason was the knowledge that they might develop lung cancer—that piece of knowledge may merely have been, so to speak, the lucky strike that broke the camel's back. Virtue may be its own reward, but the new non-smoker often finds that in escaping from the threat of cancer he has become a victim of the menace of corpulence. No won-der so many erstwhile smokers prefer to resume their chances on the merry-go-round with the possibility of cancer than continue on the swings with the certainty of corpulence.

May it not be that the great increase in smoking in this century is related to, among other things, the great reduction in breast-feeding and the inadequate satisfaction of bottle-feeding?

These remarks, made in passing, are not unrelated to the work of the practical nutritionist. But we cannot stop to de-velop them here. What I was getting round to when I began the discussion of habits was that, in view of the difficulty of unlearning early habits, it were surely the course of wisdom to create good habits in the early years of the child's develop-ment. Taking the world as we find it, and speaking for our culture alone, it seems to me that it is through education that our people can best be taught how to eat as they should.

We have succeeded in teaching pregnant mothers that the most important part of their regimen, during the 266½ days of pregnancy, for the health of the child is a good well-balanced diet. We have also succeeded in getting across to that half of the human race that is sufficiently motivated, namely women, that there are such things as calculable cal-ories and measurable vitamins, and that they affect not only the shape of things to come but also their desirability as well as durability. It has long been known that women are much more careful of the foods they eat than men. And since women are the mothers of mankind and the purchasers and preparers of food in our culture, it is principally through them that we are most likely to succeed in influencing the nutrition of the people. Hence, while by no means neglecting the male, it would seem that the most effective approach to his stomach would be via his mother and later through his wife—his mother during childhood and his wife during technical adulthood.

Since mothers are the persons in our society who are pivotally involved in the nutrition of the family, it is through them that the teaching of good nutritional habits is most likely to succeed, and this for several reasons which are almost too obvious to discuss. But discussed they must be. Firstly, mothers are most desirous of doing their best by their children. If they are told by the experts of one period that spinach is the thing, spinach will be the thing. If they are informed by the experts somewhat later that spinach is not the thing, spinach will cease to be the thing. If candy is shown to be bad for the teeth, they will do what they can to regulate the consumption of candy and purchase anticaries candy. If meals should be served which represent on the plate a good proportion of the colors of the spectrum, they will see to it that this is done. It is really quite true that since he could not be everywhere God created mothers. Thus, the first point to recognize is that insofar as nutrition is concerned mothers are probably the most educable members of the population.

Secondly, being the most educable members of the population and being the principal feeders of the young, mothers are most likely to be the ones to modify and change food habits in the desired direction.

Thirdly, not only is the nutrition of the child largely determined by the mother, but good food habits are placed on a firm foundation throughout childhood and adolescence by the mother's conduct not only in feeding her children but in feeding herself and her husband. The dietary example set by the parents plays an important role in influencing the dietary habits of the child. Hence the importance of the training of prospective parents in this regimen.

One of the greatest obstacles to the achievement of an optimum nutrition for every individual in our culture is the fragmentation of social relationships which is steadily occurring within the family itself. All but the mother's activities tend to be directed away from rather than toward the family. Instead of being family centered, the activities of the non-maternal members of the family are directed toward work, interest, and play outside the home. Children are sent off to school with their peanut butter sandwiches and apples. The husband, in millions of cases, takes his own variety of sandwiches and his flask of hot coffee to work with him, and even the mother herself, left alone as she is during the greater part of the day when her children are of school age, prefers to munch on snacks rather than prepare an adequate meal for herself. When the children return from school they are ready, not for a meal, but for some snacks and candy. In the majority of cases they will eat their dinner before the father returns from work. And when they are adolescent they will have too many outside interests to be able to adjust their mealtimes to those of their parents. Their diets are likely to consist largely of soft drinks, hamburgers, ice cream, coffee, and cigarettes. Is it any wonder that we are not a particularly healthy nation?

A recent survey, conducted by the Youth Research Institute, found that only 29 per cent of 4,310 teen-agers dined regularly with their parents, "regularly" meaning more than three times a week. Another survey of 3,517 children from five to twelve years of age revealed pretty much the same facts. I would suggest that the means of re-establishing the family meal might well be worth looking into, not merely as a contribution to better nutrition, but to better family and social relationships.

Into the psychological significances of overeating I cannot enter here. Mostly the phenomenon is due to disturbed social relationships, and these must be corrected before anything can be done of enduring value for such cases. There is, however, a form of overeating to which I would briefly like to refer—it is the overeating of the average adult.

Most of us overeat. The quantities of food we consumed during the first twenty-five years of our lives were perhaps necessary for an actively growing organism. But as we grow older we require less food to maintain ourselves in optimum health. Nevertheless, most of us persist in consuming the same or even greater quantities of food than we did in our earlier years. Here again is a fertile field for research. How can we deal with adult habits of eating?

It was Socrates who said that "bad men live that they may eat and drink, whereas good men eat and drink that they may live." Perhaps he had something there, for if we substitute for "bad" the phrase "feverishly driven" we may know where to look for the answer to this problem.

22

Embryological Beliefs of
Primitive Peoples

E MBRYOLOGY IS THE SCIENCE which treats of the formation of the embryo. If science be regarded as any branch of systematized knowledge which has been tested and analyzed by the standard of experience, then all existing peoples, advanced or primitive, may be said to have a science of embryology.

Certain members of the older schools of anthropology, such as Sir James Frazer and others, were responsible for the now widespread but completely erroneous notion that "primitive" peoples do not have any science and that magic constitutes the body of arts which precedes science and paves the way for its growth. The truth is, in fact, quite otherwise. Every people of whom we have any knowledge practices both magic and science as activities parallel with the many others which are clearly recognized as belonging to their proper places in either religious or secular life. Sometimes the borderland between magical and scientific activities is somewhat blurred, just as it sometimes is among ourselves, but, as a rule, among primitive peoples magic and science are recognized for what

From *Ciba Symposia*, vol. 10, 1949, 994-1028.

they are—the one as a manipulation of the supernatural, the other as a practical working theory of the processes of nature.

Theories of the emergence into being of the individual universally agree in that they assert the participation in the process of the supernatural as well as of the natural. At least, that is so in all social groups where creation myths or the belief in a godhead are to be found. For example, among all "primitive" peoples it is firmly believed that without the intervention of the supernatural no woman can become a mother.

A study of the embryological beliefs of primitive peoples indicates that they fall into two distinct classes, as follows: 1. Those theories or beliefs in which the act of coition is in no way causally associated with the generative process but is referred to causes altogether unrelated to it; 2. Those theories or beliefs in which the act of coition is recognized as one of a complex of necessary factors which, operating together, are capable of engendering a new being but which singly, or in the absence of any one, are incapable of producing such an effect.

Our own types of embryological belief fall into the second class, as do those of the majority of nonliterate peoples. There are differences in important details, but the general conception bears a strong family resemblance to our own beliefs.

The Australian aborigines hold what, in any evolutionary scheme of values, must be considered the most elementary beliefs concerning the genesis of the individual. Among the hundreds of tribes who, until the advent of the white man, occupied a territory slightly larger than the area of the United States, the prevailing embryological beliefs, though varying in details, followed an identical pattern, a pattern which still survives among the existing Australian tribes.

In order that the reader may develop a proper respect for the beliefs of the Australian aborigines, it may be pointed out that precisely as it is the case in our own tradition of embryological science that in embryogenesis ontogeny recapitulates phylogeny, so too among the Australian aborigines the embryological canon constitutes a complete theory of evolution. Let us, then, start at the beginning and present the

typical form of the beliefs as they are to be found among the
Arunta of Central Australia.

According to Arunta tradition, in the *Alchera* or far distant
past when there were neither men nor women, there dwelt
in the western sky two beings, of whom it is said that they
were *Numbakulla,* that is, self-existing beings who came out
of nothing. It happened one day that *Numbakulla* discovered,
far away to the east, a number of *Inapertwa,* that is, rudimentary beings, who possessed neither limbs nor senses, who
did not eat, and who presented the appearance of amorphous
human beings, all doubled into a rounded mass in which just
the vague outlines of the various parts of the body could be
seen. These *Inapertwa,* who were destined to be transformed
into men and women by *Numbakulla,* represented the intermediate stage in the transformation of animals and plants into
human beings, so that when the *Numbakulla* came down to
earth and fashioned the *Inapertwa* into men and women each
individual so fashioned naturally retained an intimate relationship with the animal, plant, or other living thing of which
he was a transformation and with which he was at one time
identical. It is this manner that men originally came into being, and it is for this reason that men necessarily possess
totems, that is to say, an animal, plant, or other object or
thing such as water, wind, sun, fire, cloud, or whatnot, with
which each individual is closely identified, since it is to that
plant, animal, object, or thing that the native believes himself
to owe his original being.

The original men created by *Numbakulla* are the *Alchera*
ancestors who banded together in totemic companies and
wandered over the land in various directions, as recorded in
the traditions associated with them. Each ancestor carried
with him one or more sacred stones which were associated
with the *kuruna,* that is, the essential spirit part of the individual, and which are called by the Arunta *churinga.* Wherever the ancestors originated, and wherever they camped
during their wanderings, there were formed *knanikilla,* or
local totem centers. At each of these spots a certain number
of ancestors went into the ground, each leaving his *churinga*
behind. His body died, but some natural feature, such as a

rock or tree, arose to mark the spot, while his spirit part, associated with a large number of other spirit individuals, or *kuruna,* remained in the *churinga.* Each totem center is, of course, associated with a particular species of totem. Thus, for example, in one locality there will be wildcat spirit individuals, in another a group of emu, then a group of kangaroos, and in another a group of hakea flower, witchetty grub, and so on. It is this conception that lies at the root of the totemic system.

These totemic spots, or *knanja,* are the abodes of the spirit babies, or *kuruna.* The *kuruna* are always on the lookout for suitable women to enter. Hence, when women wish to have children they frequent the totemic places; when they do not wish to have children they give them a wide berth. A woman knows at once when she has been entered by a *kuruna* because she feels the movement of it within her. The spirit child always enters through the loins or mouth or under a fingernail but never through the vulva.

There are many ways in which a *kuruna* may be caused to enter a woman. One way is either by means of her own or her husband's or some other person's dream. Another is by eating food into which the *kuruna* of some animal has entered. Thus, a man may be hunting a wildcat and, while chasing it, follow it into a wallaby totemic center where a wallaby *kuruna* enters it. If the man spears the wildcat near the *knanikilla* and gives some of it to his wife to eat, the wallaby *kuruna* enters her, not through the mouth but through her loins, and she will later give birth to a child whose totem will be the wallaby.

The conception of the stages of development of the embryo within the womb are very clearly defined. The *kuruna,* or spirit child, is described as being shapeless in form, having neither arms, legs, nor head, and resembling a very small, round, little pebble of a red color. The *kuruna* at the time it leaves its totemic habitation is regarded as an amorphous spiritual entity which acquires a body only after it has entered a woman. Thus, the primitive or elementary anatomical structure of the *kuruna* undergoes development within the womb of the woman into a proper body. It is probable that the *kuruna* are actually regarded as corresponding to the stage in the evolution of men and women when the latter were all *Inapertwa,* in the far distant *Alchera.* The description given by the natives of the "anatomy" of the *Inapertwa* corresponds almost exactly with that which they give the anatomy of the *kuruna.* It is reasonable to suppose, since it is a spirit of *Alchera* origin which in reality enters the woman, that it enters in its original form.

Within the womb the *kuruna* undergoes an unfolding or development into a *ratappa,* or proper baby. So clear and unequivocal is the native conception of the *kuruna* and *ratappa* that they will reject every object which may offer itself as such unless it fully agrees with their conception of it. Thus, on the rare occasions when an embryo is born at a very premature stage nothing will persuade them that it is an undeveloped human being, for it is nothing like either a *kuruna* or a *ratappa.* The embryo thus ejected is regarded as the young of some other animal which by mistake had entered the woman. Writing in 1941 of the Drysdale River tribes in northwestern Australia, Hernandez reports the case of a woman who, when reprimanded for producing an abortion, innocently replied that what she had ejected was not a child but a rat.

Every animal is regarded as having a *kuruna,* which enters the female in the same fashion as it does in the human. An emu *kuruna,* for example, enters an emu that lays an egg containing the little emu *kuruna,* which is very small and cannot at first be seen, but which grows into an emu inside the shell and hatches out from this just as a little kangaroo or human body grows inside its mother's *ekura,* or baby bag, and hatches out.

Among the Adnjamatana tribe of northern South Australia it is believed that children originate in two ancestral women known as *maudlanami* ("nami"—mother), who live in a definite place in the sky. They are large beings who have sat still for so long that they have become the color of gray weathered rock. Their long hair almost covers them and on their pendulous breasts are swarms of spirit children who secure their sustenance from them. These women are the source of all life within the tribe, each producing *muri,* or spirit children, of their own moiety. When the number of *muri* on the breasts of the *maudlanami* becomes too many, some are told to go to the world beneath and find a suitable mother. The spirits either descend on a string as fine as a spider's web or fly down in the same manner as butterflies. They are so small that only the magician or the old women can see them. The spirit child is always on the lookout for pleasant-faced and kindly mothers, particularly those with large breasts, and when a suitable woman comes near the habitat of the *muri,* it will enter her by creeping painlessly under the thumbnail, traveling up the arm, and then moving downward into the womb there to start life as a human being. Until this happens the *muri* spend their days seeking food from the gum blossoms and their nights asleep under the loose bark of the tree trunks. Late winter and early spring are supposed to be the favorite times for these little beings to visit the earth. Their arrival is announced by the presence of yellow fungi on the damp logs of the creek. These growths are believed to be the vomit of the spirit children, and when the aborigines see these they believe that someone will soon be pregnant.

Among the Australian aborigines generally, and the Arunta in particular, the human female is regarded as being a kind of incubator of the *kuruna* and *ratappa.* Her function is merely to make available the food which the spirit child is quite able to find and consume for itself, just as the *kuruna* of the emu is able to live off the nourishment it finds in the egg. The mother bears no other physiological relationship to the child than that. She bears no more genetic relationship to the *ratappa,* which is also the name for a newborn baby, or to the individual into which it grows than an incubator does either to the egg or the chicken which hatches from it. It is in this genetic sense that a physiological relationship between mother and child can be said to pass unrecognized among the Australian aborigines. This is not to say that the aboriginal does not know his own mother. He does. She is the woman who gave birth to him. He does not, however, regard himself as being physiologically related to her, but only socially. So, too, with respect to the father. The father of a child is the husband of the woman who gave birth to it. This is clearly a social relationship and is in no way conceived as a biological relationship.

These particular tribes do not recognize biological or physiological relationships, but only social relationships. The terms "mother" and "father" are used in a purely social sense. There is nothing in their meaning which denotes any genetic or blood relationship. To recognize the existence of such a thing as "blood relationship," one individual at least must be regarded as in a particular sense the cause of another; it must be recognized that some part of the one has contributed to the formation, to the genesis, of the other. The members of these tribes do not have an awareness of such things.

Of course, they are aware of the fact that a child comes into the world out of the body of the mother, but no one for a moment believes that the child was *produced* or *created* in the body of the woman from which it has issued. The belief is rather that an already *preformed* spirit child has entered her from some external source, generally, but neither always nor necessarily associated in some way with the moiety affiliation of her husband. A child is not physiologically produced in a woman, and physiologically the male has nothing to do with its production. The latter may merely be the means of causing a particular spirit child to migrate into a woman. Children are not physiologically produced by anyone; they are conceived to have been created at a far distant time, and human beings play absolutely no physiological part in their generation.

As one of the natives of a southeastern tribe put the belief as regards the mother, the mother is nothing, she is only a kind of wet nurse. In the *Eumenides* of Aeschylus this belief is recorded in the following words:

> She who is called the mother of the child
> Is not its parent, but the nurse of seed
> Implanted in begetting.

Intercourse with a male is generally, though not always, considered necessary before a spirit child will enter a woman. Trained investigators in the field have repeatedly inquired of

the natives whether pregnancy was possible without intercourse and the replies received by them have made it abundantly clear that intercourse was not regarded as having anything to do with pregnancy *in the sense of being the cause
of it.* Intercourse merely prepares the woman's womb by
opening it up, but it depends entirely upon the will of the
spirit child whether or not it will enter her. Often enough a
spirit child will enter a woman without this preliminary preparation. Pregnancy begins with the entrance of the spirit
child, not with intercourse. A virgin is incapable of conceiving
because she has not been opened up, and there is no indication to the spirit children where to go. In the nonvirgin it is
not that the vagina has been opened up, but merely that the
whole woman is, as it were, now in an open state—in a re-
ceptive condition. The seminal fluid is not regarded as having
any generative properties, but, as among the Trobriand Islanders, is looked upon simply as a lubricating fluid and nothing more.

We observe, then, that there exists among the Australian
aborigines an ignorance of physiological paternity and maternity. The true parents of childen are *Numbakulla,* the two
supreme ancestors and creators of all men.

There are many who find it difficult to understand how an
obviously intelligent people like the Australian aborigines
can have failed to grasp the connection between intercourse
and pregnancy. Since there is not the least doubt as to the
high quality of their intelligence this nescience of the facts
of procreation has seemed very puzzling. But when the conditions as they exist among the aborigines are fully understood the difficulty vanishes.

In the first place, menstruation among the women is often
very irregular and sparse; it is, in fact, generally believed that
menstruation is frequently produced by a cold or by the
scratching of some insect which has entered the vagina. But
even were menstruation understood to be a normal physiological function which occurs at definite intervals, the sexual
activities of the woman do not occur at regular intervals.
She may have had intercourse on the very day that she
noticed her menses were overdue, or she may not have had

intercourse for several days or weeks. Her sexual activities are not regulated according to any schedule, definite or indefinite, so that, even assuming that the native woman knows that her menses cease to flow at more or less regular intervals, it is certainly clear that this periodicity stands in no observable relationship to a variable number of sexual acts. Only one sexual act could normally have produced pregnancy, but what is there to lead the aboriginal woman to deduce the fact that her menses have ceased to flow as a result of one act out of a multitude with this or that man? Actually the constant relationships which it is necessary to trace before the truth can be determined are very completely obscured. Hence, there is no reason why cessation of menstruation should be associated with intercourse, or even with pregnancy, since the occasional issue of blood from the vagina during pregnancy has established the belief that menstruation may appear at any time during pregnancy or otherwise. Since quickening is felt about four and a half months after conception, and since pregnancy is assumed to have been produced at the moment it was first perceived, there is obviously no reason here why pregnancy should be associated with intercourse.

Furthermore, there are usually quite a number of women in the group who are so ugly that no man, so the natives say, would ever have dreamed of having intercourse with them, yet these very women have had children! Again, there are always several women in the group who, it is notorious, have had intercourse consistently for years and yet have never had any children. And what is more, when men leave their homes and go far away, not returning until many, many moons have passed, and on arriving home find that their wives have been presented with a child, it is, of course, the man's child as well as his wife's. It is clear from all this that intercourse can have no connection with pregnancy, that pregnancy is entirely dependent upon the will of the spirit babies. How else, then, are we to account for the children of those women who have never had intercourse with men? As for those women who have had intercourse and have never had any children, why, if it is intercourse which produces children, have these women had none?

Such evidence merely serves to refute the white man's incredible suggestions, but it is by no means the basis of the native's beliefs. That basis is, of course, experience interpreted through the alembic of traditional teaching. In his own thought the native is perfectly logical, and in relation to his own system of beliefs, his own framework of reference, his conclusions are perfectly valid. Like the philosopher he deduces results in accordance with what is implied in his own standards or measures, and through these he arrives at a logically faultless route at knowledge—or what is the same thing for him as for ourselves, justifiable belief. "Common sense" is for him what it is for us, that which is in common agreed upon as obvious to sense. It is common sense to the Australian that children are the result of a woman having been originally entered by a spirit child. Quite clearly common sense represents a process of inference from data; it is, however, not the nature of the data which determines the nature of the inference, but it is the mind, the content through which the data are apprehended or apperceived, which determines the nature of the inference. This is the reason why common sense is so often wrong; it is not that the data are at fault but the mental organization through which they are perceived which is at fault. The apperceptive equipment of the Australian with respect to the datum of childbirth conditions his common sense to see only the effects of certain causes— spirit children entering women in certain ways as a result of certain conditions and causes. The apperceptive equipment of the average bearer of Western culture conditions his common sense to see in the same datum of experience the effect of a cause which he believes to have been initiated by intercourse. It is perhaps unnecessary to add that as far as his *actual* knowledge of the matter is concerned, it is quite as much a superstition as the beliefs held in respect to the same matter by the Australians. Common sense, in short, like every other aspect of thought, is a culturally conditioned trait, and as such its form is determined in and by the culture in which it must function.

On the sociobiological plane the embryological canon of the Australian aborigines embraces a complete equivalent of the theory of the continuity of the germ plasm. Occasionally, for example, all the members of a local totemic group may die out, but this is only a temporary event, for sooner or later some woman is bound to be entered by a spirit child in the locality of the group no longer represented by living individuals because the spirits of the *Alchera* ancestors, the spirit babies, still inhabit the locality and are always on the lookout for women through whom they may be developed, and the group is in this way resuscitated.

It is evident, therefore, that every totemic group is in a very special sense a biologically determined unit, the material elements of which are represented by the *knanja* or abodes of the *Alchera kuruna,* which by their presence ensure the continuity of the totemic group, and also by means of the *churinga* with which the *Alchera kuruna* are associated. The *knanja* together with the *churinga* are, as it were, the material cellular elements of the germ-plasm of the totemic group and as long as they exist it is impossible for the totemic group to become extinct. The biological continuity of the totemic group is thus as real a biological continuity as any social apparatus devised for the purpose could possibly secure. In reality, of course, the continuity is no more than socially determined, but this is as we see it and not as the native does. For him these things are *in rerum natura* and are made clear to him by the traditions of his tribe and the everyday events of his social life, a life which embraces the complete totality of his experience.

As well as insuring the continuity of the totemic group itself, the continuity of the species of the animal or plant with which the group is identified is likewise secured and maintained by the same powers that operate in the case of man, except that in these connections the powers are usually manipulated by the performance of certain ceremonies. These ceremonies are performed at particular seasons of the year, well known to the head man and often announced to him through the medium of a dream as the most appropriate time at which to secure the increase of the totem animal or plant over whose increase ceremony he presides. Since these times are the seasons of natural increase of these animals and plants, the increase ceremonies are usually followed by the visible multiplication of the particular totemic animal or plant. Such an immediate response to the performance of these ceremonies does not fail to impress the native as a very forceful demonstration, if such were needed, of the truth of his beliefs.

The only other people, besides these Australian tribes, who are characterized by a complete ignorance of physiological paternity, and probably maternity, are the natives of the Trobriand Islands of northwestern Melanesia. The Trobriand developmental history of man runs as follows: At nighttime the child is brought as an embryonic baby and placed on top of the woman's head. For a time the baby rests within the womb and in due course is born. When it is observed that menstruation does not occur after two or three moons have passed, the woman will assume that she has been entered by a spirit child, that she is pregnant. It is believed that until the menstrual flow has ceased a woman cannot be entered by a child. Intercourse, it is held, checks the monthly flow of menstrual blood, that is to say, the menstrual flow is checked by "hammering" against the lower part of the uterus or menstrual blood. But why have the menses ceased? Because, answers the native, it is necessary for all the blood to be withdrawn to the head so that the spirit child may descend into the womb by means of it. The blood does not recommence to flow because it is retained in the body so that the child may be provided with nourishment during its intra-uterine sojourn. As the spirit child slowly descends on the tide of blood it causes dizziness, headaches, and nausea. The blood in the womb immediately begins to undergo change as soon as the spirit child is placed upon the head, and an embryo *(veguvegu)* is brought into being. The Trobrianders believe that there is only blood and water in the uterus until the third month. As the spirit child descends, the *veguvegu* is said to change again into a ratlike thing with its covering of membranes, and the name for the whole is now *kapora kikoni,* i.e., "bundle-rolled-up-rat." In this stage the embryo is described as having rudimentary limbs like a newly born rat. Many of the natives have seen the *kapora kikoni* when a woman has aborted.

When the spirit child reaches the woman's breasts it enlarges and darkens them considerably. It flows on down and enters her belly, and her bigness increases rapidly. Pregnancy is counted from the time when the breasts become appreciably enlarged. A month before confinement the *kapora kikoni* is said to assume the form of a child, to become *imilagwadi* ("it-stimulating-child").

Most Trobrianders do not go so far as to endow the spirit baby with any definite form, though some believe that it looks like a fetus, "like a mouse," and others that it looks like a minute, fully developed, child. The father helps in building up the body of the child by having intercourse with his wife during her pregnancy. "It molds the body," they say. That is why children often resemble the father. This belief is found among numerous peoples over a wide area of Melanesia, and it is of interest to note that it occurs among our own Hopi Indians. Thus, writing in 1942, in his maturity, a Hopi Indian who had been at a white man's school says:

> I thought about babies and marveled at the manner in which they are made. I had known for a long time that they are produced from the semen of a man's spinal cord and the blood from a woman's heart; and that both parents must work faithfully to complete a good offspring. I paid close attention to my wife, made a doll for her at the *Powamu* ceremony, slept with her regularly until she was large and felt strong movements, and was careful to observe all pregnancy rules. I wanted to do my part towards making a good-sized baby.

The father's part in molding the form of the child is generally considered to be achieved through the warmth of his body and through pressure. The process is thought of as a literal molding and is in many cases regarded as proceeding into late childhood. Until that period is reached the father is said to "mold" the child by the food he feeds it. As one Trobriander remarked, "Always we give food from our hand to the child to eat, we give fruit and dainties, we give betel nut. This makes the child as it is."

This influence of food upon the child's development and growth is so firmly entrenched an article of belief that, among the Australian aborigines, for example, the light skin of half-caste children is said to be due to the fact that the mother has consumed too much of the white man's flour. The really impressive fact about this particular belief is that wherever the white man has penetrated in Australia the belief grows up independently in tribes far removed from one another.

White men are regarded by the Australian aborigines as the incarnations of deceased aboriginal individuals. This belief is based on the native's observation of the fact that after a dead body has been exposed for some time to the elements the normal chocolate brown color of the skin disappears and the skin turns white; hence, when the dead man's body is reincarnated he will appear with a white skin. The aborigines frequently identify white men as long-lost members of the tribe.

While among most Australian tribes it is part of the embryologic canon that the sexes of the spirit babies were about equally divided when they were originally created, the natives of the Pennefather River region in northeastern Australia believe that their eponymous ancestor *Anje-a* fashions children out of swamp mud and inserts them in the bellies of women. Sometimes an accident befalls these infants before they get inside their human mothers, for example, they may catch one of their feet in a log and so be born with one or another deformity. When the woman has plenty of room inside, twins are sent. All children made by *Anje-a* are right-handed; those made by the other supernatural, who is named "Thunder," are left-handed.

Where, as among the Kiwai Papuans of British New Guinea, the function of semen is more or less understood, twins are regarded as being due to an abnormal splitting of the semen into two portions, or to the cohabitation between husband and wife having taken place too recklessly, or to the husband having been temporarily absent during his wife's pregnancy and then recommencing cohabitation with her. A woman will sometimes give birth to twins if she eats bananas from a tree with two bunches. Among almost all nonliterate peoples one of the twins is generally killed. It is believed that twins cannot both grow strong and well "because same life." Furthermore, it is normal for human beings to have only one offspring at a birth; only lower animals have more than that. It is again of interest to note here that the Hopi Indian previously referred to writes, "I did not want twins. But I realized that if the Mother god wished to start two babies in one womb, there was no power on earth that could stop her. Therefore I advised my wife to see the same old doctor who had twisted me into one child so that, in case she carried twins, he could put them together before it was too late."

Most nonliterate peoples believe that pregnancy lasts about five months, that is to say, it is taken to commence at the quickening. Among the Bahau of central Borneo, for example, pregnancy is reckoned from the time when it first becomes visible. Among the Sinaugolo pregnancy is reckoned from the time when the swelling of the breasts is first observed. Conception is believed to occur in the breasts since these first show signs of the mother's condition. After the child has attained a certain size it drops to the lower part of the abdomen. Morning sickness with loss of appetite is recognized as a sign of pregnancy and is stated to cease as soon as the child's bones are formed. The Kiwai of New Guinea think that the head of the embryo forms first, directed upward toward the mother's chest, then the body. Shortly before delivery the embryo turns over, head downward, this being the normal form of presentation at birth.

Among the natives of Dobu, one of a group of islands of which the Trobriands form a part, the embryologic beliefs are similar to those held by the Trobriand Islanders except that the Dobuans are aware of the part which the father plays in procreation. Semen is believed to be coconut milk which has passed through the body of the male. The semen is believed to cause the menstrual blood in the woman to coagulate and form the embryo. Among the Trobriand Islanders the semen, like the female secretions, is held to be lubricating in function. The suggestion that the essential part of the ejaculate originates in the testes is treated with derision. Women, they reply, do not have testes, yet they have a fluid like men. According to the Baiga of the Central Provinces of India, semen is manufactured in the chest. "A juice is extracted from the food in the stomach and ascends to the chest, from which a tube runs down to the penis." The Naskapi Indians of Labrador regard the semen not only as the impregnating agent but as a necessary food and stimulant for the growing embryo as it develops within the abdomen of the mother.

Among the natives of Wogeo, an island off the north coast of New Guinea, it is believed that the fetus is formed from menstrual blood and semen, but that repeated acts of sexual intercourse are necessary because the passage leading from the womb has also to be blocked up with semen to prevent the blood from escaping. Hogbin states that the whole process is thought of as being entirely physiological, that is to say, no spiritual intervention of any kind takes place. If this is true, then the natives of Wogeo are the only known exception to the rule which necessitates some spiritual intervention before a child can be born.

The Kwoma of the Upper Sepik River of New Guinea consider the fetus to be the product of woman's blood and frequent injections of semen. Growth of the fetus takes place in the womb. Ideas as to the length of the gestation period are very vague. The testicles are not supposed to possess any special function.

The natives of Ontong Java, a coral atoll in the western Pacific, until recently had no idea of physiological fatherhood. They believe that continued sexual intercourse is necessary for pregnancy, since many applications of semen eventually make a sort of stopper for the uterus and behind this the menstrual blood is held back. Out of this impounded blood the *kipua,* or presiding spirits, if they are so minded, permit the fetus to form. Every man has a spiritual entity, or *kipua,* but animals do not. The *kipua* enters the baby as soon as it is able to crawl.

Among many nonliterate peoples who are aware that some

part of seminal fluid and some essential product of the mother must come together before conception can occur, it is a common belief that impregnation cannot occur from a single sexual contact; many acts are considered necessary. This belief is common throughout Melanesia and is even to be found in America. Thus, a Chiricahuan Apache of the American Southwest states, "You have to have intercourse with a girl more than once to get a baby started. If you do it about three times a week, you will have a baby started in about two or three months."

This belief is shared by numerous nonliterate peoples who are as well informed about the facts of procreation as are the Chiricahua, but the latter's embryological beliefs are unique in one respect, namely, in that they believe that the semen which produced impregnation may actually be derived from more than one man. Thus, it is said:

> If a woman has intercourse with more than one man over a period of time, the child that comes will belong to both of them; each man contributes something to its physical make-up. The child will belong mostly to the man who has had most intercourse with the woman. If a woman has intercourse with many men and a child is born, the men say that each one has some small part in the child.
>
> It is believed that many men can be the father of one child. If a woman goes with several men, it is said that the child belongs to all of them. That is why an illegitimate child is so good-looking. He has the good points of all the men and that is why the word illegitimate child means "child of man." It can have parts from more than one man.

From such statements, and from the fact that the Chiricahua declare that children look like their parents, it is clear that they possess a well-defined conception of heredity.

The Kgatla of Bechuanaland, South Africa, believe that a woman is incapable of conceiving unless she menstruates regularly. Her blood is needed to form the child. It generally accumulates in the womb to form a large clot, which must break every month and flow out. A child is formed in the womb by the mixture of the man's semen and the menstrual blood. Some assert that a single act of coitus is sufficient to produce conception, but the majority maintain that at least three or four successive nights of intercourse are required.

As an illustration of the manner in which knowledge of these matters grows only through those who have had considerable experience in them, the following passage from Schapera may be quoted:

> Few Kgatla have any clear idea of what happens in the womb after intercourse. The men generally say that knowledge of this kind is confined to the women, or they may hazard wild theories of embryology based partly upon what they have gleaned from their wives, and partly upon guesses of their own. Some of the older women, however, whose experience in dealing with cases of miscarriage had given them opportunities of inspecting the foetus at various stages of its development, were able to give me information showing that on the whole they were fairly accurate observers. During the first two or three months of pregnancy, they said, "the womb shakes about; it mixes up the bloods of the man and the woman, so that they become thick, like cheese and form seed." "If two months pass without your menstruating after you have slept with your husband you know that his blood is fighting with yours in your intestines to make the child; you feel your stomach not sore, but palpitating, and when the third month comes you feel, near your navel, pulse-beats just like a heart." It is during this early period of gestation, "when the bloods are fighting each other," that . . . the woman's blood is particularly "hot." By the fourth month the "bloods" have coalesced completely, and the foetus has taken form. At this stage it is said to look like a lizard, with nothing to indicate that it is human. In the fifth month it acquires human characteristics, and is complete with head, body, arms and legs, but lacks hands, feet and eyes and other facial features. These appear in the sixth month, when it is fully formed. Thereafter it grows steadily in size. "In the seventh month you feel the child moving from one side to the other; in the eighth month he begins to stand on his legs and stretch himself, and then sleeps again; and in the ninth month he plays about in your stomach, waiting to be born."

It will be seen that in this account of the process of pregnancy there is contained a fair working theory of the facts.

The Kgatla hold that both parents contribute to the building of the child. Its blood, they assert, comes from the mother "because before a woman conceives she menstruates regularly, and this is nothing but blood, while after she is pregnant her menses stop, and the child starts to be molded, so it is obvious that she gives her blood to the child." The father, on the other hand, is believed to contribute the flesh "because of the heavy lumps (of semen) that he puts into the mother." In consequence, children are usually expected to resemble their father, "unless the blood of the woman has been stronger than that of the man, then the child will look like its mother."

This belief is akin to that of the Talmudists, that the father provides the *white* semen from which the bones, the brain, and the white of the eyes originate, while the mother supplies the *red* semen for the formation of the skin, flesh, hair and iris.

Some of the ideas of the members of the school of Hippocrates were not dissimilar. In the treatise *On Generation,* for example, it is stated that the embryo is nourished by maternal blood which flows to the fetus and there coagulates, forming the embryonic flesh. The proof given in support of this theory is that during pregnancy the flow of menstrual blood ceases; therefore it must be used up. Aristotle held a very similar view. Indeed, the fact is that at the time of the publication of William Harvey's *De Generatione Animalium* in 1651 the Aristotelian theory of embryogenesis from menstrual blood had numerous learned supporters throughout Europe. Many of these rallied to support the theory and attacked Harvey.

In all civilized lands there are at this day many groups and individuals whose knowledge of embryogenesis is no more accurate than that of the most isolated savage. A knowledge of such facts can be acquired only by the most painstaking observations, by means of special instruments which are possible only at a very advanced stage of cultural development.

When it is recalled that spermatozoa were not discovered

and described by Leeuwenhoek until the year 1677, that the ovum was not discovered and described by von Baer until 1827, and that it was not until 1843 that Martin Barry described the penetration of the ovum by the spermatozoon, the recency of our own achievement of accurate knowledge concerning the most elementary facts of embryogenesis should impress upon us that such knowledge is attained only at the cost of great labor, experiment, and systematic observation.

The facts relating to procreation and embryogenesis are very far from obvious. Indeed, there are perfectly normal men and women living in our own society at this moment who are unaware of the fact that intercourse is a necessary factor in producing childbirth. During the Victorian period such ignorance was much more widespread than today. We quote from the experience of an American physician and surgeon, the late Joseph W. Howe of Bellevue Hospital, New York. He wrote, in 1888:

> Married women, and men too, of much experience in other matters pertaining to the management of their physical natures, have informed me that when they entered the marriage state, they were totally unaware of the nature of the sexual relation, and that many days and nights were passed in the midst of curious sensations, doubts and fears, and ridiculous performances before the marriage was consummated. Neither did they comprehend the immediate or remote results of the new relation.

Such statements hold equally true for many persons of our own time and they serve to lend force to the truth that the facts of generation are far from self-evident. Hence, in societies where the traditional knowledge relating to these facts provides an acceptable theory, it is not in the least to be wondered at that they may persist for enormous periods of time.

23

Procreation, Paternity, and
Psychoanalysis

Róheim has endeavored to show that the so-called nescience or ignorance of the relationship between coitus and childbirth exhibited by such native Australian tribes as the Arunta and their neighbors is not due to any failure in their sciential processes but to a process of repression whereby knowledge of this relationship previously conscious is rendered unconscious, and is in consciousness replaced by a symbolic superstructure.

Why do these natives repress the knowledge of the father as the agent of procreation? Because, explains Róheim, "The identity in their minds of the child with a being who was killed by the father before the child was born is an expression of the unconscious hostility between father and son; that is, of one aspect of the Oedipus complex. The unborn child protects large game from the father's spear, because in the father's unconscious mind the large game he kills is identical with the unborn child." [1] To this explanation we shall return later. Meanwhile, it will be recalled that in 1925 Ernest Jones

From *Psychiatry*, vol. 4, 1941, 45-60.
[1] Róheim, Géza. "The Nescience of the Aranda." *British Journal of Medical Psychology*, 17, 1938 (pp. 343-560).

had already suggested that wherever the ignorance of "pro-creative paternity" was found to exist it would be found to be motivated by the wish to "deflect the hatred towards his father felt by the growing boy." [2] Jones went on to add that "repudiation of the father's part in coitus and procreation, and consequently softening and deflection of the hatred against him, a consummation desired equally by son and father . . . is what has happened where the institution of mother-right is combined with the denial of paternal pro-creation."

In 1927 Malinowski showed that in a culture which was characterized both by matrilineal descent and ignorance of physiological paternity, as among the Trobriand Islanders, anything resembling the phases of the Oedipus complex, upon the existence of which Jones rested his theory, was entirely wanting, thus disproving the basic assumption, at any rate, of that theory. [3]

Money-Kyrle quotes Malinowski's demonstration that the Oedipus complex does not exist among Trobriand children and refers to Reik's suggestion that the couvade may have as one of its functions the preservation of the child from its father. [4] Money-Kyrle goes on to ask: "May not the Melanesian matriarchy serve a similar purpose as well as that of preserving the father from the hatred of his sons, a hatred that is dangerous to society? This is the result which, according to Malinowski, has been achieved. May we not suppose that it was also the reason for the survival and development of such a social system?" [5]

The suggestion here is that in order to "soften and deflect" the hatred of father and son for one another the institution of mother-right was gradually developed and, in fact, owes its survival to the efficiency with which it reciprocally pro-

[2] Jones, Ernest. "Mother-Right and the Sexual Ignorance of Savages." *International Journal of Psychoanalysis*, 6, 1925 (pp. 109-130).

[3] Malinowski, Bronislaw. *Sex and Repression in Savage Society.* New York: Harcourt, 1927.

[4] Reik, Theodor. *Probleme der Religionspsychologie.* Leipzig und Wien Internationaler Psychoanalytischer Verlag, 1919 (pp. 30-32); and "Die Couvade." *Imago*, 3, 1914 (pp. 409-455).

[5] Money-Kyrle, Roger. *The Meaning of Sacrifice.* London: Hogarth, 1930 (p. 36).

tected the father from his sons and the sons from their father. This is essentially the view of Jones, who has in addition stated that

> it is clear that any objectionable tendencies the source of which is imputed to the act of birth can most radically be countered by simply denying this act, as is done, for example, in the puberty rites. Now, in the analysis of our neurotics we are very familiar with the wish-phantasy in which this happens in regard to the father. Many of them cherish, consciously or unconsciously, the idea that their "father" had nothing to do with their conception or birth, this being a matter entirely between them and the mother.[6]

It would be greatly interesting to know whether any of these neurotics repress the knowledge of the part played by the father in conception to such an extent that for all practical purposes they are not consciously aware of the facts. If in spite of the strength of their desires they do not succeed in bringing about such a state of repression, may not that failure be due to their inability to overcome the resistance offered by the knowledge of the facts which have so frequently been impressed upon them, and which, from the point of view of one who wishes to appear normal, must form a part of his intellectual equipment even though he cannot accept them in his own particular case? I do not know the answer to these questions, and I should strongly doubt whether any individual in our own culture has ever achieved a state of repression so complete that the fact of physiological paternity was denied. The fact is that all individuals of adult age are, in our own culture, acquainted with the role of the father in procreation, and I have yet to learn of a case which would establish an exception. If we who hated our fathers so much, and our fathers who hated us so much, have failed to repress the knowledge of our relationship to one another, why should the Australian aborigines have succeeded where we with all our beautiful systems of make-believe have failed? I do not think that any psychoanalyst has yet attempted an answer to this question.

[6] Jones, *op. cit.*, p. 122.

With respect to knowledge of physiological paternity among children in our own culture the case is different. As is well known, many children grow to adolescence without knowing anything of the elementary fact that it is necessary for a man to have coitus with a woman before childbirth can occur. I have known several such children intimately, and I have met a fair number of adults who have informed me that they were unaware of the elementary facts of procreation until they were quite grown up. Upon this point I want to make myself quite clear. Concerning the adults who informed me that they were quite old before they became aware of the facts of procreation I can only say that as far as I was able to determine they were perfectly honest and sincere in volunteering this information. I cannot say that they may not have known something of the facts in early childhood and subsequently forgot or repressed what they may have known. In this connection I may say that I do know of a case of a young man who, when he was four years of age, asked his father to tell him "how babies are born." The father then and there gave him the facts of procreation, which the boy, as he told his father more than twenty years later, promptly forgot and had to relearn long afterward. This story was told me only recently by the father. I do, however, know a number of children varying in age from four to seven years who, I have good reason to believe, never at any time in their lives knew, nor do they know now, anything of the relationship between coitus and childbirth. These children are rather better than normally intelligent, but I am afraid that they must be sadly lacking in that "instinctive intuition" which is by Ernest Jones said to play so considerable a part among infants in enabling them to divine "the main outline at least of sexual knowledge," [7] for they are completely ignorant of any such knowledge.

Experience has convinced me that in this age of enlightenment a large number of children pass toward puberty without the slightest knowledge of the facts of procreation. In a variety of ways they become aware of these facts later. Some-

[7] *Ibid.*, p. 120.

one tells them, or they read about them in a book. I have never heard of any child working the facts out for itself, in spite of Ernest Jones's statement that "a child of two years old can frame an image of genital coitus, and a year or so later connect it with the birth of another child." [8] Not only that, but to me it seems perfectly clear that no child could upon a foundation of "instinctive intuition" or upon a purely rational basis work these facts out for itself. With the latter part of this statement Ernest Jones might perhaps agree, for he speaks only of "images" which are presumably formed upon an instinctually intuitive basis, becoming only later more or less fully conscious. If, however, this process of "instinctive intuition" is postulated as a universal trait of mankind or any particular group of mankind, then I deny it, for in those human beings whom it has been my privilege to assist in developing from birth toward puberty, although I have done everything in my power to discover them, I have detected no signs of such "instinctive intuitions" or such images as Ernest Jones speaks of. This is not to say that no children exhibit such characters, as Ernest Jones asserts they do. I am merely interested here in establishing the fact that, while it may be possible that some children may by the age of two and three years become aware of the relationship between coitus and childbirth, some do not, and that it would be a methodologically unsound practice to assume a universal or even general frequency distribution among children for either the awareness or the unawareness of the facts. But that is just the sort of generalization which some psychoanalysts make in this very connection. Knowledge of the elementary facts of procreation is supposed to characterize all or most children, this knowledge developing upon a basis of "instinctive intuition" into an "image of genital coitus." Róheim, for example, is quite certain that all aboriginal Australian children possess such knowledge and that this knowledge merely becomes subsequently repressed.[9]

Now, if the fact be accepted that some children in our

8 *Ibid.*, p. 118.
9 Róheim, *op. cit.*, p. 359.

own culture pass through their early years without any knowledge, unconscious or conscious, of the relationship between coitus—or even the fact that such a thing as coitus exists—and childbirth, is it not then probable that awareness of the facts of procreation in children is not a piece of knowledge which is "divined" with the assistance of a process of "instinctive intuition"? For without the proper setting the stimuli are wanting which would "elicit" the proper responses, and the necessary images would not follow. Since we are arguing upon this level we might here cite William James's law of transitoriness of instinct.

My own observations on the development of knowledge of the elementary facts of procreation among children—that is to say, that a man and a woman must have coitus before childbirth can occur—have convinced me that this knowledge is in all those cases which I have investigated based upon empirical acquisition of empirical facts. This statement does not, of course, invalidate the generally assumed details of the process of development of the Oedipus complex in some neurotics. I am quite ready to follow Melanie Klein in her theory of the prephallic phases of the development of the Oedipus complex.[10] I cannot, however, accept the notion that the complex is of universal distribution even within our own culture area, and certainly not for all mankind. Such an assumption has been likened to that of the chiropodist's that all mankind must at one time have been martyrs to corns![11] That may well have been, though without the necessary evidence we have no right to make the assumption. With respect to the biological determinance of this complex, I think that McDougall has already said all that requires to be said upon that score.[12] And already among the ranks of psychoanalysts belonging to the Freudian school a few

[10] Klein, Melanie. "The Psychological Principles of Infant Analysis." *International Journal of Psychoanalysis*, 8, 1927 (pp. 25-37); and "Early Stage of the Oedipus Conflict." *International Journal of Psychoanalysis*, 9, 1928 (pp. 167-180).
[11] Raglan, Lord. *Jocasta's Crime*. London: Methuen, 1933 (p. 75).
[12] McDougall, William. *An Outline of Abnormal Psychology*. New York: Scribners, 1926.

heretics have begun to make their appearance.[13] Thus, Karen Horney found herself forced to reject the instinctivistic and genetic approaches upon which so many of the alleged "fundamental" concepts of psychoanalysis are based, and she came to see that the sociologically based approach is the only sound one.[14] Karen Horney has very strikingly revealed the processes of circularity of reasoning involved in the concept of the Oedipus complex and has repudiated the concept as neither a necessary nor sufficient mechanism in the development of many neurotics. She writes:

> When character trends are no longer explained as the ultimate outcome of instinctual drives, modified only by the environment, the entire emphasis falls on the life condition molding the character and we have to search anew for the environmental factors responsible for creating neurotic conflicts; thus disturbances in human relationships become the crucial factor in the genesis of neuroses. A prevailingly sociological orientation then takes the place of a prevailingly anatomical-physiological one. When the one-sided consideration of the pleasure principles, implicit in the libido theory, is relinquished the striving for safety assumes more weight and the rôle of anxiety in engendering strivings toward safety appears in a new light. The relevant factor in the genesis of neuroses is then neither the Oedipus complex nor any kind of infantile pleasure strivings but all those adverse influences which make a child feel helpless and defenseless and which make him conceive the world as potentially menacing.

Dr. Horney points out that the "contention that the Oedipus complex is not of a biological nature seems to be confirmed by anthropological observations, the results of which indicate that the generation of such a complex depends on the whole

[13] Members of the schools of Jung and Adler have, of course, never been able to attribute as much importance to sexuality and to the part played by incestuous desires in the development of the individual as the Freudian school has. Compare Jung, Carl G. *Collected Papers on Analytical Psychology.* London: Baillière, Tindall and Cox, 1916 (p. 231 ff.); *The Psychology of the Unconscious.* London and New York: Moffet Yard, 1916 (p. 463); and Adler, Alfred. *The Practice and Theory of Individual Psychology.* London: Paul, Trench, Trubner, 1924.

[14] Horney, Karen. *The Neurotic Personality of Our Time.* New York: Norton, 1937; and *New Ways in Psychoanalysis.* New York: Norton, 1939.

set of factors operating in family life, such as the rôle of authority of the parents, seclusion of the family, size of the family, sexual prohibitions and the like."

On the basis of the evidence relating to the development of the knowledge of procreation and of the development of the attitudes between parents and children in our own culture, I think it may fairly be postulated that neither this knowledge nor the attitudes subsumed in the concept of the Oedipus complex are either usual or necessary features in the development of the personality of any but the declaredly neurotic individuals. Certainly it has been demonstrated by Malinowski [15] that this complex does not develop among the Melanesian Trobrianders, and by Ruth Benedict that it does not develop among the American Zuñi Indians.[16] Nor do any evidences of such a complex appear to have been encountered by Margaret Mead among the Melanesian Manus where the father plays the part of "the tender, solicitous, indulgent guardian, while the mother takes second place in the child's affections." [17] Among the Trobrianders only avuncular authority exists for the children, among the Zuñi—not even that. These evidences—and a great many more could be quoted [18]—are alone sufficient to prove the nonbiological nature of the Oedipus complex [19] They prove that whatever

[15] Malinowski, Bronislaw. *Sex and Repression in Savage Society.*

[16] Benedict, Ruth. *Patterns of Culture.* New York: New American Library, 1950.

[17] Mead, Margaret. *Growing Up in New Guinea.* New York: Morrow, 1930 (pp. 6-7).

[18] For North American Indian peoples see the studies edited by Eggan, Fred. *Social Anthropology of North American Tribes: Essays in Social Organization, Law, Religion.* Chicago: University of Chicago Press, 1937; Lowie, Robert H. *The Crow Indians.* New York: Farrar and Rinehart, 1935. For South America see Karsten, Rafael. *The Civilization of the South American Indians.* New York: Knopf, 1926. For the relations between parents and children among primitive peoples generally see Miller, Nathan. *The Child in Primitive Society.* New York: Brentano's, 1928; and Dennis, Wayne. *The Hopi Child.* New York: Appleton-Century, 1940.

[19] For a very cogent discussion of the Oedipus complex from the anthropological standpoint see Westermarck, Edward. *Three Essays on Sex and Marriage.* London: Macmillan, 1934 (pp. 3 and 103). Some other writers who have been unable to subscribe to the "all-or-none" conception of the Oedipus complex are Myerson, Abraham. "Freud's

the complex is construed as being, one thing is certain, and that is, wherever that complex is found to occur it is demonstrable that it owes its origin to cultural factors. Moreover, the evidence strongly indicates that the Oedipus complex arises only under certain conditions, and that where these conditions are wanting the complex does not develop. It appears that individuals who grow up in families where the relations between themselves and the parents—whether in a patrilineal or a matrilineal group—are of a happy kind, a family in which there has been a minimum of situations which would be calculated to create those mental reactions which under other conditions would lead to the formation of such a complex, it appears that such individuals do not, in the absence of such conditions, develop such a complex.

In our own society, in which the father's role is still that of a tyrant, these conditions are widely prevalent, but in many primitive societies they are absent, and certainly they are absent among the Australian aborigines. It is for this latter reason that I strongly doubt the accuracy of Róheim's interpretations with respect to the occurrence of the Oedipus complex among these natives. Everyone who has ever had

Theory of Sex: a Criticism." Calverton, V. F., and Schmalhausen, S. D., editors, *Sex and Civilization*. New York: Macauley, 1929; Goldenweiser, Alexander A. *History, Psychology, and Culture*. New York: Knopf, 1933 (pp. 201-208); Raglan, Lord, *op. cit.* (pp. 70-75); Kretschmer, Ernst. *A Text-Book of Medical Psychology*. New York: Oxford University Press, 1934 (pp. 135-139); Burrow, Trigant. *The Biology of Human Conflict*. New York: Macmillan, 1937 (pp. 78-79); Ellis, Havelock. "Eros in Contemporary Life." Cattell, R. B., and others, editors. *Human Affairs*. London and New York: Macmillan, 1937 (p. 197); and "Perversion in Childhood and Adolescence." Calverton, V. F., and Schmalhausen, S. D., editors. *The New Generation*. New York: Macauley, 1930 (p. 539); McDougall, William. *An Outline of Abnormal Psychology*. London and New York: Scribners, 1926; Stern, William. *General Psychology from the Personalistic Standpoint*. New York: Macmillan, 1938 (pp. 350 and 356); Allport, Gordon. *Personality*. New York: Holt, 1938 (pp. 12-13). The only anthropologist who seems to have encountered no difficulty in giving his wholehearted support to the concept of the Oedipus complex as a developmental process among primitive children is my old friend and teacher, Prof. C. G. Seligman. "Anthropological Perspective and Psychological Theory." *Journal of the Royal Anthropological Institute*, 62, 1933 (pp. 193-228). See also Laubscher, B. J. F. *Sex, Custom, and Psychopathology*. London: Routledge, 1937; and New York: Robert McBride, 1939.

anything to do with these natives has been greatly impressed by the extraordinarily affectionate relations existing between parents and children. The evidence up to 1913 has been dealt with by Malinowski,[20] and I have brought it up to date in the book which prompted Róheim's article.[21] Under the conditions existing in the Australian family group, with suckling of the children being continued for at least three years, with no training as to bodily cleanliness and, thus, without the frustration of weaning and the anal frustrations postulated by Melanie Klein as the determining influences in the formation of the Oedipus complex,[22] the conditions necessary for the development of this complex hardly seem to be fulfilled. The fact alone that so many observers have thought it worth recording that the most impressively affectionate relations exist between children of all ages and the father would strongly suggest that at no time are the conditions favorable for the development of any jealousies, unconscious or conscious, between them. Similarly, these relations appear to hold true for the female members of the family.

I think, therefore, that there are good grounds for believing that anyone who goes to central Australia and finds that the natives, in their cultural structure if not in themselves, show evidences of a repressed Oedipus complex, is simply forcing an interpretation of the facts to fit the demands of a predetermined theory. It is these facts which we shall here have to consider, but before doing so I should like to make certain general remarks in connection both with comments by psychoanalysts on my book and with the relation of psychoanalysis to anthropology in particular.

In the book which called forth Róheim's article, I was interested in discovering what the Australian aborigines *con-*

[20] Malinowski, Bronislaw. *The Family among the Australian Aborigines.* London: University of London Press, 1913.

[21] Montagu, Ashley. *Coming into Being among the Australian Aborigines.* London: Routledge, 1937; and New York: Dutton, 1938.

[22] "The Oedipus tendencies are released in consequence of the frustration which the child experiences at weaning, and . . . they make their appearance at the end of the first and the beginning of the second year of life: they receive reinforcement through the anal frustrations undergone during training in cleanliness." Klein, *op. cit.*

sciously believed and said concerning the nature of their own and their fellows' genesis. As an anthropologist relying, for better or for worse, upon the accounts of anthropologically trained field workers I could hardly do otherwise. Róheim points out that without the psychoanalytic perspective the anthropologist is here at a disadvantage. With this statement I am strongly inclined to agree; but where, may one inquire, is the psychoanalytic data which I might have utilized in my analysis of the aboriginal procreative beliefs? There is, of course, the outstanding work of Róheim himself. This, I thought I had examined and treated in as impartial and rigorously scientific a manner as it was in my power to do. In a very kind unsigned review of my book in *The International Journal of Psycho-Analysis* [23] the anonymous reviewer states that I have neglected to take into consideration the "complexities of the unconscious mind" and points out my failure even to "refer to the psycho-analytical critique of the evidence" published by him.

Now, the only psychoanalytical critiques with which I was acquainted which bear on the Australian problem are those of Róheim.[24] On the general question of ignorance of physiological paternity I knew of only two works written from the psychoanalytic standpoint by Ernest Jones.[25] These latter works I had read at least twice before my book ever came to be written, and during the preparation of my book I must have read them on three or four separate occasions, each time coming to the conclusion that the views there put forward had no direct bearing upon the evidence I was considering. For the same reason I decided against any discussion of Malinowski's *Sex and Repression in Savage Society*, a work to which no reference is made in my book. I need not point out that in the writing of a book such as mine

[23] 19, 1938 (pp. 156-157).
[24] Róheim, Géza. *Australian Totemism*. London: Allen and Unwin, 1926; "Psychoanalysis and Primitive Cultural Types." *International Journal of Psychoanalysis*, 13, 1932 (pp. 1-224); and "Women and Their Life in Central Australia." *Journal of the Royal Anthropological Institute*, 54, 1933 (pp. 207-265).
[25] Jones, *op. cit.*; and review of *Sex and Repression in Savage Society*, by Malinowski, Bronislaw. *International Journal of Psychoanalysis*, 9, 1928 (pp. 364-374).

very many more works are read and consulted than ultimately find a place in the author's text or list of references. Had I adopted the principle of including everything which others might consider relevant to the problems I was discussing, my book would have been swollen to impossible dimensions. It is big enough as it is. The material dealt with and the evidence discussed in various sections and chapters have already been made, and are even now being made, the subject of separate and more elaborate studies by me.[26]

But, it may justly be inquired, is the question of the complexities of the unconscious mind, of the possibility of repression, merely of indirect relevance to any treatment of the procreative beliefs of the Australian aborigines? Are these things of such slight importance as to merit no consideration in a work which claims to be something of a study in the psychology of belief? To these questions I can only answer that I consider that such light as psychoanalysis would be able to throw upon the problems of aboriginal nescience would obviously assume relevance and importance only under conditions which, in the opinion of all informed students, would render it so. I have never for a moment entertained the slightest doubt that when psychoanalytic methods came to be applied to the study of nonliterate peoples, in addition to the methods commonly employed by the field anthropologist, our understanding of such peoples, and particularly of the individuals comprising them, would be greatly enriched. Róheim's later Australian studies are an interesting beginning, but it would be an uninformed judgment, aware neither of the complexities of the problems involved nor of the methodo-

[26] "The Origin of Subincision in Australia." *Oceania*, 8, 1937 (pp. 193-207); "Infertility of the Unmarried in Primitive Societies." *Oceania*, 8, 1937 (pp. 15-26); "Physiological Paternity in Australia." *American Anthropology*, 39, 1937 (pp. 175-183); "The Future of the Australian Aborigines." *Oceania*, 8, 1937 (pp. 343-350); "Social Time: a Methodological and Functional Analysis." *American Journal of Sociology*, 44, 1938 (pp. 282-284); "Adolescent Sterility." *Quarterly Review of Biology*, 14, 1919 (pp. 13-34 and 192-219); "Climate and Reproduction." *Science*, 89, 1939 (pp. 290-292); "Ignorance of Physiological Paternity in Secular Knowledge and Orthodox Belief among the Australian Aborigines." *Oceania*, 11, 1940 (pp. 110-122); "Physiology and the Origins of the Menstrual Prohibitions." *Quarterly Review of Biology*, 15, 1940 (pp. 211-220).

logical difficulties to be overcome, which would hazard the opinion that Róheim's work represented more than such a beginning.

Cultures are extremely complex systems of phenomena, and not less so are the individual minds functioning within them. To learn to understand fully the culture in which we ourselves are born and live is a difficult enough task, not to mention the difficulty of learning to understand oneself or another individual. How much more difficult is it, then, to gain even an inkling of the character of a native culture and of a native mind! Those who have had the rare opportunity of studying the languages of several so-called primitive peoples are, in my opinion, the only persons, with the exception of those anthropologically trained investigators who have been able to live among such peoples, who can form any real idea of the extraordinary variety of ways and the profoundly different manner in which minds functioning in cultures other than our own are capable of being organized. It is not merely a matter of difference in language but a profound difference in the orientation and organization of thought.[27] These differences are, of course, merely the reflection of the differences in cultural organization. They have no demonstrable relation to any gratuitously assumed biological differences. Now, it is quite evident that the anthropologist with his usually foreign cultural background is at a great disad-

[27] On this subject see Boas, Franz. Introduction to the *Handbook of American Indian Languages*. Washington: Bureau of American Ethnology, Bulletin 40, Part I, 1911 (pp. 5-83); Boas, Franz, editor. "Language." *General Anthropology*. Boston: Heath, 1938 (pp. 125-145); Sapir, Edward. *Language, an Introduction to the Study of Speech*. New York: Harcourt, 1921 (reprinted 1929); Bloomfield, Leonard. *Language*. New York: Holt, 1933; Malinowski, Bronislaw. "The Problem of Meaning in Primitive Language." Ogden, C. K., and Richards, I. A., editors. *The Meaning of Meaning*. London: Paul, Trench, Trubner, 1923 (pp. 451-510); Malinowski, Bronislaw. "An Ethnographic Theory of Language and Some Practical Corollaries." *Coral Gardens and Their Magic*. Vol. 2. London: Allen and Unwin, 1935 (pp. 3-74). Compare also Elkin, A. P., editor. *Studies in Australian Linguistics*. Sydney: Oceania Monograph No. 3, 1938; Cassirer, Ernst. "Philosophie der Symbolischer Formen." *Die Sprache*. Vol. 1. Berlin: Bibliothek Warburg, 1923; and *Das Mythische Denken*. Vol. 2. Berlin: Bibliothek Warburg, 1925; and Sapir, Edward. "Language." *Encyclopaedia of the Social Sciences*, 9, 1933 (pp. 155-169).

vantage when, in the field, he commences the study of the culture of a nonliterate people. Unless he can acquire the language of the people he is investigating, he can at best hope to obtain only a superficial acquaintance with that culture. In order to understand what individuals really think he must be able to think with them. He must be able to take down native conversations, discussions, songs, myths, and so on in a systematic manner, and in interpreting his texts he must be able to find not so much the right word as the right *meaning*.[28] It is only within relatively recent years that anthropologists have been able to do this in any satisfactory manner.

Concerning such matters psychoanalysts have not often shown themselves to be fully aware. I believe I am correct in saying that it has generally been assumed among psychoanalysts that the method and theory of psychoanalysis which have been developed in our own European cultures are universally applicable not only to all peoples and cultures,[29] but to all peoples and cultures of all times. *Totem and Taboo* is the best example of this latter assumption. The fundamental assumption is that all human minds are organized upon the same fundamental plan and operate in much the same way, whereas the findings of ethnology abundantly demonstrate that among existing peoples, at any rate, cultures and minds are organized in a great variety of different ways. What is profoundly meaningful to the individual in one culture may be, and frequently is, completely meaningless to the individual of another culture; and what may mean one thing to the individual in one culture may mean a very different thing to the individual of another culture, even though they may live cheek by jowl with one another. Meanings and significant relations are clearly the functions of cultural organization. This seems to me to hold true for unconscious as well as for conscious mental functions.

When the psychoanalyst applies his European methods of analysis to the Australian aborigines and their culture, and

[28] For an excellent example of this see Cushing, F. H. *Zuñi Folk Tales.* New York: Knopf, 1931.
[29] This is the viewpoint adopted by Ernest Jones in his valuable article on "Psycho-Analysis and Anthropology," *Journal of the Royal Anthropological Institute,* 54, 1924 (pp. 47-66).

interprets his findings by a theory elaborated upon the basis of his observations among European peoples, neurotic or normal, he is, in my opinion, guilty of an elaborate process of self-deception. It is an elementary principle of scientific experimentation that results obtained on animals of the same species and strain cannot be assumed to be comparable unless the conditions under which the experiments were carried out were comparable. Of course, the results may eventually prove to be comparable even though the conditions under which the experiments were carried out were not, but such a fact can be established only by repeated experiment—one cannot assume it, for the simple reason that one may be wrong. Psychoanalysts, however, are content to dispense with such experimental procedures and at once assume that, whatever the conditions in different cultures, psychoanalytic findings hold good for all mankind, and, naturally, if one grants the validity of this premise, everything works beautifully. My point is that this premise requires to be repeatedly tested by dispassionate observers who are interested only in establishing the truth and not by observers who are anxious to establish the fact that psychoanalysis is or is not applicable to the investigation of nonliterate peoples.

With substantial modifications adapted to the particular culture to be investigated, there can be no shadow of doubt that the psychoanalytic approach could be made to do good service in illuminating the problems revolving about the personality of the individual, as well as about the "personality" of the culture itself. Anthropologists have too long neglected the study of the individual in nonliterate cultures and have paid too much attention, perhaps, to the type. In the study of the individual, psychoanalysis will, it is to be hoped, render great service to the anthropologist. But what should we say of the anthropologist who used an anthropological approach which attacked the problems of nonliterate culture with the methods used by the sociologist in the study of European cultures? Precisely, I think, what we should have to say of the application of psychoanalytic method in a culturally untested situation to the study of nonliterate culture and personality, namely, that being the study of *cultural* effects as reflected in mind and behavior in a European culture or cultures, the method and the theory were not—as they stand —applicable to the analysis of mental functions and behavior in any culture other than that in which they were elaborated.

That was my view when I wrote my book, and it is still my view. If I am wrong I shall be only too glad to have the fact demonstrated to me. But until psychoanalysts with a thorough training in anthropology have gone into the field and have tested out the theory and the method of psychoanalysis in situations which are more or less comparable, or for which all due allowances have been made, and which are amenable to scientific treatment, I think it hardly reasonable of them to take the view that they are being unduly neglected because their contributions to European psychology are not taken into account when a student of a field which includes their own happens to be inquiring into the psychology of a people of a totally different culture. Had I, in my book, entered into any discussion of "unconscious processes" of mind and their "symbolic" reflections in culture, I should have been committing a scientifically unpardonable error. I would have deserted the realm of factual data, by which alone I was steering my course, for an adventure in speculation—and that was not my purpose.

As a student of psychoanalysis of long standing, my view of the present status of psychoanalysis is that it is still very much in process of development as regards its most fundamental concepts and that it is still far from being as readily usable a method of investigation in the field as Róheim thinks it is. These remarks will make clear, I hope, my reason for not devoting more space than I did in my book to the consideration of the problem of Australian aboriginal nescience of the facts of procreation from the psychoanalytic standpoint. I do not, in short, believe that a method and theory of mind based upon the treatment of European individuals suffering from some form of psychoneurosis can be safely utilized in interpreting the individual and collective phenomena with which we have to deal in primitive societies. Boas stated this position quite clearly nearly forty years ago. I am not aware

that any psychoanalyst paid any attention to the challenge
of his remarks. He wrote:

> While I believe some of the ideas underlying Freud's psycho-
> analytic studies may be fruitfully applied to ethnological
> problems, it does not seem to me that the one-sided ex-
> ploitation of this method will advance our understanding of
> the development of human society. It is certainly true that the
> influence of impressions received during the first few years of
> life have been entirely underestimated and that the social
> behavior of man depends to a great extent upon the earliest
> habits which are established before the time when connected
> memory begins, and that many so-called racial or hereditary
> traits are to be considered rather as a result of early exposure
> to a certain form of social conditions. Most of these habits do
> not rise into consciousness and are, therefore, broken with
> difficulty only. Much of the difference in the behavior of
> adult male and female may go back to this cause. If, however,
> we try to apply the whole theory of the influence of sup-
> pressed desires to the activities of man living under different
> social forms, I think we extend beyond their legitimate limits
> the inferences that may be drawn from the observation of
> normal and abnormal individual psychology. . . . While,
> therefore, we may welcome the application of every advance
> in the method of psychological investigation, we cannot accept
> as an advance in ethnological method the crude transfer of a
> novel, one-sided method of psychological investigation of the
> individual to social phenomena the origin of which can be
> shown to be historically determined and to be subject to in-
> fluences that are not at all comparable to those that control
> the psychology of the individual." [30]

In my book I devoted what I considered to be a great deal
of space to the consideration of Róheim's findings among the
Australian aborigines insofar as they had any bearing upon
their procreative beliefs. In other connections I quoted
Róheim as my authority more than once. Since, in his article,
Róheim offers a single sentence from my book as my "critical
observation" on his account of the enaction by the Pindupi,

[30] Boas, Franz. "The Methods of Ethnology." *American Anthropologist*,
22, 1920 (pp. 319-321).

Pitchentara, and Nambutji children of the whole process of coitus, conception, and childbirth, I may be allowed to quote the whole paragraph here:

> The fact that Róheim observed children enacting "the whole process of coitus, conception, and childbirth" does not, of course, mean that these children were aware of the fact, as Róheim implies, that intercourse is causally related to conception and childbirth, nor does it even necessarily mean that they recognized that intercourse was in some way connected with childbirth. The observed fact alone that in play they go through the "whole process" tells us very little concerning their ideas about that process. If, as all observers including Róheim are agreed, it is generally known that intercourse serves to prepare the woman for the entry of a spirit child into her, the rôle of intercourse will, in the case of the children's play, be quite clear—it is but the mirror of what is officially believed, namely, that intercourse is a necessary preliminary condition of the entry of a spirit child into a woman. Róheim's statements cannot be too easily dismissed. As an experienced psycho-analyst he could be relied upon to discover and faithfully report those nuances of meaning and behavior which might perhaps escape others. His statements concerning the western central tribes, namely, that they believe the unborn child to enter the mother through the penis, are certainly somewhat novel, for no other investigator had been previously able to secure similar statements from the natives. These statements are, of course, not in question, and although they were secured from informants who had never seen a white man it is none the less possible for all that that some white influence had been at work here, though this is to be doubted. If then Róheim's report is to be relied upon it would seem probable that until the native is initiated into the social interpretation of the nature of things he is under the impression that intercourse is closely connected with childbirth; when, however, he has been initiated into the traditional teachings he discovers his former elementary knowledge to have been incomplete, and he gradually shifts the emphasis from a belief in material reproduction to one in favor of spiritual reproduction. The inference from this being that in certain groups the shift in emphasis, the displacement, may become so complete that any connection between intercourse

and childbirth may eventually come to be altogether obscured.[31]

Surely, it should be clear that what I was saying in this passage, and what I now repeat, is that Róheim's analysis of the nature of the native nescience may be quite correct, but that until further evidence becomes available it would be more compatible with the principles of scientific method to await the further evidence before drawing any definite conclusion.

Róheim has claimed that a true knowledge of the facts exists in secular belief side by side with the spirit conception beliefs of orthodox teaching but that the former is simply repressed in favor of the dominant orthodox beliefs. Upon the basis of his own findings Warner has independently arrived at a similar conclusion,[32] and Thomson has recently also made a similar suggestion.[33]

It may at once be said that all this is possible, particularly in view of the fact that the field worker does not generally succeed in obtaining any information other than that which is orthodox. Secular belief is for the most part determined and dominated by orthodox religious teaching, and it is unusual for the investigator to obtain any data relating to the genesis and development of belief in primitive cultures. We do know, however, that many of the childhood beliefs of the Australian undergo an appreciable modification by the time he becomes a fully initiated member of the tribe, and there is no particular reason to believe that his notions concerning the nature of procreation should not be among those affected. There is, however, no positive evidence that this is so, but it is a possibility to be borne in mind, for it may be pointed out that there is no necessary reason why the Australian should not pass from a childhood belief in the virtues of intercourse to the adult belief in the virtues of spirit children, just, for

[31] Montagu, op. cit.

[32] Warner, W. L. "Birth Control in Primitive Society." *Birth Control Review*, 15, 1931 (pp. 105-107); and *A Black Civilization*. New York: Harper, 1937 (pp. 23-24).

[33] Thomson, D. F. "Fatherhood in the Wik-Monkan Tribe." *American Anthropology*, 38, 936 (pp. 374-393).

example, as we ourselves advance from the uninitiated childhood belief in the stork to the esoteric adult belief in intercourse as the true cause of children. But we must be on our guard against such analogies. Until further intensive researches have been carried out with reference to this problem, preferably on Australian peoples uncontaminated by foreign influences, the question as to whether or not the Australian aboriginal is *completely* ignorant of the facts of procreation cannot be definitely settled.

The passage quoted from my book can be found on pages 200 to 201. Róheim states that "The main thesis of Ashley Montagu's book is the ignorance of natives with regard to physical paternity." [34] Throughout his article Róheim conveys the impression that my book was written to support the thesis that the natives were ignorant of physical paternity.

I may remark that thus far Róheim happens to be the only critic who has detected such a thesis in my book. My book has no thesis. What it pretends to be is an impartial and critical analysis of the evidence relating to the procreative beliefs of the Australian aborigines. Certainly I tried to prove that such a complete nescience of the facts of procreation was a possibility not to be lightly dismissed, but that was not my thesis. If anyone has a thesis to support it is Róheim, not I. Róheim is concerned to show that the natives do understand the relationship between intercourse and childbirth. Having examined the evidence, I admitted the possibility and pointed out that there were also other possible explanations for the facts described by Róheim.

As a scientist I am unable to accept the view that, because Róheim states he observed certain children enacting the process of coitus and childbirth, these children were therefore actually aware of the meaning of what they did. In his earlier study Róheim stated that the children enacted the whole process of coitus, conception, and childbirth; now, writing from his notes, he finds that they enacted the process of coitus and childbirth only. Róheim quotes from his field notes of August 5, 1929:

[34] Róheim, *op. cit.* (p. 346).

The realism with which Wili-kutu imitates the process of cohabitation cannot be surpassed. He fits the *kalu kurari* (a paper trumpet I gave them to play with they called *kalu-kurari; i.e.,* penis of a boy. The other objects mentioned in the text—serpent, monkey—are the toys I gave them to play with) to his own penis and adds the ball sideways as an additional *ngambu* (testicle). Then he puts the ball to the opening of the *kalu* (trumpet) and takes it out again. "This is how the semen comes out," he remarks. Then he fits the serpent right into the hollow part of the trumpet, pulls it out again and says: "The child comes out of the penis." Muluru, a smaller Nambutji boy, uses the serpent as a penis and copulates with the monkey. The monkey, he declares, is a very big woman, a *kunka mamu* (demon woman), and the serpent *tarpangu, i.e.,* goes into it, he says, when he imitates the movements of coitus, using the serpent as a penis. (This performance of Muluru is interesting because *tarpangu*, the technical term for the final "going in" of the ancestors, is here used to denote coitus.)

"By this performance," writes Róheim, "they proved that they were fully conscious of the rôle played by the penis and by semen as a fecundating agency." [35]

Dr. Róheim will no doubt be thoroughly shocked when I state that I am quite unconvinced by this account or his interpretation of it. From what he reports I still do not know of what the children were conscious or thinking when they did and said these things. As for the Pitchentara story, one phrase of which goes:

> Copulate, copulate, children make,
> Copulate, copulate children with with.

I have quoted several similar instances in my book where copulation is closely associated with the finding of babies. And, as I have shown in the same place, such sexual activities are not regarded by the natives as the cause of children. The fact that a little Australian boy said that "the child comes out of the penis" may mean merely that that particular child had but the most confused of ideas as to the manner in which children really are created. In my book I pointed out *ad nauseam* that practically everywhere in Australia, contrary

[35] *Ibid.* (pp. 351-352).

to the common belief, intercourse is associated with conception, *but not as a cause of conception or childbirth.* That native boys enact the process of coitus and childbirth is not therefore a matter for surprise. It is what we should expect. What is of interest, however, is that Róheim now clearly states that they did not enact the process of coitus, *conception* and childbirth. This may be significant; that is, that the process of conception was not included in their dramatization. As I showed in my book after an exhaustive examination of the evidence, the Australian aborigines have no notion of physiological conception, but they do believe that a woman must be opened up by the male penis before a spirit baby can enter her.

Róheim says, "The facts stated in this paper prove beyond doubt that the rôle of the male in procreation is known to Australian children." And in a footnote he adds, "I do not say that they are professors in physiology." [36]

Róheim's facts prove nothing of the sort. In my opinion all that they prove is what everyone already knows, namely, that children are conscious of the fact that such activities as intercourse and childbirth exist; that semen comes out of the male penis; that one boy said that the child comes out of the penis. But what these children understood or understand by all these things remains doubtful.

Róheim quotes several cases in which small children from our own culture area rejected the "real" explanation after having accepted it for a few months. "Thus a little girl of three rejected the real explanation after having accepted it for a few months. The reason as revealed by analysis was that she desired the little brother to grow in her own stomach and not in her mother's stomach. After a year she had 'forgotten' whatever she knew regarding the natural causation." [37]

[36] *Ibid.,* p. 359.
[37] *Ibid.,* p. 358 and Bernfeld, Siegfried. "Uber sexuelle Aufklärung." *Zeitschrift für psychoanalytische Pädagogik,* 1, 1926 (p. 195). Compare also: Zulliger, Hans. "Eltern, Schule, und sexuelle Aufklarung." *Zeitschrift für psychoanalytische Pädagogik,* 1, 1926 (pp. 230 and 235); and Graber, G. H. "Zeugung und Geburt in der Vorstellung des Kindes." *Zeitschrift für psychoanalytische Pädagogik,* 1, 1926 (p. 278).

Now what, it may well be asked, does Róheim mean by a little girl of three rejecting the "real" explanation of the facts of procreation? What can the "real" facts mean to a little girl of three? Róheim quotes Zulliger's report of "the case of a little girl of four who first accepted the natural theory, and then, after seeing the picture of the stork with a child in a picture book, reverts to the stork theory. The same child also evolved absolutely 'Australian' theories on the subject, for the little girl believed that the father gives the mother something to eat and that is how she gets a child." [38]

It might be argued that in quoting this case Róheim is putting himself in a vulnerable position, for it may be said that in the case of this little girl he is presenting an argument in favor of the notion that the Australian beliefs are founded upon an early desire to find a really workable explanation of childbirth!

But the Australian children, according to Róheim, are aware of the role of the father in procreation and only later repress this childhood belief in favor of a belief in spirit children immigrating into women, and as adults have only "a latent concept of" the connection. From all this we infer that the adults are consciously unaware of the relationship between coitus and childbirth. If this is what Róheim really means, we may well ask where did the children obtain their knowledge of the facts of procreation which they subsequently repress? By "instinctive intuition"? By working it out for themselves? Or did some unrepressed individual let the cat out of the bag?

Róheim writes, "How far the official doctrine succeeds in supplanting this view one cannot exactly say—but it does not go very far. The process is probably merely like repression, a skin-deep repression. 'It would be nearer the truth to say that some of them go so far in the acceptance of the official doctrine as to *deny* this connection.' [39] I agree entirely with Professor Warner, who remarks that probably the physiolog-

[38] Róheim, *op. cit.*
[39] This is undoubtedly what Warner means, but it is not, as Róheim suggests, a direct quotation from Warner.

ical knowledge is not considered important by the native when he is talking to the anthropologist, for it is the official doctrine of spiritual conception that looms large in their thinking." [40]

Now, I have already shown in my book that the tribes discussed by Warner, and others nearby by Thomson, show the clearest evidences of having undergone the most radical changes as a result of contact with at least one Melanesian people. Also they have been for a considerable period of time exposed to contacts with the white man. Their knowledge, therefore, of "the facts of procreation" may have been acquired from a Melanesian source or, still more recently, from a white one. When speaking to an investigating anthropologist it is not unnatural that they should vaunt their knowledge of these "facts" before him. However this may be, the suggestion that the orthodox teaching looms so large in native thought that it completely overlays the facts when the native is speaking to the anthropologist [41] is, of course, of the greatest interest in itself as showing what the natives do consider important even in a group in which the elementary facts of procreation are said to be understood.

It may be that these facts are everywhere in Australia understood. I should not be surprised to find that they were, but thus far satisfactory evidence has not been forthcoming that they are understood. On the other hand, there is a great deal of evidence which suggests that the relationship between coitus and childbirth is not understood. This evidence is fully discussed in my book.

Róheim raises the question: "If the father has nothing to do with the child why must he find it? And why does he place it on his wife's navel? For as we happen to know in the sex theories of European children the navel is the symbol of the vagina, and in Central Australia the *tjalupalupa* (navel) in the songs or ceremonial ground drawings is definitely ex-

[40] Róheim, *op. cit.*
[41] This view was first put forward by Lang, Andrew. *The Secret of the Totem.* London: Longmans, 1905; and subsequently was independently maintained by Read, Westermarck, Porteus, and others.

plained as being a euphemism and meaning really the vagina." [42]

In the first place, it must be pointed out that the "finding"
of the child by the father and his placing it on the wife's
navel is a process which occurs only in dreams. In the second place, it requires to be pointed out even more strongly
that this process is only one of many ways in which babies
may come to enter a woman. Thus, for example, a woman
may dream that she has been entered by a baby, or another
woman may dream the spirit baby has entered a certain
woman to whom she will then tell her dream, and only then
will the woman thus informed know that she has been entered by a spirit child. In other cases the woman becomes
aware that she has been entered by a spirit baby only at the
quickening which is always taken to be the instant of entry
of such a child into the woman. She may be miles away from
her own or her husband's horde country. In such a case the
conceptional totem of the child may then be that of the
locality in which its mother knows it to have entered her.
Spirit children may enter women from whirlwinds which have
overtaken the latter, or they may enter women by merely being told to do so by a man, not necessarily the father, or
even by a woman. In western Australia the father of the child
is not necessarily the husband of the mother but the man or
woman who "found" or dreamed it, the *wororu.*[43] In other
cases, where it is obligatory for the father to "dream" the spirit
baby, there is no shadow of a suspicion of a physiological
relationship between them. Nowhere is this better brought
out than in a book by Mrs. Daisy Bates, who for more than
forty years lived in intimate contact with various tribes of
Australian aborigines. Among the tribes of Broome, in northwestern Australia, Mrs. Bates describes the spirit child, or
ngargalulla, beliefs, which in general follow the usual pattern
of these beliefs throughout Australia. She writes:

> So firm was the belief in the *ngargalulla* that no man who
> had not seen it in his sleeping hours would claim the paternity

[42] Róheim, *op. cit.*
[43] Radcliffe-Brown, A. R. "Beliefs concerning Childbirth in Some Australian Tribes." *Man,* 12, 1912 (pp. 180-182).

of a child born to him. In one case that came under my observation, a man who had been absent for nearly five years in Perth proudly acknowledged a child born in his absence, because he had seen the *ngargalulla*, and in another, though husband and wife had been separated not a day, the man refused absolutely to admit paternity. He had not dreamed the *ngargalulla*. Should a boy arrive when a girl came in the dream, or should the *ngargalulla* not have appeared to its rightful father, the mother must find the man who has dreamed it correctly, and he is ever deemed to be the father of the child.

The *ngargalulla* is still a spirit in the first months of its existence, but when it begins to laugh and cry, to touch and talk, and to manifest its personality as a little human being, its link with the dream world is gone, and it becomes *cobajeera*—in other words, a normal baby. Thenceforward, through its whole life, the fathers who have dreamed its existence are the controllers of its destinies, within the relentless circle of tribal law. There is no glorification of maternity, no reverence of woman as woman, in the dark mind of the aboriginal. Apart from the natural affection between mother and son, sister and brother, and apart from her physical fulfillment of certain dominant needs, a woman is less than the dust. Her inferiority is recognized by the very youngest of the tribe.[44]

From this account it appears clear that these natives have no notion of physiological conception or, if they do, that they have succeeded in concealing it pretty thoroughly from Mrs. Bates. It is also made quite clear why the father must "find" or "dream" the child—whether he be the husband of the mother or not. It is because a definite man must be secured in a socially acceptable manner to stand in the relation of father to a definite child—*pater*, not *genitor*—and to be responsible to it in a socially obligatory manner. This was one of the principal facts which I tried to make clear in my book,

[44] Bates, Daisy. *The Passing of the Aborigines.* London: Murray, 1938 (pp. 27-28). Compare also: "The Marriage Laws and Some Customs of the West Australian Aborigines." *Victorian Geographical Journal*, 23, 1905 (pp. 36-60); and "Social Organization of Some Western Australian Tribes." *Report of the 14th Meeting of the Australian Association for the Advancement of Science*, 1913 (pp. 387-400 and footnote 25, pp. 181-188).

the fact that in Australia such a thing as physiological paternity is not recognized, but only social paternity, which is the
important thing. I also put forward the view that the same
was true of maternity. What Mrs. Bates says of the native
attitude toward maternity and the lack of regard in which
women are held in the tribes with which she is acquainted is
in accordance with that view. Róheim finds this latter view
absurd, one not even worth troubling to refute. Professor
A. P. Elkin, who knows the Australian aborigines as few
anthropologists have ever known them, takes a view of this
suggestion of mine which I should like to recommend to the
attention of Róheim. He writes:

> The point of Dr. Ashley Montagu's book, however, is not
> just to reaffirm the native nescience of physiological pater-
> nity,[45] as a result of a re-examination of the old sources and a
> critical examination of the more recent evidence of which
> there is a considerable quantity; he also maintains that the
> evidence shows that the Aborigines are and were ignorant of
> physiological maternity. This is a thesis which justifies the
> vast labor expended by the author, whether we finally agree
> with him or not. Even those who know the Aborigines well
> have probably not bothered to analyse or to ascertain the na-
> tive conception of motherhood. In the light of Dr. Ashley
> Montagu's thesis, we are now challenged to do this. Possibly
> the difference between himself and some others will turn out
> to be one of definition only or mainly, but he will have done
> a good service if his argument causes clarity of thinking on
> this matter.[46]

I can only regret that Róheim has not been inspired to
clarity of thinking, and that he altogether failed to understand what I meant by ignorance of physiological maternity.
I, of course, meant nothing so utterly imbecile as that "an
Australian child does not know its own mother." [47] What I
tried to show in my book is that, while everyone knows that

[45] In this connection Elkin writes, "In my own experience, assertions of
the procreative effect of sexual intercourse have only been made by men
who have been in long and close contact with whites." *Oceania*, 8, 1938
(p. 377).
[46] *Ibid.*
[47] Róheim, *op. cit.*

a certain child was transmitted into the horde or tribe through a certain woman, no one believes or thinks in terms of the child having been actually *produced* by her in connection with a particular man. The belief is rather that a spirit child, already preformed, has entered her from a spirit center, generally situated in her husband's territory, and that in due time it makes its appearance through her medium among them. This view of the process of coming into being is certainly unphysiological, and since the natives are continually asserting that the "mother nothing," that she acts merely in the capacity, as Howitt suggests, of a wet nurse,[48] I am inclined to take their word for it.

My point, in brief, is that from the purely physiological or biological standpoint the natives think of the relationship between mother and child in much the same way as we do of the relationship between the incubator and the egg. The incubator makes possible the development of the egg into a chick, and the woman makes possible the development of a preformed spirit baby—*kurunna*—into a fully formed infant—*ratappa*—but neither of them have any connection whatsoever with the generation of the egg in the one case and of the spirit baby or the infant in the other. *The mother has no part in the generation of the individual.* This is what I mean by ignorance of physiological maternity. The fact that a child "comes out" of the body of a woman is socially important and physiologically without any significance whatsoever. The woman is a kind of necessary incubator for the spirit child but biologically no more than that. Socially, of course, the association of a particular woman with the child to which she has given birth is of the very greatest significance. Now Róheim, like Radcliffe-Brown,[49] assumes that the fact of "coming out" of the body of a particular woman is a physiological and inescapable fact. Inescapable the fact is to everyone and it is of the greatest importance that it should be so, but physiological it is only to those who think in such terms.

[48] Howitt, A. W. *The Native Tribes of South-East Australia.* London: Macmillan, 1904 (p. 195).
[49] Radcliffe-Brown, A. R. *Man,* 38, 1938 (pp. 15-16).

My point is that the evidence strongly suggests that the Australians do not think of this obvious physical relationship as a physiological one any more than we think of the relationship between the egg and the incubator as such.

Radcliffe-Brown has stated that "The Australian aborigines do not recognize physiological but only social relationships." [50] In an earlier part of the same work, Radcliffe-Brown claims that the "obvious physiological relationship between a woman and the child to which she gives birth . . . is recognized by the Australian native." These statements are obviously contradictory but the contradiction is not necessarily a serious one. As I have pointed out in my book, the difference of opinion here may ultimately be reduced to a matter of definition. If it can be agreed that a relationship between a woman and a child which she does not generate but to which she merely gives temporary lodgment until it issues from her does not constitute a physiological relationship in the eyes of the native, the contradiction is, I think, resolved.

Among the Australian aborigines the woman out of whom an individual has issued into the world is that individual's *own* mother *because* he has issued from her. The notion of generation does not enter into the matter in the least. The process of issuance is a fact but it is not regarded as a physiological fact, no more than the entry of a spirit child into a woman is regarded as a physiological fact. This is, however, not really a point of great importance, the important fact is that the woman is not held to play any part in the generation of the child. And this, I repeat, is what I mean by ignorance of physiological maternity. Future researches in the field will alone prove whether such a nescience exists among the Australian aborigines or not. I can only hope that I have provided a few ideas which may be considered worth testing.

I may now briefly refer to Róheim's theory that the native nescience of paternity is due to repression of the knowledge of the father as the agent of procreation because "The identity

[50] Radcliffe-Brown, A. R. "The Social Organization of Australian Tribes." *Oceania*, 1, 1930 (p. 43).

in their minds of the child with a being who was killed by the father before the child was born is an expression of the unconscious hostility between father and son; *i.e.*, of one aspect of the Oedipus complex. The unborn child protects large game from the father's spear, because in the father's unconscious mind the larger game he kills is identical with the unborn child."

Now, this whole generalization is based upon a single one of the many ways in which children are believed to come into being among the Australian aborigines. Róheim's theory can at best, therefore, be applied only to a particular belief; it obviously cannot be extended to embrace those cases in which the father actually dreams or finds the child, or to those many other cases in which the child enters the woman independently of any activities on the part of the father, or to those other cases which I have briefly touched upon in this paper. Hence, as I see it, Róheim's theory cannot be accepted without doing violence to the facts as a general explanation of the aboriginal nescience of physiological paternity. I conclude, therefore, that while it is possible that aboriginal children know, as everyone of course does, that coitus is a necessary factor in the production of childbirth, such children realize after they have undergone initiation into the esoteric beliefs of adulthood that it is by no means an important factor and that it is certainly not the *cause* of conception. What they believe to be the *truth* as adult thinkers is that immigration of spirit children from a source independent of the bodies of a particular man and wŏman is the cause of conception and childbirth. Such adult knowledge is really an extension and clarification of the childhood notions relating to procreation, not a suppression or obfuscation of them. There hardly seems to be any necessity to invoke the mechanism of repression here. In any event, if children actually know that coitus and/or seminal fluid makes babies, how are we to explain the alleged fact that these children have already succeeded in repressing —for this is what Róheim suggests—the knowledge of their physiological relationship to a particular man? Or are we to understand that repression occurs only later, during or after initiation? If the mature aboriginal is convinced that coitus is not the cause of childbirth, whatever he may have believed as a child, and whatever the elements involved in the development of that conviction, we can do no other than accept his own testimony to that effect.

ABOUT THE AUTHOR

ASHLEY MONTAGU was born in London, England, in 1905, and studied anthropology at the Universities of London and Florence, and Columbia University, where he was awarded the degree of Doctor of Philosophy for a thesis on the Australian aborigines. Professor Ashley Montagu has been scientific worker at the British Museum (Natural History), Curator of Physical Anthropology at the Wellcome Historical Medical Museum, London, Assistant Professor of Anatomy at New York University, Anthropologist to the Division of Child Research at the same university, Associate Professor of Anatomy at the Hahnemann Medical College and Hospital, Philadelphia, and Chairman and Professor of Anthropology, Rutgers University. He has also been a visiting lecturer and professor at Harvard University and the University of Delaware, Senior Lecturer in Anthropology on the Veterans Administration Postgraduate Training Program in Psychiatry and Neurology, and was Rapporteur of the UNESCO Committee of Experts on Race which drafted the famous UNESCO Statement on Race. He has been Family Affairs and Anthropological Adviser to NBC, and has appeared on many radio and television programs in his capacity as an anthropologist. He is Chairman of the Anisfield-Wolf Award Committee which awards annual prizes for meritorious works in the field of race relations, and he is an associate and advisory editor of *Acta Geneticae Medicae et Gemellologia* (the study of twins and twinning), and *Child-Family Digest*. Professor Ashley Montagu is a member of many scientific and learned societies, and is the author of some eighteen books, mostly in the field of anthropology. He has also contributed several hundred articles to the scientific and general periodicals of this and other countries. His hobbies are gardening and book collecting.

This book was set in

Times Roman and Caledonia types by

Harry Sweetman Typesetting Corporation.

It was printed and bound at

the press of The World Publishing Company.

Design is by Larry Kamp